European Institute of Education and Social Policy

Trentham Books

The EEC and Education

by Guy Neave

© Trentham Books 1984

First published 1984 by
Trentham Books
30 Wenger Crescent, Trentham,
Stock-on-Trent, ST4 8LE

ISBN paper: 0 9507735 4 9

All rights reserved. No part of this publication may be reproduced, stored in retrieval system, or transmitted in any form or by any means, electronic, mechanical, photocopying, recording or otherwise, without the prior permission of Trentham Books.

cover design by Cal Swann FSIAD

Set and printed in Great Britain by:
Bemrose Press Ltd./Cheshire Typesetters, Chester.

Contents

Chapter One:
The Background   1

Chapter Two:
The education of migrants and their family   21

Chapter Three:
Transition from school to work   41

Chapter Four:
Education and training   57

Chapter Five:
Cooperation in higher education   77

Chapter Six:
Equality of educational opportunity   101

Chapter Seven:
The European dimension in education   117

Chapter Eight:
Education and training for disabled children and young people   137

Chapter Nine:
The micro-electronic revolution   151

Chapter Ten:
Information and policy development in the European Community: EURYDICE   163

Chapter Eleven:
International Relations   177

Chapter Twelve:
Conclusion   189

Foreword
By Lord Briggs of Lewes

This is the first printed record of the educational interests and activities of the European Community and as such it will be an invaluable work of reference. It is more than a work of reference, however, for it explains as far as possible why as well as how the Community has become involved in education.

Equally important, it suggests why and how the range of Community interests and activities in the educational field has changed from one period to another. There have been continuing concerns on the part of the Commission, but there have also been shifts of emphasis and interest. For example, while there has always been a continuing interest in education and work, the emphasis has necessarily been different since the sharp rise in youth unemployment.

A study of the why as well as the how of Community activity is particularly important in that the Treaties of Rome did not specifically mention education in their provisions. Indeed, it was not until 1969 that education began to figure significantly on the Commission's agenda. In the intervening years there have been major national changes involving greatly increased expenditures and, in many cases, substantial structural reforms. When ministers of education met during the 1970s, they were exchanging experience and ideas of a very different kind from those they would have been exchanging twenty years before.

The hope of developing educational activity focussing on Europe, seeking to influence the perspectives of an emerging generation, has not been easy to realise. All European problems and potentialities have an educational dimension, and without such a dimension, it is difficult to see how it will be possible to bring up an enlightened citizenry. Yet the dimension is not always recognised and when it is recognised, it is sometimes viewed with very guarded reserve. By contrast, the sense that national educational problems and potentialities have a European dimension, has been strengthened and it is acknowledged that those concerned with them can benefit greatly from discussing them within a European (but not an exclusively European) context.

Educational developments in different European countries since the Treaties of Rome were signed in 1957 have transformed educational systems as they existed then. These developments have had significant economic, social and cultural consequences both through changes in access and numbers and through changes in course content and impact. There have also been changes in the educational process as a result of the development of continuing education and the use of new educational technologies. While national systems retain their distinctive identities, and some of the influences that have changed them during the last twenty years are national in origin, others are common to many, if not all European countries. They deserve to be studied, therefore, not only in parallel or comparatively, but together, as they are done in this book. It should be of interest and concern to educational policy-makers and administrators everywhere, therefore, and the material presented in it will provide a basis for further monographs, national and European, in the form of both articles and of working papers. The book points also to the need for further synthesis, increasingly necessary as educational horizons tend to narrow and there are limitations to the resources available for further educational advance. There are other reasons for synthesis too, given that not all the changes of the last twenty years have produced the results expected of them. The search for value for money is bound up with concern for quality.

There is obvious value in the development of an independent critical opinion in educational circles on what has been achieved as a result of Community involvement and on the tasks — they are many — which may be, could be, or ought to be done in the future. The European Institute of Education and Social Policy in Paris, of which the author of this book is a member, provides both a research centre and a forum where facts — and processes — can be studied free from operational or political preoccupation. It can also look at long term processes as well as immediate issues. Its title reflects the impossibility of dissociating educational policy from other branches of social policy which have themselves been transformed since 1957. Yet it affirms the strategic importance of education in achieving change, and through its own links with the Commission and with the Community it has played its own part in the history chronicled and analysed in the pages that follow.

Acknowledgements

In writing this account of the educational activities of the Commission of the European Communities, I have had the help, encouragement and advice of many people, both inside and outside the Education Services of the Commission. To them, my special thanks. Particular mention should be made of Hywel C. Jones, Director of Education and Vocational Training, Guiseppi Porcasi, Counsellor to the same service, Pat Daunt, Head of Division in charge of action on behalf of the Handicapped, Domenico Lennarduzzi, Head of Division in the area of Cooperation in Education. To the desk officials who interrupted their schedules to explain the subtler points of detail and the finer nuances of the programmes and activities for which they are responsible, special acknowledgement is due. It is a real pleasure to be able to mention Henriette Bastrup-Birk, André Kirchberger, Lucien Jacoby, Hans Kairat and Ron Martin.

Much of the work was carried out within the context of EURYDICE, the Education Information Network in the European Communities. So, it is only right that debts of hospitality and assistance, incurred whilst with the Central Unit at Bruxelles, be acknowledged. To the members of the Central Unit and to its Head, John Richardson, much more is owed than can be mentioned here.

Nearer home, I have drawn heavily on the resources and ingenuity of Alan Smith, Edward Prosser and Martine Herlant at the Office for Cooperation in Education in Bruxelles, not just for documentation and a cross Community perspective on cooperation in higher education, but also for space and other assistance. Ladislav Cerych, with typical generosity, made sure that the time spent outside the European Institute of Education did not result in a backlog of unfinished responsibilities.

Finally, all enquiries reach the point where they must make the change from manuscript to document. This task befell Eliane Godefroy of the European Institute of Education and Social Policy. Her attention to detail and skills at decyphering the unintelligible went beyond all reasonable limits.

It remains to be said that those who, in various ways, contributed to this undertaking, are absolved from any unhappy interpretations or errors this book might contain. As theirs has been the generosity in time and courtesy, so the responsibility in this latter domain remains mine.

Guy Neave
Bruxelles February 21st 1984

Chapter One

The Background

Structure:
Introduction
The Legal Background
Towards a Community Education Action Programme
Principles of cooperation in education
Resolution of the Council and Ministers of Education February 9th 1976
Decision-making machinery
   The Commission of the European Communities
   The Council of Ministers
   The European Court of Justice
   The European Parliament
Decision-making machinery in the educational domain
The Planning context
Structure of the report

SOURCES

Introduction

Few subjects are more controversial than 'Europe'. This is scarcely surprising since there are almost as many interpretations of what 'Europe' was, is and ought to be as there are interests arguing about such matters. To some, amongst them the founding fathers of the European community itself such as Jean Monnet and Robert Schuman — the vision of 'Europe' sprang directly out of a reaction to and a distaste for, the rise of militant nationalism. Such nationalism, it has been argued, brought about two World Wars and the decline of Europe's place in the world. The vision of a United Europe is, in fact, an old and generous vision that may be traced back to the 18th century and more particularly to the Proposal for a Perpetual Peace, put forward in 1713 by the Frenchman, the Abbé de Saint Pierre. But this is not the only view that exists. To others of a less historical bent, Europe appears less as a challenge to construct a new political, economic or social order than as a direct threat to those already established. If such views may be ascribed to the 'Little Englander' or the French patriot, they should not be dismissed for all that. Concern over the issue of who and how social, political and economic institutions should be controlled has been a fundamental issue since the Revolution of 1789 and has coloured both the practices and beliefs that, in their turn, underwrote the emergence of nation-state democracy. It is then, understandable that the emergence of a Community with supra-governmental powers of legislation may seem a diminution of the sovereign powers of Parliament and as such, yet another example of the alienation of political influence from the base. After all, the emergence of democratic institutions was coterminous with the rise of the nation-state. Finally, there are those who agree with the notion of 'Europe of the Peoples' but point out that it is not necessarily limited merely to Europe of the Ten. The latter definition, they argue, is far wider than just the major industrial powers of the Western European peninsula.

Even within the relatively narrow definition of Europe as Europe of the Ten there are innumerable different interests and alignments, each with its own interpretation and imperatives. Europe of the Regions is as different from the Europe of the steelworkers as Europe of the herring fisherman is from the Europe of the Liberal Professions. Yet, whether steelworkers, fisherman or liberal professions, all have to decide what type of Europe will emerge in the future. And in this, no less than in the original task of nation-building, the role of education is paramount.

It is not the purpose of this study to examine the development of education systems within the Member States of the Ten. This task has already been undertaken by Lionel Elvin in his book, *The Education Systems in the European Community*. Rather the burden of this investigation is to provide an account of the place of education within the European Community seen from the standpoint of Brussels. It is, primarily, concerned with the development of actions less at the level of the Member States, than at the level of the Community and its focus is essentially upon those events taking place within the Education services of the Commission itself. What are the formal powers of the European Community in the field of education? How does it go about reaching those decisions that relate to education? What have been the main points of interest to Member States and how has the Education service sought to meet them? What are the major areas of Community concern in education and how has Brussels set about the development of Community action? How are priorities determined?

These questions are all the more important for the fact that a belief exists which holds that membership of the European Community means that such matters as curriculum, school structure and practice, will ultimately be determined by the Commission. It is a notion as erroneous as it is powerful. Being part of Europe does not mean the imposition of educational uniformity. Still less does it mean the replacement of diversity and pluralism by stultifying enactments from distant technocrats. Rather the contrary. Education systems in Community countries display a variety in their structures, practices and customs that are almost bewildering. Such variety — the result of factors historical, political and cultural that first moulded the education systems of individual Member States — is a highly valued source, providing alternative perspectives and experience to supplement the knowledge and experience of the individual country. The exchange of such experience between Member States is an important dimension to Community action in the field of education. To this extent therefore, educational development in the Community as perceived by Brussels is very much intended to foster, where not to further, such diversity. Indeed, it forms the bedrock on which Community policy rests.

Yet, despite the myriad differences in administrative control, institutional structure and curriculum content, countries in Western Europe have had to face issues over the past decade that are broadly similar. The need to take into account the particular requirements of 'minority' groups, the creation of equal opportunities for girls, the drive on the part of all young people to obtain education beyond the formal limits of compulsory schooling — these issues are generic to all Member States irrespective of the particular national context in which they emerged. Thus, throughout the Ten, the number of school students in upper secondary education rose from 6,343,000 in 1970/71 to 9,525,000 in 1980/1. ('Education and training', *EUROSTAT Bulletin 2/1982*, Luxembourg, 1982, Statistical Office of the European Communities, p.5). Staying on beyond compulsory schooling in the Ten rose from 49.8 percent of all 16 year olds in 1970/71 to 60.5 percent a decade later; for 17 year olds, the corresponding figures are 30.1 percent and 44.5 percent whilst for 18 year olds 28.1 percent continued with full time education in 1970 compared with 35.8 percent ten years on. If in 1970, participation in upper secondary education was a minority experience in all but two Member States — the Netherlands and Belgium — ten years later it had become the norm. And, in certain countries — France, the Netherlands, Belgium and Denmark — upper secondary education had assumed all the characteristics of moving towards a 'universal system' of schooling with participation rates varying between 74.4 percent of 16 years in the case of France to 91.5 percent for the Netherlands. (*Impact of demographic change on education systems in the European Community*, Brussels, 1981, EURYDICE, p.7; *EUROSTAT Bulletin, op.cit.*).

More recently, the Community has had to face another set of difficulties which have placed enormous strain on national systems of education. On the one hand, there is the question of falling rolls and demographic decline in primary and lower secondary education with all the implications this has for the teaching profession. And, on the other, there is the growing problem of youth unemployment and the transition from school to adult life. To be sure, not all Member States of the Ten are faced with the problem of falling pupil numbers. Greece and the Irish Republic are notable exceptions in this respect. (Guy Neave, 'Education systems under pressure: the planning response of certain Western European countries to the demographic and economic crisis', *Paper presented to the Annual conference of the British Educational Management and Administration Society,* London, September 17th 1982 (mimeo). But there is no exception to the difficulties involved in the latter.

In these, as in other areas of educational development, governments have been placed under considerable pressure to devise suitable measures to meet such problems. How the Education and training services of the European Commission have sought to assist Member States to meet these challenges is the main concern of this study.

The Legal Background:

The legal basis of the European Community rests upon three treaties: the Treaty of Paris, signed on April 18th 1951 which set up the European Coal and Steel Community and the *two* Treaties of Rome signed on March 25th 1957 which created two Communities — the first being the European Economic Community and the second, the European Atomic Energy Committee. The first treaty of Rome laid down the institutional framework of the EEC which then consisted of a Commission, a Council of Ministers, a European Assembly and a Court of Justice. The prospect of the Six expanding to form the Nine gave rise to a further Treaty, signed at Brussels on January 22nd 1972. Known as Treaty of Accession, it provided for those countries acceding to the EEC to be bound by the previous Treaties, subject always to the amendments and adjustments agreed at Brussels. (Dennis Evans, *Accountant's Guide to the European Community,* London, 1981, Macdonald and Evans, p.1). Britain, Denmark and Ireland joined the Community on January 1st 1973 and, on January 1st 1981, Greece entered as tenth Member State.

Though there are many examples of international organisations that bring states together for closer cooperation, few have the legislative powers of the European Community. The Community has four instruments by which action may be forwarded. These are Regulations, Decisions, Directives and Recommendations. Regulations apply directly and have the force of Community law. Decisions, though binding, apply only to those Member States, companies or individuals to whom they are directed. Directives are used to set down agreed and compulsory objectives but leave the way in which they are to be attained to the discretion of the individual Member State. And, finally, there are Recommendations and Opinions which are not binding in an EEC context, but merely register agreement amongst Member States.

If the Treaty of Rome acted as the foundation stone for the subsequent development of community policy, legislation and practice, (Hywel C. Jones, 'Education in the European Community', *Address to the North of England Education Conference,* Liverpool, January 1st 1983 (xerox), p.1) it is a fact that formally education did not figure as part of it, though provision for vocational training was included under articles 118 and 128, as was the mutual recognition of academic qualifications under article 57 — the latter as a means of facilitating professional mobility across Member States. Recently, it has been argued that article 57 did imply Community involvement in education policy. (R. Gwyn, 'Towards a European policy of initial teacher education', *European Journal of Education,* vol. 14, no. 4, 1979, p.361). But niceties of interpretation do not always prevail when national sensitivities are concerned.

Developments in the field of education:

The twelve years from 1957 through to 1969 were a period when education remained a taboo subject within the corridors of the European Community. Indeed, Member States seem to have adopted toward education the same attitude that the French politician, Leon Gambetta, once suggested his compatriots adopt towards the loss of Alsace Lorraine in 1871: 'Think about it always. But speak of it — never!' A number of explanations have recently emerged to account for this strange silence. By some, it was assumed that cooperation in such areas as culture and education could be more usefully carried out within the framework of a wider grouping of European States such as already exists in the Council of Europe (Jones, *op.cit.,* p.2). Others, linking education to the question of national sovereignty, have pointed out that the particular view of *l'Europe des Patries,* developed by General de Gaulle made states extremely sensitive to interventions in those areas not covered by the Treaty of Rome of which education was one.

By the early Seventies, however, attitudes began to change both in the Member States and in the Commission itself. Symbolic of this was the first meeting in Council of the Minister of Education, in November 1971, the first of its kind since the establishment of the Community in 1957. The importance of this meeting lay in its recognition of the need to establish a basis for cooperation in the specific field of education. This move took place against a background of other Community level developments, principally in the area of vocational training. Earlier, in July 1971, the Council of Ministers had adopted a series of general guidelines for a Community level programme in this latter field. The purpose of such a programme was seen, inter alia, as providing '... the population as a whole with the opportunities for *general* (our italics) and vocational education, further education and life long education which will adequately allow indi-

The Background

viduals to develop their personality and to follow a skilled occupation in an economy of which the needs are constantly changing' (quoted in Education in the European Community', *Bulletin of the European Communities*, 3/74, p.5).

Though firmly anchored in Articles 11 and 128 of the Treaty of Rome, the long term significance of this action was not that it gave added impetus to vocational training — though that in itself was important. Rather, its significance lay in the fact that for the first time *general* education was mentioned as an area of interest to the Community. Though it should also be noted that such mention was made in conjunction with that area which did fall under the Treaty, namely, vocational education and training.

This theme was taken up by the meeting of the Ministers of Education of the Six in November 1971. In their final communiqué, the Ministers pointed out that the Treaty of Rome already made provision for actions involving vocational training. It was now appropriate to complete these actions by increasing cooperation in the field of education as such. (Secretariat General of the Council, *Press release No. 2257/11*, November 16th 1971). A number of suggestions were made about the form this cooperation might take, amongst them a proposal by the French Minister of Education, then Olivier Guichard. M. Guichard put forward the notion of a European Centre for Educational Development. Though, ultimately, this proposal was not taken on board, its feasibility was examined by a Working Party of Senior Officials set up in the aftermath of the Ministers' meeting to review ways by which cooperation in the field of education might be achieved. The Working Party completed its report in November 1972, just after the pre-enlargement Summit conference of Prime Ministers and Heads of State held in Paris on October 19th and 20th 1972.

If the Heads of State meeting made no mention of education as such, it did mark a significant change of emphasis in the future path to be hewn by the Community. It set up the first Community level social action programme, laid down a policy and a fund for regional development and agreed upon the first environmental protection programme. The future of the Community did not lie solely in the field of economic expansion as an end in itself. Waxing almost lyrical, the communiqué that resulted from the meeting stated: 'Economic expansion . . . must as a priority help to attenuate the disparities in living conditions. It must emerge in an improved quality as well as an improved standard of life. In the European spirit, special attention will be paid to non material values' (quoted in Jones *op.cit.*, p.3).

In truth, attention to the 'non material values' — not least of which education was already under way. In July 1972, the Commission asked Professor Henri Janne, formerly Belgian Minister of Education, to undertake a personal review of those areas that might lend themselves to a future programme of action in the field of education. The Janne Report, 'For a Community Policy on Education' was presented in February 1973. Strictly speaking, it is not a formal expression of Community policy, though some have pointed out that it stands as the only published statement that one might equate with a blueprint for action (Gwyn, *op.cit.*, p.362). The Janne Report, which was the summation of discussions held between some 35 leading experts in the field, started from two premisses. The first took as its point of departure that an irreversible recognition of an education dimension of Europe had begun and that this initial movement led to an education policy at European Community level ('For a Community policy in education', *Bulletin of the European Communities Supplement 10/73*, Luxembourg, 1973). The second reiterated the view already noted by the first meeting of the Ministers of Education, namely that the Treaty of Rome could be interpreted in such a way that those clauses dealing with vocational training could be extended to cover a rather wider ambit. 'The Treaty of Rome', Janne noted, 'postulates taking over the whole problem of the training of young people and adults as far as it is related to the needs of optimum economic development' (*ibid.*, p.11). Amongst those matters touched upon in the report were education with a European dimension, foreign language teaching, mutual recognition of school leaving certificates and the development of permanent education, the latter being particularly stressed. The Janne Report provided an important intellectual impetus to the long range discussion of possible areas of action. To this extent, it was a noteworthy contribution to breaking down the taboo which, hitherto, had been set around the area of education in Community affairs.

Towards a Community Education Action Programme:

Within the Commission itself, the formal decision to include Education as one of its services was taken in January 1973 when the responsibility for this area, combined with Research and Science Policy, was placed under the ambit of Directorate General XII. For the first time Education figured as part of the responsibility of one of the 13 Commissioners. Professor Ralph Dahrendorf assumed this task.

Draft proposals for future development in the field of education continued to flow into the Commission. One, dealing with the activities that might be undertaken by the Directorate for Education, Research and Science was presented in May 1973 and in March the following year, a further communication was laid before Council by the Commission. Entitled 'Education in the European Community', it set forth a certain number of issues that might be seen as the starting point for action at Community level. Broadly speaking, its suggestions fell into three main areas:

— the need to improve opportunities for teachers, research staff and students to move among the countries of the Community in the interests of scholarly research, the broadening of professional experience and generally to extend their studies into a European environment. An important element in this was the recognition of academic qualifications across Member States;
— the education of children of migrant workers;
— the development of a European dimension in education. Particularly important in this were held to be the teaching and learning of foreign languages, the study of Europe as part of the normal school curriculum, the

strengthening of cooperation between establishments of higher education. The idea was also mooted of extending the development of so called 'European schools'.

These suggestions were presented to the Ministers of Education in June 1974 — their first meeting since the enlargement of the Community to Nine Member States. The Resolution that resulted from this meeting marked an important step in laying down the ground rules for cooperation at Community level in the educational sphere. Cooperation, the Ministers agreed, should proceed by progressive stages — an important detail since it left room for subsequent negotiation. No less relevant was the agreement that cooperation itself should apply to specific priority areas. These were:

- better facilities for the education and training of nationals and the children of nationals of other Member States of the Communities and of non member countries;
- the promotion of closer relations between education systems in Europe;
- the compilation of up-to-date documentation and statistics on education;
- increased cooperation between institutes of higher education;
- improved possibilities for academic recognition of diplomas and periods of study;
- the encouragement of freedom of movement and mobility of teachers, students and research workers in particular by the removal of administrative and social obstacles to the free movement of such persons and by the improved teaching of foreign languages;
- the achievement of equal opportunity for free access to all forms of education (*Official Journal No. C 98 2,* August 20th 1974).

Principles of cooperation in education:

Agreement having been reached on the strategic guidelines as to the substantive content basis for cooperation, equally important were the fundamental principles of cooperation itself. Even at this early stage of the discussion, the Commission under the influence of Professor Dahrendorf, set its face resolutely against using the principle of 'harmonisation' in the educational arena. This emerges clearly in the three principles on which future cooperation in the field of education was to be grounded.

The first of these recognised the right of every citizen to education. No less crucial was the notion that education ought not to be made subservient to the ups and downs of the economic cycle. Nevertheless, it was felt to be important that education should reflect major changes in the economic and social spheres of Community policy. Thus, on the one hand, the need to uphold the autonomy of education and educational practice was borne in mind whilst on the other, the need to bring education, training and employment systems more closely in tune with one another was recognised.

The second principle enunciated at the Ministers meeting of June 6th 1974 was the importance of upholding the diversity and particular character of Member State education systems. 'Cooperation', the Resolution stated, 'must make allowance for the traditions of each country and the diversity of their respective educational policies and systems' (*Official Journal No. C 982, op.cit.*). Thus, the varying patterns of power, responsibility and control and – in some cases, long established conventions which placed certain limitations on the ability of central government to intervene in specific areas of educational activity – were to be safeguarded. From the very first, the field of education departed from one of the major objectives that hitherto had been seen as part of Community policy in such areas as agriculture and customs duties. The idea of Community policy tending towards the standardisation of practice and curriculum across Member States was rigorously excluded. 'Harmonisation of these systems or policies', the Resolution of June 6th 1974 pointed out, 'cannot be considered as an end in itself'.

The third and final principle was no less crucial in setting the base-line for policy development in education. If cooperation was to involve the statement of specific objectives as part of Community policy, then the manner in which they were achieved was to remain firmly the responsibility of the individual Member State.

With the statement of these principles, the task of working out the finer details of a future action programme in education was passed over to an *ad hoc* Education Committee, drawn from representatives from the Nine Member States and Commission Officials. It reported its suggestions towards the end of 1975. The document produced by the *ad hoc* committee served as the basis for discussion between the Ministers of Education at their meeting of February 1976, when the first Community Education Action Programme was adopted. The Ministers' agreement to this is enshrined in the Resolution of February 9th 1976.

The Resolution of the Council and Ministers of Education of February 9th 1976

The Resolution of February 9th 1976 provides the specific basis for Community level action in education. It set out the objectives of the new programme together with the machinery for controlling and overseeing its implementation. With the framework provided by the main heads agreed at the June 1974 Ministers meeting, the Resolution of February 1976 set out a series of actions to be undertaken both at the level of Member States and at the level of the Community itself. Amongst the latter was a series of pilot projects to evaluate and compare teaching methods for migrant children, efforts to increase understanding between Member States of each others systems of education, with provision for study visits to assist in this directed at administrators in school systems, higher education whether at local or regional level. The development of a 'European dimension' in the thinking of both pupils and teachers was also seen as especially relevant. The programme accordingly made provision for studies to be made on extending the practice of recognising periods spent abroad as part of the individual's educational experience. And the possibility for teachers to spend part of their career abroad was touched upon. In the sphere of higher education, the Community was to undertake measures intended to strengthen contacts between individual establishments, whilst other measures such as the mutual recognition of academic qualifications were to be investigated. The teaching of foreign languages also formed an essential part of the Action Programme. In this field the programme envisaged actions at Community level to organise meetings between organisers and researchers in this area.

The passing of the Resolution of February 9th 1976 brought to a close the protracted and often difficult quest to find a basis for cooperation in education. It set down the areas in which such cooperation should concentrate and develop. It constitutes, even today, the principal foundation for research, action and development between the Community and the Member States. A further and no less interesting characteristic of the Resolution is its 'dual' character which emerged in the distinction placed between those actions to be carried out at Community level and those which fall under the purlieu and responsibility of individual Member States. The issue of foreign language teaching may serve as illustration of this division of responsibility. If the general objective laid down in the Resolution was to offer all pupils the possibility to learn at least one Community language, the measures intended to attain it are split into two. The Community was given the task of examining at Community level research findings relating to language teaching methods. The task falling to Member States involved the organisation of regular and extended periods abroad for language teachers or language assistants (*Journal Officiel des Communautés Européennes No. C 38/4,* February 19th 1976).

This 'dual' nature of the Resolution reflects some of the particular difficulties that arose in the course of negotiating the place that education should occupy in the affairs of the Commission and the establishment of procedures to underwrite it.

Decision-making machinery

Before examining the implications of the 'dual' nature of the February 1976 Resolution for the role and competence of the Commission acting in the area of education, it is as well to make a brief description of the main Community institutions. These are: The European Commission, the Council of Ministers, the Court of Justice and the European Parliament.

The Commission of the European Communities has the main responsibility for drawing up proposals for action and, if accepted, has the power to see they are carried out. It is responsible for seeing that the decisions arising from the Treaties of Paris and Rome are correctly applied. It proposes to the Council of Ministers all measures in the fields of agriculture, energy, external trade, economic and monetary union, industry, environment, research and social and regional issues likely to advance Community policy. The Commission has extensive powers to implement those Community policies that derive from the Treaties or are the basis of Council decisions. With the exception of action in the field of coal and steel, competition and nuclear energy — which are specifically covered by the Treaties — the Commission acts on mandate from the Council. It also administers common funds — the European Agricultural Guidance Guarantee Fund, intended to modernise and assist agriculture — the European Development Fund, designed to assist development in Third World countries signatory of the Lomé conventions and the European Social Fund — designed to assist young people, migrant workers, workers in the declining industries or those moving out of agriculture to find new jobs.

Headed by 14 Commissioners — two from each of the following countries: United Kingdom, France, Germany and Italy with one from each of the remaining Member States — the Commission is divided into 20 Directorates General. The Directorates General may be divided into two groups — those with a horizontal function such as the Legal, Budget and Personnel services, others with a vertical function dealing with specific policy sectors such as agriculture or external relations (Evans, *op.cit.*, p.27).

The Council of Ministers constitutes the highest decision making body. It decides the main Community policies and, within the European Community, is the supreme executive and legislative authority. Following the Greek entry to the Community on January 1st 1981, the Council now has ten members. It is composed of ministers from each Member State. The Presidency of the Council rotates between Member States, each country acting as president for a six month period. The agenda determines the type of attendance. On agricultural matters, for instance, meetings will be attended by national Ministers of Agriculture, unemployment issues will bring together Ministers of Labour. Preparatory work for these meetings is coordinated by a Committee of Permanent Representatives (COREPER) which in turn is assisted by working parties of senior civil servants from Member States. In addition, the Council has a general secretariat of some 1,900 persons (*Fifteenth General Report on the activities of the European Communities in 1981*, Luxembourg, 1982, p.29). Member States may exercise a veto if they consider their vital interest threatened.

The European Court of Justice is the final arbiter in interpreting legislation arising from the Treaties or that passed by the Community. The obligations and duties that are imposed on Member States as a result of passing of legislative instruments — Directives, Decisions or Regulations — may, after due process, be upheld by the European Court. The Commission may take a Member State before the Court if it considers, for instance, that it has broken its treaty obligations, but only after the Member State has been informed of the reasons why the Commission deems it in breach. The European Court of Justice which has ten judges, one from each of the Member States, is concerned solely with Community legislation and should not be confused with the Court of Human Rights at Strasbourg or the International Court in the Hague.

The European Parliament is the direct expression of the citizens of Europe, democratically represented. It has 434 members who sit in seven political groups in addition to which is one non-affiliated group of 10 Euro MPs (*Sixteenth General report on the activities of the European Communities,* Luxembourg,

1983, pp.24-25). In addition to political groupings, the Parliament is organised into specialised standing committees, each of which has a permanent staff in Luxembourg. There are 12 standing committees which deal with such matters as Political affairs, Legal matters, Budgets, Agriculture, regional policy. The Commission is answerable to Parliament for its action and policies. Formally, the European Parliament has the power to dismiss the 14 Commissioners, provided it can summon a two thirds majority and 50 percent of those participating back such a proposal. The role of this institution in making Community laws is mainly consultative. Prior to reaching a final decision on a proposal from the Commission, the Council of Ministers usually consults Parliament. However, under the terms of the Treaties, the Council of Ministers is not *obliged* to take note of parliamentary opinion. This is not to say that Parliament is devoid of influence. This is often exercised indirectly. Since the Commission has the power to modify its proposals at any point in the procedure prior to the Council of Ministers reaching a final decision, Parliament can often obtain modifications or even significant initiatives in the area under discussion by influencing the thinking of the Commission. Parliamentary control over the Community budget is increasing. Whereas earlier, control was exercised over some 3 percent, today it is in the region of 25 percent (Evans, *op.cit.,* p.40). Significantly, in 1982, the Parliamentary President, Pieter Dankert (Netherlands, Socialist) signed a joint declaration with the Presidents of the Council of Ministers and the Commission with a view to ensuring a more effective development of the budgetary procedure (*Sixteenth General Report . . . op.cit.,* p.25).

Decision-making machinery in the educational domain:
Because education does not figure in the Treaty of Rome, the administrative relationships and responsibilities between the main community institutions such as the Commission, the Council of Ministers and the Member States rest on a slightly different footing. This explains the notion of the 'dual' nature of the February 9th 1976 Resolution, which springs from the need to stress the voluntary agreement entered into by Ministers of Education of Member States to discuss matters pertaining to education. Thus, if Community level action is agreed upon by Ministers, they still reserve the right to draw up policy within the framework of their own countries. As in other areas of Community activity, the Council of Ministers acts as the highest executive and legislative authority, but the fact that Ministers of Education meet does not imply that their discussions have implications for Community level activity. If matters engaging a budgetary responsibility are raised this requires the use of a complicated formula, designed, once again, to stress the voluntary nature of their decision. In Education, therefore, the formula used to describe the meeting of the Council of Ministers having decision making powers that the Commission subsequently acts upon is 'The Meeting of the Council of the European Communities and of the Ministers of Education meeting within the Council'.

A further difference between Education and other areas of responsibility inside the Commission is the presence of the Education Committee. The

Education Committee was placed on a regular and permanent footing by the Resolution of February 9th 1976 (*Journal Officiel des Communautés Européennes No. C 38/1*, February 19th 1976). Having worked in an *ad hoc* capacity to draw up the details for a proposed Education Action Programme, it was given the main task of exercising general oversight on the Programme once it had been accepted by the Ministers. The Education Committee has a unique place in Community structures. Procedurally, it operates along lines usually associated with the Council of Ministers. This is reflected in its composition which is drawn from representatives of the ten Member States and Commission officials (Council note on the Education Committee, *Document R/2723/75 (EN 118)*, November 6th 1975). Delegations from Member States are nominated from the national Ministries of Education or, in the case of Belgium and the Federal Republic of Germany, are chosen in keeping with the particular way in which education is organised in those two countries. Since Belgium has two Ministries of Education, one for the French speaking parts of the country and another for the Flemmish speaking parts, both Ministries are represented. Similarly, delegations from the Federal Republic of Germany include representatives from the *Laender* as well as the Federal Ministry of Education. The United Kingdom delegation often contains officials from the Scottish Education Department, the Northern Ireland Department of Education, representatives from Wales and the Department of Education and Science in London.

Like the Chairmanship of the Council of Ministers, that of the Education Committee rotates every six months and is held by the country currently presiding over the Council. Its secretariat is drawn from the staff of the Council Secretariat. If, from a procedural point of view, the Education Committee follows the pattern set down in the Council of Ministers, its existence serves to underline once again, the voluntary nature of the agreement by Ministers of Education to work together on a continuing basis that, formally, remains outside the legal framework of the Council of Ministers.

Vis-à-vis the Education Committee, the Commission, which has full membership of this body, has a dual role. This stems from the fact that in some instances, items for consideration fall within the terms of the Treaty of Rome. In others, they do not and therefore require intergovernmental agreement. In relation to the Education Committee, the role of the Commission is to prepare proposals for consideration and, in the case of Community level actions, to see that they are carried out. The Commission also administers the Community's education budget. In this, as in the matter of commissioning research, designating expert consultants, awarding scholarships, the Commission exercises complete autonomy *vis-à-vis* the Committee ('Comité dé l'Education: modalités de fonctionnement', *Document T/136/ 76 (EN)*, February 16th 1976, p.5).

For its part, the Education Committee reports to the Council and to the Ministers of Education meeting within the Council ('Council note on the Education Committee', *Document R/ 2723/75 (EN 118)... op.cit.*). In addition to its responsibility for coordinating and monitoring the progress of the Community

The Background

Education Action Programme, the Education Committee prepares the meetings of the Council and of the Ministers of Education. It may also make proposals, where appropriate, for further action in the field of cooperation. On average, the Education Committee meets every six weeks.

As we have already noted, the Commission's Education services were originally located inside the Directorate General XII, being sectorally linked with Science and Research. Vocational training, already established since 1963, occupied a separate place within the ambit of Directorate General V, being linked with Social Affairs. This separation of powers continued until 1981 when, following the establishment of a new Commission and a redistribution of portfolios in 1980, education and vocational training were brought together under the ambit of the Directorate General for Social Policy – Directorate General V. The Directorate General, which comes under the responsibility of the Commissioner for Social Affairs, Mr Ivor Richard, is sub-divided into four directorates. These are i. Employment, Living and working conditions and welfare, ii. Education, vocational training and youth policy, iii. the European Social Fund and, finally, Health and Safety.

The Planning Context

The administrative reshuffle which brought education and training together under the same Directorate has sometimes been presented as marking a third stage in the development of Community education activities (Jones, *op.cit.*). Certainly, it allowed a closer link to grow up between the planning of education measures and the setting up of new training initiatives. And, to this extent, it does indeed mark a new point of departure. But the prime force that led to this step — namely the rise of youth unemployment in the Community as a whole — was not a new phenomenon. Quite the contrary, the effects of the economic crisis had been visible since the time the first Community Education Action Programme was first drawn up and had not been without influence upon the subsequent development of that Programme.

If we take the period from the Ministers of Education meeting in June 1974 up to the amalgamation of the Commission's education services with the Social Policy field in January 1981 as a whole, it is possible to see more precisely the way in which Community action in education was affected by the economic crisis and, more to the point, how the crisis forced the Commission fundamentally to rethink the assumptions on which its educational planning rested.

Already during the run up to the promulgation of the Education Action Programme in February 1976, the Commission had to face the possibility that the Programme could not be implemented in its entirety. Towards the end of 1975, therefore the Commission opted for a rather more limited action than was first envisaged. Particular importance was attached to those measures aimed at easing the transition of young people from school to working life ('Mise en oeuvre du programme d'action au niveau communautaire', *Document SEC (76) 216*, January 1st 1976). In discussion with the Education Committee, it was decided that the Action Programme should be divided into six priority

15

sectors of which the last should be left to the second stage of implementation. These sectors were:

- the exchange of information on the organisation of appropriate measures in education for the children of migrant workers;
- regular confrontation meetings between educational administrators with a view to discussing such matters as the possibility for teachers to spend part of their careers in an EEC country other than their own;
- development of documentation and statistics;
- joint study projects and the elaboration of criteria on which they could develop;
- equality of opportunity with particular regard to the preparation of young people moving from school to working life and the provision within the framework of 'formation continue' of complementary studies to permit young workers and those unemployed to improve their chances of finding work;
- preliminary work on the national administration of grants for students, researchers and teachers with a further report on the existing position as regards the recognition of academic diplomas by other Member States and means to improve it (*ibid.*).

The Ministers' meeting of February 1976, however, attached special weight to one section of the Community Action programme — namely, the preparation of young people for work and the transition from school to working life. A report on this was asked for which, after consideration by the Education Committee, was presented to the Council and Ministers of Education meeting in December 1976. It was subsequently incorporated into the Resolution passed by the Ministers on December 13th 1976. A more detailed analysis of the subsequent development of the Transition Programme — one of the more powerful vehicles for cross national cooperation to emerge from the Commission — will be undertaken in Chapter Three.

At the time of the February Resolution of 1976, youth unemployment was assumed to be 'conjunctural' — a passing phenomenon that would disappear as the economy picked up. Thus Commission planning tended to emphasise the identification of particular groups more vulnerable than most to the effects of the recession. Its focus lay upon relatively short term measures — reinforcing the vocational training element in education being one. This did not necessarily require a rethinking of the Commission's strategy, though several sources indicate a growing awareness of the need to coordinate education and the different elements in the social policy field ('Preparation of young people for working life and for transition from education to work', *Document R/ 32290 E/76 (EN 52)*, October 8th 1976). By the latter part of 1978, belief in the short term nature of youth unemployment could no longer be sustained. Commenting on the implications for educational planning, a Commission document pointed out: 'Even the overall objectives of employment policy are being revised in relation to the development potential of the education sector. The Community Action Programme in the field of education has therefore more far-reaching implications than originally envisaged in 1976' ('Cooperation in the field of education: a progress report', *Document R/ 2797/78 (EN 61),* November 31st 1978). If the emergence of long term youth unemployment gave added weight to the Transition Programme, it also called for radical rethinking in the Commission's approach to the question. The view taken by the Education services was that once-off modifications to education on the one hand and vocational training on the other were no longer credible as ways of alleviating short term pressures on the labour market. Rather, what was required was a closer, integrated planning between the two sectors of education and training. Both systems, it was argued, should serve as instruments for long term adaptation to those developments both in society and in the economy which, at present, could only dimly be perceived (*Document 6844/84 (EDUC 18) Annex 1,* May 12th 1981).

Officially, the call for a new approach to educational planning, the development of a strategy rather than a series of tactical measures, emerged at the meeting of Ministers of Education in Luxembourg on June 22nd 1981. If the integrated approach to educational planning received added impetus with the displacement of the Education Services of the Commission from Science and Research and their inclusion in the Social Policy Directorate in 1981, the change in perspective antedated this move.

This qualitative change in the Commission's approach to planning its educational activities has taken a number of forms. In the first place, the new approach to bring education and vocational training closer together was given a further boost in 1982 with the proposal, set before the Council, for new guidelines in the vocational training field. In the second place, changes in the terms of reference of the European Social Fund stand in the offing. The Commission has put forward the notion that young people under 18 should be eligible for support immediately after completing compulsory education. Hitherto, the Social Fund was restricted to supporting initial training schemes for youngsters over 18 years officially registered as unemployed. And, finally, one effect of the new planning context has been to move education from the periphery to the centre of the Community's preoccupations (Jones, *op.cit.,* pp.28, 5).

Structure of the report:

It is against such a background that this account of the European Communities' activities in education should be seen. Chronologically, the main period covered runs from 1976 until 1982, though in the case of Chapter Four, Education and Training, this has been broadened, going back to 1963 since it is from this time that the first initiatives were taken. In essence, the areas and topics covered correspond to the major points laid down in the Community Education Action Programme. Thus, Chapter Two deals with activities relating to the education of Migrants and their families, Chapter Three with Transition from school to working life, Chapter Five with Cooperation in higher education, and Chapter Six with those developments associated with that part of the February 1976 Resolution that touched upon Equality of Educational Opportunity. Chapter Seven examines what is often termed 'The European Dimension in education'. This, in effect, encompasses a relatively wide-ranging series of activities, designed in the main, to improve the knowledge of young people about Europe, its culture, history, languages and civic traditions. These aspects represent what might be called 'the first generation' activities of the Commission in the educational field. At the time of writing, others are being developed, amongst them, the new programme for the handicapped and initiatives dealing with the implications of the new information technologies for both education and training. Chapters Eight and Nine give an account of developments in these two domains. They are of particular interest since they show clearly the emergence of a new approach to Community action projects, an approach that tends to emphasise not merely the issue of integration between different areas of social and educational administration, but also the importance attached by the Commission to activities firmly rooted in the local community. Chapter Ten traces the main developments in the Community's Education Information Network EURYDICE. EURYDICE is one of the main instruments by which policy makers in one Member State may be kept abreast of the latest developments in others. It is, then an important instrument for cooperation in education. However, the Community is not alone in sharing many of the current preoccupations that beset the world of education. Chapter Eleven shows the working links that exist between the Commission's Education services and the major international organisations such as the Council of Europe in Strasbourg and the Organisation for Economic Cooperation and Development in Paris.

In recent years, it has become fashionable to argue that innovation and educational change do not go well with economic stagnation. If this might be true in some countries or appear true to certain groups within them, it is not true for all. Indeed, the Community Education Action Programme, launched at the onset of the economic crisis, has not merely evolved, but also provided the vehicle for significant innovations at grass roots level as well. It has, in short, shown that contraction is not necessarily inimical either to change or to those efforts required to rethink the type of provision that the future may require us to envisage. How this has been tackled, the findings and results of the various projects studies and programmes that the Commission has sponsored over the past six years, the ways in which interests have been fostered and action undertaken — the reality of Community action in education, rather than the myth — these are the subjects of this account.

The Background

SOURCES:
i. Primary: internal Commission Documents.
Document R/2489/ 75 (EN111), October 10th 1975
'Council note on the education Committee', *Document No R/ 2723/75 (EN 118),* November 6th 1975.
'Mise en oeuvre du programme d'action au niveau communautaire', *Document No SEC (76) 216,* January 21st 1976.
'Comité de l'éducation; modalités de fonctionnement', *Document No T/136/76 (EN)* February 16th 1976.
'Preparation of young people for working life and for transition from education to work', *Document R/32290/ e 76 (EN 52),* October 8th 1976.
'Cooperation in the field of education: a progress report', *Document No R/ 2797/78 (EN 67),* October 31st 1978.
Document No 8638 (EDUC 33), July 10th 1980.
Document No 6844/81 (EDUC 18) Annex 1, May 12th 1981.
'714 ième session du Conseil et des Ministres de l'Education réunis au sein du Conseil', Luxembourg le 22 juin 1981 (xerox).
Secretariat General of the Council, *Press Release No 2257/11,* November 16th 1971.

ii. Secondary: printed sources, official documents
'For a community policy in education', *Bulletin of the European Communities (supplement), 10/73,* 1973.
'Education in the European Community', *Bulletin of the European Communities supplement 3/74,* 1974.
Official Journal No C. 98/2, August 20th 1974.
Official Journal No. C 38/1, February 19th 1976.
Impact of demographic change on education systems in the European Community, Brussels, EURYDICE, 1981.
'Education and training', *EUROSTAT Bulletin 2/1982,* OSCE.
Fifteenth General Report on the activities of the European Communities in 1981, Luxembourg 1982.
Sixteenth General Report on the activities of the European Communities in 1982, Luxembourg 1983.

iii. Tertiary: pamphlets, articles from non-Commission sources:
Dennis Evans, *An Accountants guide to the European Communities,* London, Macdonald and Evans, 1981.
R. Gwyn, 'Towards a European policy for initial teacher education', *European Journal of Education,* vol. 14, No. 4, 1979.
Hywel C. Jones, 'Education in The European Community', *Address to the North of England Education Conference,* Liverpool, January 1983 (xerox).
Guy Neave, 'Recent trends in education policy in Western Europe' in Colin Brock, Patricia Broadfoot & Witold Tulasiewicz (eds.), *Politics and Educational Change,* London, Croom Helm, 1981.
Guy Neave, 'Education systems under pressure – a wider perspective: The planning response of certain Western European countries to the demographic and economic crises', *Educational Management and Administration,* vol. 11, No. 2, June 1983, pp.120ff.

Chapter Two

The Education of Migrants and their Families

Structure:

Introduction
The extent of migration in the European Community
Commission thinking on migrant policy
Community activities
Mechanisms of policy and development
Specific pilot projects
   1. Reception methods
   2. Teaching the language and culture of origin
   3. Development of specialised programmes for teacher training
   4. Diffusion of teaching materials
Links with the Council of Europe and UNESCO
Research studies
Development of information exchange
Eurydice (The European Community's Education Information Network)
Role of the European Social Fund
Conclusion

Notes
SOURCES

Introduction:
To seek work in other Member States on the same terms as those enjoyed by the citizens of such countries is one of the fundamental rights of nationals in the European Communities. Mobility of labour is then, one of the touchstones of Community policy. However, this principle cannot be viewed solely within the areas of employment and social policy. There are many sorts of migrants. Some for instance are seasonal workers moving into France to help with the grape harvest. Others, from Britain for instance, cross the North Sea to the Netherlands or to Germany to work on short term contract labour. Eventually, both will return to their homelands. But there is a third group for whom migration is not a short spell in foreign parts, earning good money to be spent at home. For this latter group, migration means permanent settlement abroad. They bring with them wife and children who also have to adjust to the culture and customs of the host country, learn its language and acquire its ways.

The phenomenon of permanent settlers, seeking a new life, is of course well established in the United States, Canada and Australia. And, as a result, their education policy has been heavily influenced in dealing with the inflow of new citizens. This has not been the case in most Western European countries. Rather their education systems have been attuned to the demands of relatively homogenous populations, speaking the same language — or its derivative dialects — and sharing broadly the same cultural values.

The necessity for education systems to adjust to large movements of population is not, in itself, new. In the course of the 19th and early 20th centuries, industrialisation and the flight from the land which accompanied it, placed immense strain on the national education systems of Europe. For all that, transnational migration has given rise to a new situation. It has brought in its wake large numbers of people whose culture, values and languages differ profoundly from those of the host country. Such a situation has brought about considerable debate at all levels of society. How far should education explicitly undertake cultural assimilation? To what extent should the host country assume the responsibility of ensuring that children and young people of migrant origin remain in touch with their home culture? What should the schools do to avoid creating an alienated sub-proletariat living on the margins of society?

The extent of migration in the European Community:
By 1975, some 13,500,000 immigrants resided in the Member States of the European Community. Since then this figure has fallen and stands today at some 12,000,000. In short, one inhabitant in twenty in Community countries has immigrant origin. Within the more precise field of education, the total enrolments of migrant children in schools throughout the Community is in the region of one and a half million. More than two thirds of these children come from countries outside the Ten from Spain, Yugoslavia, Portugal and Turkey. Taken

overall, the number of migrant children in the age group 0-14 for all Community States with the exception of Greece and Italy amounts to 8.1 percent of that age cohort in 1981. This population is not evenly distributed across the different countries. There are considerable variations in the proportion of immigrant children aged 0-14 which range from 1.8 percent in Ireland to 31.8 percent in Luxembourg. And though the birth rate amongst migrant families is falling, it still tends to be higher than the native population. This means, in effect, that over the next few years both the numbers and the proportion of children with this background will tend to rise. Indeed, some estimates reckon that between 1980 and 1990, the major urban areas of the Community will have to come to grips with the fact that second and third generation migrants will account for between 20 to 40 percent of all young people leaving school and seeking places on the job market.

At present, pressure to meet the requirements of migrants and their families is concentrated on the pre-school and primary level of Community education systems. Over the next few years, this will change and the main burden of adaptation will come to bear on secondary schools as the bulk of migrant children work their way up the school system.

Commission thinking on migrant policy:

Thus the development of migrant communities across Western Europe is an important element not merely for social policy in general but also for education in particular. Community policy on the issue of migrant education has undergone considerable alteration over the past few years, with the result that current thinking inside the Education Services of the Commission now tends to associate the specific problems of education for migrants and their families with the rather broader issue of social deprivation in general, on the grounds that if not all migrants are deprived neither are all the deprived migrants. Indeed, recent Commission studies suggest that some 350,000 children across the Community may be reckoned to suffer deprivation. 200,000 of these are children of migrant workers. The remaining 150,000 are children of the so-called 'Fourth World' – the twilight zone of transmitted and intergenerational deprivation existing on the edge of most industrialised societies.

But even if migrants do share many aspects of deprivation with certain groups in the home population, nevertheless, they face very specific problems of their own that tend to amplify such disadvantage. Prime amongst these are often inadequate command of the host country's language, a mismatch between the schooling received prior to emigration and that provided in the country of settlement and, in consequence, both a low level of achievement and a high level of grade repeating. In addition, there are particular difficulties faced by second generation migrants. Though straightforward linguistic problems may be less amongst this group, there still remains the acute problem of competing with young nationals of the host country for places on the labour market. To the extent that second generation migrants face the same situation as their native counterparts between the ages of 15 and 25, they cannot be said to form a group apart. Though their situation may be more exaggerated, as a result of a 'tighter labour market', their difficulties are essentially the same as any young person with a similar level of qualification from that particular age range.

The essential similarity between the obstacles faced by young people in general and migrants no less so, has changed the policy perspective within the Commission. The view is now held that measures designed to alleviate some of the difficulties of migrant workers and their families are inseparable from a more wide-ranging strategy the general purpose of which is to bring relief to the problem of economic and social deprivation, shared by migrants and native populations alike.

Community activities:

Community education activities in the area of migrant families have a dual basis, the first being contained in the Social Action Programme set out in the Council Resolution of 21st January 1974, the second in the form of the Education Action Programme endorsed by the Ministers of Education at their meeting of 9th February 1976. Until the reorganisation of the Commission's services in 1981, these two programmes involved close cooperation between the two Directorates concerned, the Directorate General XII (Education) and the Directorate General V (Social Affairs). Together, both Resolutions cover all migrant workers, irrespective of whether they are nationals of Member States or third countries, though certain aspects such as freedom of access to employment and social security may not pertain in the latter category.

The Education Action Programme identified a series of measures to be carried out first by Member States and second, by joint action at Community level. For their part, Member States agreed to undertake the following measures:

- the development and organisation of reception centres to provide accelerated language courses for migrants in the tongue of the host country;
- they would, as appropriate, provide more facilities for teaching such migrant children their mother tongue and culture, if possible in school and in collaboration with the country of origin;
- they would provide more information for migrant families about the training and educational facilities available to them.

The first two measures were taken up in Directive 77/486/CEE passed on July 27th 1977. They came into force in July 1981. Specifically, the Directive requires the host country to facilitate the initial reception of children who are nationals of a Member State, through tuition in either the official language or one of the official languages of the country. The host country must ensure that teachers responsible for the education of these children have appropriate initial training and, where necessary, further training. Finally, it must also ensure that the teaching of the migrant children's mother tongue and culture is promoted in cooperation with the country of origin and in coordination with normal education.

The Directive is binding only where it concerns children who are dependents of another Member State's nationals who have been — or are currently — employed in the state where the children are resident and in coordination with normal education. The Council adopted a declaration in which it expressed its resolve to extend this to all categories of immigrants irrespective of their country of origin. Nevertheless, taken in conjunction with the Resolution passed at the 9th Session of the Standing Conference of European Ministers of Education held in 1975 at Stockholm, this directive is a major step towards creating those educational structures able to meet the particular requirements of migrant workers' children. Furthermore, it opens up a new perspective to cooperation in education by requiring that the host country's policy in the teaching of the mother tongue and culture pay some regard to the practices found in the homeland.

If we look at the broad lines of Community strategy towards migrants and their families however, it is possible to detect two main lines of development. The first of these emerged from the original purpose of the Communities as an economic entity. It is enshrined in Regulation 1612/68[1] governing the freedom of movement for Member State nationals and their families within the Community. Article 7 states that a worker who is national of a Member State shall *'by virtue of the same right and under the same conditions as national workers, have access to training in vocational schools and retraining centres'*. Article 12 stipulates that *'the children of a national of a Member State who is or has been employed in the territory of another Member State shall be admitted to that State's general educational, apprenticeship and vocational training courses under the same conditions as the nationals of that state if such children are residing in its territory'* and further, that *'Member States shall encourage all efforts to enable such children to attend these courses under the best possible conditions'*. Thus, the educational rights of migrant workers' children were, because education did not feature then as an aspect of Community policy, subsumed as one of the conditions under which the economic construction of the Community took place. In this respect, it is significant that the educational aspect of what remained basically a policy of vocational training, was couched in terms of *access* to education. It is clear, however, that Regulation 1612/68 had direct educational implications and constituted a direct legal instrument which Directive 77/486/CEE later elaborated upon in more specific detail and form.

This perspective changed with the passing of the Education Action Programme in February 9th 1976. From that moment, education policy began to focus more specifically on those issues of a linguistic, cultural and pedagogic nature that conditioned, not so much *access to education*, as the *determinants of successful participation* in education by such children. Its attention turned to the type of structures, provision and facilities, teaching methods and techniques specific to various levels of the incoming child population.

1. *Official Journal C. 2572,* October 19th 1968.

Prepartion for this move began already in 1974 as part of the more detailed elaboration for future fields of action of the Education Action Programme. Expert groups brought together by the Commission discussed various models of reception systems and reception methods. The following year, in 1975, discussion was broadened to include teaching the mother tongue, issues contained in basic education and the in-service training of teachers. In 1976, amongst the topics broached were pre-primary education as well as educational and vocational guidance. With the groundwork thus laid, the Education Action Programme set out vehicles for the development of policy in this domain. These were:

- 'pilot projects' based on an action research procedure;
- research studies;
- the development of information exchange;
- EURYDICE (The European Community's Education Information Network).

Mechanisms of policy and development:

Pilot projects are designed to act at three separate levels between individual Member States and the Commission. First, at the level of local school structures and teaching methods. Here, the stated aims of the projects are seen as stimulating the adaptation of the former and the improvement of the latter. Second, being linked with the Ministry of Education, they may influence action carried out at national level. One particularly striking instance of this is the decree published by the Danish Ministry of Education in October 1981. As a result of the Odense pilot project (*details of which see p.II, infra*) children of immigrants now have the possibility of being taught in their mother tongue in pre-primary school. They will also have the right to continue primary education in the same school where they received pre-primary education. Third, the development of good relationships at the local level between the respective national research teams responsible for the probject. This often creates new channels through which alternative possibilities and solutions developed elsewhere may interact. Particular weight is attached by the Commission to the development of the second and third levels of policy development. The heuristic value of interplay between researchers, and those involved in individual pilot projects at the local level, is underlined by increasing the budget for study visits among these groups of individuals.

The purpose of the pilot projects is to show, by means of experiments whether the various schemes outlined for further research and evaluation, are practical so that conclusions may be drawn that are valid for all Member States.

Research studies follow a more classical mould in the Commission's approach to policy development. They are designed to elicit an overall view of the state of knowledge in a stipulated domain as a means of developing specific ideas that may later be incorporated into pilot projects. Rather than being addressed to practitioners and researchers who may form the principle constituency in the case of the pilot projects, they are aimed at administrators and researchers.

Such was the case, for example, of the colloquy that met in May 1976 which brought together experts — sociologists, linguists and educationalists — from both Europe and the United States and Canada to discuss vocational and pre-vocational training for migrants' children. It was organised by AIMAV, an international research association for applied linguistics, based at the University of Ghent (Belgium) and took place under the auspices of the Commission.

Information exchange, by contrast, may be looked upon as the basic level, though no less important for that, in the ascending hierarchy of educational policy and action. Such an approach is intended to identify the general problematic as conceived by those affected by it or their representatives, in this instance, migrants associations. They are often regarded as key to assessing the needs of this group and in overcoming any distrust or lack of knowledge that prevents them from benefitting from facilities already placed at their disposal. One such instance was the meeting held on October 13th-14th 1981 at which the association *Information, Culture et Immigration France* presented an outline of its activities and working methods in the area of cooperation with the media, with ministries and migrants' associations. Another, which took place three years previously in November 1978, involved an exchange of views between senior civil servants of the national Ministries of Education and representatives of the media in which the British Broadcasting Commission showed programmes designed for migrants and their families. A further meeting on this topic took place in December 1979. The role that radio and television might play in the social integration of migrant workers and in maintaining the language and culture of origin were the principal topics of discussion.

Unlike other areas of Community education policy, projects dealing with the education of migrant workers' children rely on a slightly different model of diffusion. This is carried out by a series of seminars and colloquies with the projects themselves acting as a vehicle for diffusing good practice. Learning by example is thought to be a particularly potent way of developing more sensitive insights into alternative strategies for innovation. By this means, participants from other projects may test out the developments learned in the context of one particular region and apply them to other circumstances. Two such meetings were held in the course of 1982 in Limbourg (Belgium) and Marseille (France) during April and June. Based on the findings of the two projects in these areas, they discussed developments in integrated teaching of both the language and culture of origin and inter-cultural education.

Specific pilot projects:

Pilot projects, launched in September 1976, have centred on the following issues: ways for receiving and 'acclimatising' the young migrant into his new social, cultural and linguistic environment; teaching the language and upholding the culture of origin; the development of specialised programmes for teacher training; the diffusion of teaching materials.

1. Reception methods:

Four pilot projects to investigate various models of reception techniques have so far been undertaken, at Winterslag/Waterschei (Belgium) between 1976-1979, Leiden (the Netherlands) between 1977-1979, Enschede (the Netherlands) on going from 1979 and, finally in the Odense area (Denmark) between 1979 and 1981. The first of these, at Winterslag/Waterschei had four objectives: to provide intensive language teaching in Dutch, to maintain fluency in the mother tongue, to integrate new arrivals into their host environment and to develop the basic skills in reading, writing and arithmetic. The foreign classes were made up of 2/3 migrants' children — Turkish, Greek and Italian in the main — and 1/3 Belgian. Language competence tests were administered at the beginning of the project and progress regularly monitored, against two control groups. Foreign pupils in the experimental group at Waterschei made clear progress in vocabulary, command of the spoken language and reading Dutch, though less in the written language. Interestingly, the immigrants tuition in their mother tongue had a positive influence on their progress in Dutch.

The psychological gains of this approach were especially important. The fact that their language was taught in school appeared to enhance migrant children's self esteem and, no less relevant was the fact that weaker pupils showed a higher gain score in the areas tested than their abler peers. The crucial factor accounting for this encouraging result is felt to be the high degree of coordination between class teachers and foreign teachers as well as a highly effective educational backup.

The Leiden project was designed to test a reception model for new arrivals and involved bringing all such children together in a single school acting as a reception centre. For the first three weeks the youngsters, mainly Moroccan and Turkish, are taught by someone of their own nationality. Dutch language teaching is based initially, on short periods and subsequently becomes more intensive. After two years, the children join a class of their own age group in a neighbourhood school. Subsequent observation after one year's integration in the neighbourhood school showed that little problem existed for 6-8 year olds. 8-10 year olds, however, showed some difficulty with Dutch.

Another variation in reception techniques has been tried out at Enschede from 1979 onwards. In the first stages, it involved creating a separate class for Moroccan and Turkish children though linked with a class of Dutch youngsters. At first, teaching is conducted in the native language. Dutch is taught by Dutch specialist teachers to small groups of 4 to 5 pupils, this taking place between the two twinned classes. Both classes, Dutch and immigrant follow a common core which, beginning with singing and gymnastics, is gradually extended as the latter begin to master Dutch. This system of associated classes ends after two years and Dutch becomes the main medium of teaching.

The Odense experiment was intended to deal with problems of reception for immigrant children in areas of low immigrant density. Here, youngsters are taught the rudiments of Danish by intensive methods and, after six months, are placed in the class corresponding to their age group. In contrast to the other pilot projects, there is no period of linguistic or cultural transition. The child's home language is not taught and, during the reception period, he is surrounded by people who have no knowledge of his mother tongue. This experiment is relatively limited and involved around 20 migrant children. The intensive use of audio-visual material is thought to be a most efficient method.

2. Teaching the language and culture of origin:

Five pilot projects have been involved in maintaining the language of origin and its accompanying culture. These took place in Paris (France) between 1976 and 1979, Bedford (England) between 1976 and 1980, London (England) between 1980 and 1981, Marseille (France) and the Belgian area of Limbourg, the latter two continuing still.

The Paris project, covering 15 experimental classes spread over 7 schools, involved five classes of Italian, four each of Spanish and Portuguese and two of Serbo-Croat. Each class enjoyed three hours per week devoted to the home language and culture. The purpose of this exercise was to keep children in contact with the life and culture of origin, to improve their reinsertion in the event they should return home, to make them more sensitive to the norms and values of French culture, hopefully, in order to facilitate their learning of French. Two types of studies were carried out. The first provided a description of pupil behaviour in different school classes and during play periods. The second was an analysis of behaviour, controlling for nationality, the schools attended, and assessment by teachers, both French and foreign, of each individual pupil. Interesting divergences were found between the assessment by French and foreign teachers of the same pupil. However, it seems that, insofar as the objective of the programme was to make French teachers, parents and pupils more aware of and open to the presence of young immigrants, it has been successful. If, at the start French teachers showed some hostility towards the project, an inquiry in 1977 revealed that 80 percent were in favour of teaching the language of origin and an extremely high level of those replying were in favour of continuing it on into secondary education.

In Bedford, Italian and Pundjabi were taught for five hours a week to around 100 Italian and Pundjabi pupils, spread over four primary schools. The experiment, continued over four years had similar aims as the Paris project. In addition, assessments have been carried out in the areas of cognitive development, development of the child's self image, his relations with his peers and with teachers, the level of attainment in the mother tongue and the extent to which he has integrated with the school.

The London experiment, carried out through the Inner London Education Authority involves teaching Greek and Bengali integrated as part of the normal school curriculum.

The pilot project in Marseille, started in September 1979, may be seen as a continuation of the Paris pilot project. Run in three primary schools, it involves teaching for one period per week in Portuguese, Turkish and Arabic. Class teachers are given assistance by foreign colleagues during this period.

The Limburg experiment is centred around the integrated teaching of both language and culture of origin. Two school centres at Maasmechelen (Limburg) joined up with those at Winterslag/Waterschei. The principle aim of this project is to improve coordination between Belgian teachers and their foreign colleagues in the drawing up of lessons to ensure that the base disciplines (*activités d'éveil*) contain an intercultural element. In first and second grades, foreign teachers also take part in mathematics teaching.

3. Development of specialised programmes for teacher training:

It is self evident that innovations such as language teaching to young children, the pedagogic problems associated with bilingual classes or a multicultural curriculum demand equally important changes in the training of teachers to carry them out. Initiatives in this direction were undertaken in the two school years 1977-78 and 1976-77 by the Schools Branch of the French Ministry of Education in collaboration with the *Centre de Recherches et d'Etudes pour la Diffusion du Francais* (CREDIF, or the Research centre for the study and dissemination of the French language). In 1976-77, three in-service training courses were put on at Douai, Grenoble and Lyon. They concentrated on the problems of initial reception for children of kindergarten age as well as the problems of remedial education for incoming migrant children. The following year, particular emphasis was placed on the development of teaching techniques and the preparation of suitable curriculum materials. An evaluation of these courses was carried out by CREDIF in 1976.

A similar initiative was taken during the academic year 1980-81 by the Belgian Ministry of Education. In-service training for teachers of migrant children was set up. It revealed a pressing need for the establishment of in-service courses as well as documentation centres for this category of teacher.

But, as we have seen, the problem of bilingual education cannot concern the teachers from the host country alone. It must also involve those involved in imparting the language of origin. One such scheme, developed in the school year 1976-77 by the Research Group *Ausbildung von Lehrern von Ausländerkinder* – ALFA, jointly sponsored by the North Rhine Westphalia Ministry of Education and the Italian Consulate-General in Dortmund, brought together Italian teachers working in both reception and normal classes. The seminar covered such topics as teaching Italian as a first language, and the development of suitable methods and materials. The culture and geography of the host country were also touched upon. The following year, similar courses were organised for Greek teachers.

Despite the Commission's sustained and active commitment to developing teacher training programmes in this area, it remains nevertheless a fact that one of the major difficulties is to obtain qualified teachers from amongst the migrant community itself. This is essential if the use of the mother tongue in schools is to be maintained. Even in established teacher training programmes, though the situation is slowly changing, little attention is paid to the problems of immigrant children either in initial or in in-service programmes. The Commission has called for the strengthening of existing courses in this field and for new ones to be set up to meet this need.

4. Diffusion of teaching materials:

Though in many of the examples already examined, the question of preparing suitable materials to accord with bi- or multi-lingual education has figured in an ancillary position, in the long run no teaching technique, however inspired, can go very far on outdated and irrelevant material. Since 1980, the development of primary school materials for the integrated teaching of Italian culture and language is being undertaken by the Italian Institute for the Encyclopaedia, supported by the Commission. These materials in the first instance, will be used for the education of immigrant Italian youngsters in conjunction with the French Ministry of Education and the Belgian Ministry of Education for the French-speaking areas.

In this connection, a two day meeting was held on December 9th and 10th 1981 at which the *Istituto della Enciclopedia Italiana* presented its products to representatives from the Education Ministries of Italy, France, Belgium and Luxembourg. Also in attendance were experts from Germany, France and the United Kingdom. The presentation of audio-visual and printed materials for Italian pupils following integrated language and culture of origin classes at primary level, marked the completion of the first phase of this project. The second phase, launched in 1983, provides suitable material for the children of Italian immigrants in Germany.

The Commission is also planning to participate with the German Federal and Land authorities in a project designed to develop programmes and teaching material for Turkish-language pupils at secondary level. This is intended to replace English as a first optional foreign language for young Turkish speakers.

In the United Kingdom, the Commission is also associated with the London-based Linguistic Minorities Project undertaken by the London University Institute of Education, and sponsored by the English Department of Education and Science. This project has *inter alia,* the task of preparing teaching materials for staff involved with such groups. In addition, the Commission has funded a Language Information Coordination Network, a unit whose purpose is to improve ways of disseminating information in this area across the European Community. This unit, funded by the Commission for two years from January 1981-December 1982, works in close collaboration with the Linguistic Minorities Project.

The purpose of the pilot projects is to try out, develop, evaluate and to disseminate good practice.

What then may be said to be the most important points of general application thrown up by these projects? The first is that it is perfectly possible to educate together groups of children from different linguistic and cultural backgrounds. Second, that the development of integrated curricula is especially important, not merely for the educational progress of incoming migrant children, but also for their self esteem. Third, that the preparation of lessons in all subject areas is enhanced by sustained coordination between host country teachers and their foreign colleagues. Fourth, that parental participation in primary school and more particularly in pre-school activities is highly important.

Links with the Council of Europe and Unesco:

Throughout the development of the pilot project programme, the Commission has followed closely the progress made by similar undertakings, carried out under the Council of Europe in countries both within and outside the European Communities. Coordination between the programmes of the two institutions takes place on the basis of an annual meeting. Direct cooperation is maintained through two research bodies — the Essen-West German based *Ausbildung von Lehrern für Ausländerkinder* and the *Laboratoire de Recherche en Sciences Sociales de l'Ecole Normale Superieure de Saint-Cloud* (LARESSO) in Paris. Each is involved in projects on the education of migrants for both the Council of Europe and the Commission. Resolutions passed by the Council's Committee for Cultural Cooperation continue to influence the Commission's work in this field.

Equally helpful to the Commission in deciding which direction its activities should take, have been contacts with Unesco. Several meetings between the two organisations took place on questions relating to multi-cultural teaching and bi-cultural education for the children of migrant workers.

The Commission is also working with the Council of Europe in the development of a pupil profile system (*livret scolaire*). It is designed to help teachers in host countries evaluate the previous achievement of pupils coming from other Member States. The *livret scolaire* will, as far as possible, be based on standardised items of evaluation (see *infra,* Chapter XI, pp.000).

Research studies:

Research-based enquiries, in contrast to development-based projects, form the second of the three elements in drawing up the Commission's education strategy in this area. A review of the background literature on learning difficulties faced by migrant children in acquiring the language of the host country was undertaken by the International Association for Applied Linguistics (*Association internationale pour la recherche et la diffusion des méthodes audio-visuelles et structuro-globales*) based at Ghent University (Belgium). Carried out in 1975-76, it also included reference to the role of the mother tongue and to the sociolinguistic dimension of bi-lingualism in children of migrant workers.

Amongst other research was an analysis of bi-lingual education programmes used in different Member States. The purpose of this project was to assess such programmes as a means for developing bi-cultural education for young migrants. One of the major questions to which such research was addressed was whether it was possible to develop a profound knowledge of two languages without overburdening the timetable. The general conclusion from this series of enquiries which involved schools in Luxembourg, Ireland, Wales and the German American school in West Berlin, was that the use of two languages as parallel teaching media was indeed possible without either lowering standards or placing overdue strain on the timetable.

Also in this context was the development of a diagnostic test of language competence in Dutch for 11-12 year-olds. It is designed not only to test current competence but also to outline a future teaching profile for individual children. The test, developed by the *Centraal Instituut voor Toetsontwikkeling* of Arnhem (Netherlands) was presented to the Commission at an expert meeting on the 4th and 5th December 1980.

Important though they are, language difficulties are not, unfortunately, the only obstacle facing youngsters from migrant families. Guidance and vocational counselling are no less significant in the contribution they can make to the successful emergence of such children as independent, self-supporting beings. Therefore, from the outset of the Education Action Programme much weight was also attached to analysing the various methods used to develop guidance counselling for a slightly older group of young migrants. This took the form of a series of four studies centring on the cities of Bradford (Northern England), Brussels, Müchengladbach-Cologne (West Germany) and Roubaix (France).

The Bradford study, unlike the remaining three, was less an investigation of the dimensions of disadvantage, than an enquiry into procedures designed to overcome such difficulties. By setting up individual dossiers for all migrant children under the age of 14, the guidance counselling service could give specific advice on such matters as continuing study, full or part time, the problems associated with changing jobs or the ways of applying for study grants.

Both the Brussels and the Roubaix enquiries revealed some of the consequences of linguistic handicap. In the former instance, young migrants, compared with their Belgian counterparts, showed a backwardness in attainment reckoned at some 12 months. Though directly correlated with social class background, in both the Roubaix and Brussels studies, the cause was thought to lie in lack of adequate language training. As a corrective, remedial education was introduced in three Brussels classes, designed to increase understanding of words and phrases. This brought about spectacular results in that the most disadvantaged subsequently showed a better performance than the average attained by the control group. The enquiry conducted at Müchengladbach/Cologne centred on the vocational training of migrants' children. In 1975, only 30 percent of migrant school-leavers reached the level of the *Hauptschulabschluss* — the minimum of school leaving certificate, with some 3 to 4 percent entering vocational training. The call for pre-vocational training for this group, the main conclusion of the Müchengladbach-Cologne report, received additional backing from a study carried out in 1977-78 by the *Internationaler Bund für Sozialarbeit Jugensozialwerk* of Frankfurt. It concluded that young migrants entering the country between the ages of 14-16, those who faced failure in school, or who dropped out early, had little prospect but the dole queue. It, too, recommended additional measures in the area of pre-vocational and vocational training.

Development of information exchange:

Information exchange forms the third element in the Commission's process of policy elaboration. We have seen that this part of the policy formulation procedure was an integral part of drawing up the more detailed aspects of the Education Action Programme in the shape of the various discussions between experts held during the two years from 1974 to 1976. But it also forms an equally important role in the assessment and evaluation of the pilot projects. The discussions that take place as follow-up to more sustained and long-term development or research undertakings which have been described earlier, perform two specific, though interrelated, functions: the first is to identify those common points in all projects or research undertakings, the second, as a logical consequence of the first, to draw up a broad line of options or recommendations that, in turn may either be fed back into a second stage pilot project or, passed up to the Education Committee. The Education Committee may then consider such recommendations as a range of options some of which may, after discussion, be passed up to the Council of Ministers.

As regards the first function, that of identifying common features across different national pilot projects arranged around the same theme, the Commission requested the ALFA (*Ausbildung von Lehrern für Ausländerkinder*) from Essen University and the Landau Teacher Training College in 1978, to carry out an evaluation of the pilot projects on reception methods and on the teaching of the language and culture of origin. Its report, presented to the Commission in June 1980, was discussed at a joint meeting of experts from Member States and officials from the respective Ministries of Education on November 8th and 9th of that year. The main conclusions were presented to the Education Committee in the later part of 1981. An abridged version of this report is to be published shortly.

A similar evaluation of the Odense, Enschede, Luxembourg, London and Marseille pilot projects has been conferred jointly on ALFA and the *Laboratoire de Recherche en Sciences Sociales de l'Ecole Normale Supérieure de Saint-Cloud* in June 1981. The final report was received in 1983.

The second function, that of defining a series of policy options, forms the last phase of the pilot projects and takes place in the form of a number of colloquia between participating research staff, administrators and participants from the Commission's services. Thus the follow-up discussions of the reception methods project, assessing the Waterschei/Winterslag experiment took place in 1978, that of Leiden the following year, the Luxembourg study was discussed in 1981, and the Odense project in 1980. The series of pilot studies on teacher training were the subject of two colloquia in 1979 and 1981 with a third planned to examine the findings of the Landau team in the later part of 1981. The Paris and Bedford projects formed the subject of colloquia in 1978 and 1980 respectively, whilst the Limbourg and Marseille studies were scheduled for debate in 1982.

EURYDICE (The European Community's Education Information Network):

A key role in disseminating the results of these undertakings is played by EURYDICE, the European Community's Education Information Network. The education of migrant workers is one of the four areas on which the network concentrates. To underline the importance of information exchange, a meeting with senior officials responsible for questions related to the education of migrant workers and their families was held on December 8th 1981 at Brussels. It was agreed that a need existed to set up closer links between the various national units of the EURYDICE system and those centres run by Ministries in charge of migrant affairs. In some Member States such links already exist.

Role of the European Social Fund:

In addition to policy elaborated within the framework of the Education Action Programme, complementary support for the training of migrants and their families is also provided by the European Social Fund. According to the Council decision of December 20th 1977, the Commission was authorised to provide assistance from the Social Fund to set additional expenditure incurred by Member States, particularly in the provision of teaching directed specifically towards the children of migrant workers. Furthermore, the Social Fund may also provide financial assistance for initial and in-service training of those personnel, teachers and social workers in the main, engaged in this task. The Social Fund may cover up to 50 percent of the cost of measures coming under this head, whether carried out by public or private organisations. Financial support from this source has been considerable. In 1974, some 4,800,000 Units of Account were given over to this heading which rose to 16,100,000 the following year, to 12,800,000 in 1976, to 20,800,000 in 1977 and fell slightly to 16,000,000 in 1978.

The guidelines of the Social Fund at present operating, gives first priority to the following fields of action:

– projects to improve the conditions of internal Community migration, essentially involving Italian immigrants, though the entry of Greece to the Community will extend this field;
– training for personnel involved in teaching the children of migrant workers, or welfare counsellors catering for immigrant families;
– pilot projects designed to improve methods of teaching for the children of migrants.

New measures and the extension of existing ones in the field of educating migrant workers' children have been given second priority in the operations undertaken by the Social Found as a whole.

Research enquiries and pilot projects may also be funded from this source insofar as they serve to define further and future policy options in the area of intervention included under the remit of the Social Fund. Some idea of the importance of this parallel realm of the Commission's activities can be gathered from a short statistical overview. In 1977, projects assisted from the Social Fund involved some 80,000 migrant children. In addition, a further 150,000 adult migrants followed training courses in vocational training and language education. Some 3,500 teachers and social workers were enrolled in various in-service or initial training programmes assisted from this source.

To date, seven pilot projects and research studies have been undertaken within the framework of the Social Fund. Broadly speaking, they may be divided into three groups, each corresponding to the various populations concerned. These are the children of migrant workers, migrant workers themselves and teacher/social worker programmes for personnel who will be involved with the migrant population in the future.

In the first category is a study carried out jointly by the *Institut für Sozialforschung und Sozialwirtschaft* of Saarbrücken (West Germany) and the *Centre d'Information et d'Etudes Humaines* of Metz (France). It concentrates on both educational and vocational training for the children of Italian migrant workers in these two particular regions.

In the second category, devoted to the problems of migrant workers themselves, are three projects. The first of these, carried out in 1974 by the *Centre d'Animation Sociale Italien* of Brussels, developed training courses and adult education programmes to assist migrant workers in an urban environment to improve their integration and mobility in this new setting. A similar undertaking, this time by CEPPAC of Brussels, examined the needs of Italian migrant workers, especially in the area of social and economic integration as well as both linguistic and vocational training. The Paris-based organisation, AMANA analysed the specific requirement of first-time immigrants in terms of developing audio-visual aids designed to assist primary linguistic competence and the introduction of recently arrived immigrants to social life in their new setting.

In the third category, are two projects dealing with various aspects of teacher training. The first provided training for bi-lingual Italian/German teachers and social workers. It was undertaken by the Institute for the Training and Guidance of Migrant Workers of Rome with the approval of the Italian Ministry of Labour and Social Security. The second study, commissioned from the *Centre de Préformation* of Marseille (France), prepared a teacher training programme the purpose of which was to enhance the adaptation and the pre-vocational training of migrant workers.

One of the major conclusions to emerge from these projects is that much of the material currently used to introduce migrants to their host country, whilst comparatively well suited to those with more than a modicum of 'cultural capital', are less appropriate for the majority of newly arrived immigrants. This calls for radical innovation in the whole approach not merely to adult education and the development of compensatory education for this particular group, but also in the field of teaching methods, educational materials and their contents.

As this brief overview shows, considerable headway is already being made under the auspices of both the Commission's Social Action Programme and also the Education Action Programme.

There are, however, other areas in the education of migrants and their families where an important contribution may be made by the European Social Fund. One of these is thought to be in the provision of financial support to media-based and other government activities which underwrite language and literacy courses for this particular group. Recent assessment of the potential for social integration furnished by radio and television programmes also suggests that the Social Fund might subsidise pilot schemes to improve language teaching methods for migrants and their dependents.

Conclusion:
What may one conclude from the various experiments, pilot projects and other research the results of which have been described in this Chapter? So far, Community policy towards migrants and their families has concentrated on setting up structures, developing and testing different methods and practices and this on a basis which is largely empirical in approach. Clearly, much effort and resources are being put to use in assisting the various migrant communities to find their place in their new countries of settlement. But the way ahead is a long one and much still remains to be done. Recently, the Advisory Committee for the Free Movement of Workers, a tri-partite body composed of representatives of government and from both sides of industry from each of the Member States, pointed out that two areas in particular deserved closer attention. These were pre-school provision for the migrant community and the issue of education and vocational guidance.

At present, pre-school education is not compulsory in any of the Member States of the Community therefore it cannot be subject to a binding Community directive. In other words, this area remains outside the competence of Directive 77/486/CEE of July 1977. Yet, without pre-primary provision for such children, the transition to primary school is particularly difficult. By contrast, studies have shown that children who regularly attended nursery school from the age of 3, see their chances of benefiting from primary education considerably increased.

The Commission's thinking on the matter is that, as a first step, a Resolution might be passed calling for pre-school education to be provided free of charge, where possible, for all children of migrant workers. At the same time, more efforts should be made to give migrant families adequate information about the purposes of such schools. Second, from the standpoint of implementing such a policy, it is held that greater emphasis be placed on coordinating all those services which, at local level, have responsibility for the education and social welfare provision for small children.

Nor are the problems any the less pressing in the field of education and vocational guidance. There is much evidence to suggest that in those Member States where vocational training takes place inside firms — for instance, the Federal Republic of Germany, the United Kingdom and the Netherlands — young foreigners are under-represented amongst trainees. Where vocational training is part of the full-time education system — as it is in France, for example — these young people tend to be channelled into short-course options leading to manual occupations from the end of primary education. Since the vocational elements of such courses are often inadequate, outmoded or of low level, they make for considerable difficulty in moving from school to work. Though already urgent, given the particular economic climate, this issue will become more acute in the next few years as the numbers of second generation migrants reaching this point in the education systems of their host countries, grow.

The Commission is to call upon Member States to adapt their education and vocational guidance services as well as those facilities dealing with vocational preparation and training more fully to the needs of the immigrant population. Amongst the various measures envisaged are the setting up of suitable structures to deal with language problems, and the introduction of remedial programmes to bring immigrants up to a level required for entry to skilled occupations. No less significant is the need to develop provision for language training aimed at the adult members of the families of migrant workers. This latter topic was discussed at a symposium held in Berlin between June 9th and 12th 1981 at the European Centre for the Development of Vocational Training. It was attended by government representatives and by both sides of industry.

These are just some of the immediate and practical implications that have emerged from the various experiments and development projects the Commission has supported in the area of the education of migrants and their families. Others are likely to arise as the evaluation of these undertakings identifies further areas of action and intervention. Nevertheless, the lesson one may retain from the Commission's activities to date is this: if measures for assisting migrants to come to terms with their new social environment are to be introduced successfuly, the structures and provision through which they are carried out must be laid down beforehand.

SOURCES

i. **Primary: internal Commission documents.**
'Mise en oeuvre du programme d'action au niveau communautaire', *Document SEC (76) 216*, January 21st 1976.
'Memorandum of the decisions reached on the Action Programme at Community level', *Document 340/76 (EN 15)*, March 23rd 1976.
'Note from the education services of the Commission to the Education Committee: Activities at Community level in conjunction with education of children of migrant workers', *Document 856/77 (EN 33)*, March 1977.
'Activités en faveur de l'éducation des travailleurs migrants et des membres de leur famille: projet de programme triennal 1979-1982, *Document CAB VIII 108-79 REVISE*, 1979.
'Note to the Education Committee from the education services of the Commission: The pre-school education for children of migrant workers', *Document XII/888/80 EN REV*, January 27th 1981.
'Outcome of the proceedings of the Education Committee', *Document 6502/81*, April 29th 1981.

Education and the European Community

Rapport sur les activités communautaires en faveur de la formation culturelle et professionnelle des travailleurs migrants et des membres de leur famille 1975-1981, Septembre 1981 (xerox).

'Note from the services of the Commission to the Education Committee: Report on the activities for the education and vocational training of migrant workers and their families in the European Community 1975-1981', *Document V/192/82 (87/en)*, March 16th 1982 (official version of former source).

'Note to the Education Committee: activities for the education of migrant workers and the members of their families: activities in progress and proposed for the 1982/3 school year', *Document V/254/82 EN*, January 24th 1982.

'Note from the services of the Commission to the Education Committee. Radio and Television and the needs of migrant workers families in the European Community', *Document XII/213/81 (89/en)*, March 11th 1982.

'Second generation of migrant workers — vocational training and employment: Note from the services of the Commission to the Education Committee', *Document V/127/82 EN*, March 16th 1982.

'Note to the Education Committee from the services of the Commission: summary record of the meeting between the heads of national units for the Information Network EURYDICE and senior national officials responsible for matters related to the education of migrant workers', *Document V/238/82 EN (90/en)*, March 10th 1982.

ii. **Secondary: printed sources, official documents.**
Official Journal C. 2572, October 19th 1968.
Official Journal C. 280, December 8th 1975.
Official Journal L. 199, August 6th 1977, p.32.
Official Journal L. 337/12, December 27th 1977.
Official Journal C. 159, June 26th 1979.
Formation d'enseignants français accueillant des enfants étrangers: évaluation des stages du Centre d'études et de la formation des instituteurs au service des enfants migrants, Paris, CREDIF/Ecole Normale supérieure de Saint-Cloud, 1979, 3 vols.
Linguistic minorities Project: second progress report, London, April 1981, (typewritten).

iii. **Tertiary: pamphlets, articles of a non-official nature**
'Forsogsprojekt aendrer dansk bekendtgorelse', *EF Avisen*, No. 10, 1981.
The impact of demographic change on education systems in the European Community, Brussels, EURYDICE, September 1981.
Guy Neave, 'Urban education in Europe', *Secondary Education*, (Journal of the British National Union of Teachers), vol. 5, no. 2, Summer 1975.

Chapter Three
Transition from School to Work

Structure:
Introduction
Community Policy
   1. Pilot projects
   2. The Purpose of the pilot projects
   3. The final phase
   4. Some of the main findings of the pilot projects
   5. Impact of the pilot projects
Study visits
Statistical Guidelines
Conclusion
SOURCES

Introduction:
One of the more remarkable changes in educational thinking in the course of the Seventies has been the notion of educational efficiency and the indicators used to ascertain it. At the start of that decade, the belief was commonly held that one pointer to the performance of education systems was the number of young people who chose to remain beyond compulsory schooling. Another was the proportion of the age group attaining that level of qualification which permitted access to higher education. In fine, efficiency was judged on the ability of schools to retain and to qualify their pupils. Those who either left school early, untrained or unqualified were assumed to have found a place on the labour market. They did not, however, constitute a measure of efficiency. Today, this perspective has changed, and the criteria of performance at a systemic level have also altered. Increasingly, the performance of education systems is not exclusively measured by the attainments of its brightest and most talented — though this is not forgotten. Rather it is measured in terms of how far its leavers are suitably qualified for the existing labour market and how far education is capable of providing remedial and other facilities for those who are likely to face considerable difficulties in the transition from school to work.

This change of perspective is largely a function of the massive rise of youth unemployment in the latter part of the decade. And such a change has also revealed the paradoxical situation that those systems which may be seen as efficient in the terms of the traditional criteria are not necessarily those which do best in terms of assisting the less able. In certain Community countries of which France and Britain are perhaps the best examples, the rise of youth unemployment has had profound effects on the structure, provision and strategy in the field of education. The rise of *de facto* parallel education and training services run by the *Ministère de la Formation Professionnelle* in the case of the former or the Manpower Services Commission in the case of the latter are both examples of profound structural change, itself based on the recognition that more needs to be done to assist the unqualified school leaver. Improvements in the counselling and guidance system, currently envisaged in the Legrand Report for the 11 to 15 middle school in France are part of a rather broader strategy to try and reduce the numbers of those who emerge from the school system without formal qualification. And in the Federal Republic of Germany, the basic vocational training year (*Berufsgrundbildungsjahr*) introduced in 1976 though with varying degrees of success, may be seen in the same light, namely as part of that major shift in priority towards the less able pupil.

If the rise of youth unemployment has ushered in new issues — for instance the place of vocational preparation as part of the common education of all young people prior to the end of compulsory school — in a sense, it has also accelerated certain changes already implicit in educational development prior to its onset. Amongst the most important has been the issue of the relationship between general academic education on the one hand and vocational training on the other. The historical structures of education systems in Western Europe have tended to draw a line between those schools dispensing academic education and those, generally of shorter duration, courses of a vocational nature. Over the past decade, this distinction which grew up in the course of the previous half century, has tended to become less rigid. A prime factor in this has been the 'democratisation' of upper secondary education mainly as a result of more young people staying in school beyond the end of compulsory education. During the ten years' from 1970 to 1980, the proportion of 16 year olds in the Member States of the Ten remainining in school beyond compulsory schooling rose from 46.5 percent to 62.7 percent; for 17 year olds from 32.6 percent to 46.7 percent and from 23.0 percent to 36.0 percent for 18 year olds.

The fact that a majority of young people now remain at school in that area of upper secondary education hitherto reserved mainly for those destined for academic education not only entailed a greater diversification in the type of instruction required, but also recognition of the diverse ambitions, goals and needs imposed by adolescents who, earlier, would have left as soon as possible. Full-time upper secondary education can, therefore no longer be associated wholly with the interests of those destined either for higher education or for the professions. This development has sometimes been associated with the 'vocationalisation' of upper secondary education. It is, in effect, an attempt to cater for a new diversity of claims upon secondary education by linking its courses more closely with the perceived requirements of the labour market. It can be argued that vocationalisation at the upper secondary level was an inevitable response to the increasing staying on rate and would, then, have occurred even if youth unemployment had not assumed such proportions as it did from the mid Seventies. Problems associated with the transition from school to work may have accelerated this process. They did not, however, give rise to it.

A second factor involving a gradual reorientation of the curricular structure in the lower secondary school derives specifically from the need to ease the transition from school to work. Experience in many Member States has shown that the factors contributing to a relatively successful transition from school tend to operate far earlier than the last year of compulsory schooling. Rather, they are to be found amongst those decisions taken around the age of 12 or 13 whether by teachers, parents or pupils, which affect the type of 'stream' or 'track' in which a young person is placed. The introduction of various forms of 'pre-vocational training' as part of the common curriculum — a feature already noted in France, the Federal Republic of Germany and Great Britain — was the response to this difficulty.

Community Policy:

It is against this background of changing structures and perspectives within the education systems of Member States that Community policy is placed. The importance of this programme can be judged from the fact that each year some 4,000,000 young people leave the schools across the EEC. Many of them face a daunting prospect and one which continues to get no better. Over the five years from September 1978, the number of people out of work in the Community increased from approximately 6,000,000 to around 11,430,000. And just as general unemployment has grown, so too has the number of young unemployed under 25 who constituted around one in three of all those out of work in 1978. By September 1981, they accounted for 41.4 percent. If general unemployment is increasing, it is accelerating even faster amongst young people.

This general situation is further complicated by such factors as the state of industry in the particular region, irrespective of the type of qualification or the absence of qualifications held by school leavers. Amongst others are the gradual decline in the traditional outlets for training through the apprenticeship system, particularly in those countries like West Germany, France and the Netherlands where this has been a major element in post school provision. And finally there is a marked differential, present in all Member States of the Community, between the unemployment rate for girls which in all cases tends to be higher than for boys. This latter feature is due in part to the limited range of occupations open to girls and in part, because those jobs that are available for girls tend to be of an unskilled or semi-skilled nature.

The origins of Community policy in the area of the transition from school to work may be traced back to the closing months of 1976, when the Education Committee drew up a report setting out the main issues posed and the difficulties currently facing Member State education systems.

The report argued in favour of a major change in the perspective of social policy. Previously, it pointed out, social policy was directed more to alleviating grievances after they had occurred than to developing measures to prevent them taking place. Unemployment amongst young people in the Community started to develop in 1973 and continued to deepen thereafter. The setting up of a preventive strategy to meet this problem required two conditions: the establishment of an integrated social policy, the better to coordinate efforts undertaken by different agencies; second, the identification of those groups of school leavers particularly vulnerable to unemployment. This latter point was highly important since the identification of such groups might enable appropriate measures to be taken before they left school.

The report provided the background to the Resolution adopted on December 13th 1976 which set down a series of measures to be taken both by Member States and the European Communities over the period from 1978 to 1980. At Community level, they comprised:

— the setting up of a series of pilot projects;
— the organisation of study visits for specialists and discussion workshops for key personnel in the area of teacher training;
— the preparation of statistical guidelines.

The Commission exercises oversight of these measures, working in close liaison with the Education Committee. Further linkage with the Member State education systems is provided by a liaison official designated by each national Ministry of Education to act in consultation with the Commission. The purpose is not simply to maintain an overview of developments taking place in the area of transition at Member State level, but also to enable Member States to compare their experience and exchange views on the matter in the Education Committee.

1. Pilot projects:

The pilot projects may be said to form the core of the Community's work in the field of transition from education to working life. First approved in Autumn 1977, there are today some 28 projects ranging from Denmark to Sicily, from Berlin to Ireland, involving several hundred different educational establishments and some 10,000 young people across the Community. 50 percent of the costs are born by the European Community. The pilot projects are intended to run for 3 years with a further year to allow the results to be evaluated. They were completed by the academic year 1981-82.

The Community's financial contribution towards the cost of the pilot project was set at some 2,400,000 Units of Account for the first year of operation — the academic year 1978-79 — with budgetary estimates of some 4,705,000 Units of Account proposed for 1980-81 and a further 1,600,000 for 1981-82. Complementary finance has come from local, regional and national authorities and, in a few instances, from the European Social Fund. Some Member States, preferred to make a more substantial contribution than the usual 50 percent of the costs as a means to uphold the original scope of the projects. Overall, the budget during the first year of operation from all sources amounted to some 6,000,000 EUA.

The focus of this 'action research' is on the following six themes:

— the educational and training needs of school leavers who find difficulties in obtaining employment;
— the problem of poor motivation towards study and work that many young people show and means of stimulating greater participation;
— compensatory action to provide better chances for specific groups of young people, for instance, girls, young migrants, or the handicapped;
— the association of educational guidance, training and placement agencies in the development of continuing guidance and counselling services;
— the improvement of vocational preparation both before and after school-leaving age through cooperative active between the education and employment sectors;
— the improvement of the initial and in-service training of teachers the better to equip them to prepare young people for both adult and working life.

During the preparation period in the early part of 1977, great care was taken to ensure a geographical balance in the distribution of the projects and to devise them in such a way that all six themes were adequately covered. Also included in the investigation was the question of curriculum and structural development inside compulsory education. The projects are intended to span both the final years of compulsory education and the immediate post compulsory period, effectively the age groups 16-20. There is considerable variety in the range, type and scope of the enquiries undertaken. Some are limited to single communities, industrial as well as rural. Others, for instance, centre on a single educational establishment. There are some covering what amounts to whole regions. For example, the Orientation and Guidance enquiry in Trento (Italy), involves virtually all lower secondary schools in the area. A further category, based on the development of particular subjects in the curriculum, brings together 100 or more institutions.

The purpose of these projects is, first, to create a network of institutions and individuals which can learn from the experience of activities in a similar field in other countries. The potential for transferability of experience between Member States is a key area of development. Second, their aim is to stimulate ways of setting up coordinated policy across the various agencies responsible for education, training and manpower services and to involve trade unions and employers as well. A first step in this direction was taken with the setting up of management or advisory committees for all projects which also include teachers and parents.

How are the projects structured? Some divide into separate sub-projects which is the case in Denmark, for example. There, four sub-projects are under development, one of which involves many different types of schools and technical institutions on a county basis. A second group breaks up into independent elements, similar in some respects to sub-projects. The enquiry in Shannon (Ireland) is based on five separate types of intervention in five different schools. The cooperative guidance and counselling project at Ludwigshaven (West Germany) and the Sheffield (UK) 'transition school-working life' programme are also of this type. A third model involves investigating a common theme, but on different sites. In France, for example, the project involving the integration of 16 to 18 year olds into working life is based on 10 establishments throughout the country, whilst the Inner London Education Authority's Bridging Course investigation brings together 5 consortia, made up of two secondary schools and a College of Further Education, located in different parts of the city. A fourth group is either state or country wide. Such is the dimension of the development of the project on cooperation between lower secondary and vocational training schools in Baden-Wurtemberg.

An analysis of the content of the projects shows that, there are four main areas of activity: the reform of vocational training, the development of new models for educational and vocational guidance, the setting up of new links between compulsory and post compulsory education and, finally, the various experimental systems alternating work with further education. As examples of the first, are two projects in Belgium and France. Their main concern is the development, in the area of vocational education, of more flexible course structures based on a system of credit units to provide students with greater choice of subject. Evening courses, based on three widely separated colleges

– Bruges, St Nicholas and St Genesius-Rode – have been introduced with the support of local industry. They involve such areas as welding, technical drawing, construction and workshop organisation, following a modular format that allows wide individual specialisation. In France, teams from six regions are working to improve the contents of a mechanical engineering course and making it more relevant to real industrial practice. The course, defined in terms of operational objectives, seeks to develop new methods of teaching and learning. In the field of educational and vocational guidance, the project located at Chieti (Central Italy) is particularly interesting. In collaboration with local industry, the project is building up a data bank to provide local information for teachers to develop an appropriate guidance strategy. Previously, no careers service existed in the area. In Luxembourg there is a project aimed at helping young people to form firm proposals for their future. It includes a system of follow-up contacts for up to three years after they have left the project site. When necessary, they will receive further guidance during this period. The strengthening of links between compulsory and post compulsory education is the object of the project carried out in Baden-Würtemberg. Some 65 groups comprising nearly 2,000 contact teachers drawn from both the *Hauptschule* (non academic lower secondary school) and vocational schools are engaged in curriculum development, the purpose of which is to coordinate the content and presentation of subjects taught in both types of school, improve advice given to students about the type of vocational preparation available, and to exchange teachers across the two areas of the education system. Amongst examples of different forms of alternating work with further education are the Clydebank (Scotland) and Ludwigshaven (West Germany) projects. In the former, lower secondary school pupils work one day a week in a vocational education institute. Those in the building department, for instance, are involved in constructing a miniature house. The experience, it is argued, is a considerable help in creating self confidence amongst the participants and gives new impetus to acquiring some of the basic skills in numeracy and literacy. In the latter, pupils from special schools spend half a day's practical work in various training workshops in the neighbourhood; such work is then integrated into the curriculum. Thus practical activities underline the development of manual skills and act as vehicles to acquire other competencies.

2. *Purpose of the pilot projects:*

The purpose of these pilot projects is not merely to ascertain the feasibility of new models and methods – thereby contributing to the extension of good practice – but to provide concrete examples that may in future serve as the basis for wider developments. Central to this has been the introduction of a system of continuous evaluation of the projects as they develop. This feature, which is perhaps unique in an undertaking of this size and scope, is seen as crucial in two respects; first, because it is seen as underlining the Community dimension of these projects and second, as a method of Community interaction. At another level, the use of an evaluation network, set up in the Autumn of 1979 and consisting of some 50 people distributed across 19 evaluation teams, is to intensify the exchange of information amongst the various projects thereby reinforcing the internal dynamic of learning within the venture as a whole.

The central coordination of the pilot project development, the creation of facilities for efficient exchange of information has, since 1978, been the responsibility of a Central Animation Evaluation Team — a body of 4 experts — working in association with the Educational Services of the Commission. It is based on the Social Research Institute, IFAPLAN, in Cologne which is directed by Dr Gerhard Welbars.

Both in the evaluation of projects individually and the programme as a whole, the Community dimension is of prime importance. In September 1977, the Education Committee agreed on the general framework of this part of the undertaking. Tasks for evaluation, ranging from the initial analysis of objectives through to the assessment of further measures for wider application within the national framework of policy or across national frontiers, were drawn up.

In-built to the structure of the pilot project programme is provision for exchanging ideas and experience between individual schemes, especially those dealing with similar topics. To this end, several meetings were held for those working on the various projects at national level. At Community level the same approach is used, by means of small colloquia on specific areas of interest linked to the six priority areas of the projects. Amongst the issues discussed were:

- unqualified school leavers disenchanted with school, held at Cannes (France) in April 1978;
- unmotivated, less able students in the last years of compulsory education, held at Edinburgh (Scotland) in November 1978;
- teacher training for transition to working life, held at Stuttgart (West Germany) in March 1979;
- work experience and alternating forms of training, held at Amsterdam (Netherlands) in April 1979;
- vocational guidance and counselling, held at Ludwigshaven (West Germany) in June 1979;
- guidance and orientation, held at Dublin (Ireland) in September 1980;
- final phase of the programme, held at Brussels (Belgium) in December 1980.

A rather broader forum was provided in the form of workshops which bring together experts and administrators working in the field. The first of these was held in November 1977 under the auspices of the Commission at Harrogate (England) and was devoted to the theme 'Teacher training for the period of transition'. This subsequently developed with the various Ministers of·Education in the Member States assuming the main responsibility. The meeting held in May 1979 in Luxembourg dealt with the problem of preparing girls for working life, followed by a similar occasion in Kassel (West Germany) in November of the same year when the topic under discussion was the interface between general and vocational training. It also considered possible areas for joint action between the Member States.

'Groups at risk in secondary education' was the theme pursued at the Noordwijkerhout (Netherlands) workshop held in May 1980. The final event in this series took place under the joint organisation of the Irish Departments of Education and Labour in Dublin from September 22nd to 26th 1980. It was devoted to examining vocational guidance and career oriented educational advice.

Following the entry of Greece into the European Community, an informal meeting was held in March 1981 at Athens. It examined the various themes that would allow the new Member States to contribute to and benefit from the programme. Several fields for possible further action were identified. They were:

— the training of teachers for special vocational education;
— the retraining of teachers in technical subjects for compulsory schools;
— staff training in guidance and careers education in the final years of compulsory education;
— the preparation of staff in technical and vocational education with the view to provide specific opportunities within vocational training centres for young people leaving general upper secondary education and not finding employment.

The issues involved in the transition from education to working life are of concern to other organisations as well. Such seminars provide useful occasions to exchange views on work being carried out on this topic in other contexts. Thus, the meeting at Luxembourg also included representatives from the Council of Europe and the Organisation for Economic Cooperation and Development, Paris.

3. The final phase:

As from the academic year 1980-81, the programme of pilot projects entered its final phase. In March 1980, the Central Animation and Evaluation Team presented its interim report to the Education Committee. The final report was presented to the Education Committee in 1983. It included an overall evaluation of the programme as a whole as well as an evaluation of individual projects. Originally, it was envisaged that the Community would support the programme financially over a three year period from 1977 to 1980. The complexity of some of the projects together with the importance of securing at least one, if not two, student cohorts passing through — an important consideration if the evaluation was to have credibility — led the Council and Ministers of Education to extend the programme for a further year.

The final phase of the pilot project involved a qualitative shift in focus. If some projects have reached the end of their lives, others will continue either as 'permanent projects' or be transformed at the first element in a series of undertakings at regional or national level, based on their results. It is thought particularly important that the key activity in this phase — dissemination of the results and findings — should take place during the life time of the projects, because the experience and ideas they represent will have greater impact if they can be verified against concrete and living examples rather than through written reports alone.

The activities in this period of the projects' development may be summarised under four heads:

- the identification and analysis of the results of the pilot projects and the exploitation of the material they have produced;
- the presentation of these results in the national context whilst relating them to policy developments within Member States;
- the identification of implications for future action and development at different levels;
- the stimulation of debate on innovation and change in this field, more particularly through the dissemination of information and material from the projects.

4. Some of the main findings of the pilot projects:

It is, of course, extremely difficult to summarise the major findings from a programme that stands as one of the most complex exercises in international co-operation in the history of educational development. That remains the task of the final report. Nevertheless, it is interesting to see what have been the interim lessons that might be drawn from the work undertaken so far.

The first of these involves what might be termed the 'in school dimension' and consists, essentially, of methods of teaching and learning, relationships between staff and students and the content of the curriculum. The enhancement of motivation, initiative and self-confidence amongst young people appears to be influenced favourably by the use of active methods of learning in which students 'do' rather than remain as passive recipients. Small group work, discussions and project work seem especially effective. Equally important in fostering positive motivation have been the changes in relationship between staff and students, most of which tend towards a less authoritarian model. Understanding the world of work and developing the ability to meet it, can be introduced by re-focussing some of the more traditional school subjects — for example, geography, history and economics — as well as introducing new working material with an orientation to the world of work in these subjects. These might be said to form some of the more immediate remedies. In the long run, however, the issue at stake is whether, without a major reform of the school curriculum to take into account the necessity to develop many of the important competencies such as initiative, ability to get on with one's peers and self knowledge, reasonable adjustment to transition, even by normal students, let alone the highly unmotivated, will not continue to pose considerable difficulties.

The second lesson one might derive from the pilot projects is the need to integrate guidance and counselling into the school as part of the global process of education rather than having it remain, as it still tends to do, in a position of isolation. This aspect of transition is highly important, not merely because it should act as the vehicle linking schools and the outside world, but because it is becoming recognised to an increasing extent that the traditional sources of information — parents and friends — do not necessarily dispose of that type of information which will allow a young person to make a judicious choice of subject, job or career, particularly in a time of rapid economic change. Sustained and continuous guidance, information about local opportunities and conditions of employment are prime requisites in this area.

The third conclusion that might be drawn is the need to integrate work into the school. The use of work simulation, particularly for the less able or difficult student, is an important means of developing both basic skills — such as literacy and numeracy — and affective attitudes — such as cooperativeness and individual as well as group decision-making — by dint of showing how such skills relate directly to the real world. The Shannon (Ireland) experiment of creating mini-companies in which the production line was planned, developed and the goods marketed, is unusually interesting in this respect.

The fourth conclusion is that transition from education to work can be made less fraught if the resources of the community outside the school can be brought in to stimulate learning. In the past, the traditional emphasis in education, whether lower or upper secondary — has been to divorce theoretical work from the practical. Many of the projects, however, have shown that by using the community to illustrate how these two in fact link together, a new sense of relevance is imparted to students. It also allows them to make an easier transition quite apart from fostering communication, interpersonal skills, and motivation.

Generally speaking, these may be said to constitute the 'upstream' part of the problem of transition from education to work. They are, essentially, school-based. 'Downstream' issues, those which are posed in the context of young people who have already left school, require a different approach, not least because participation in such programmes is entirely voluntary which means that no small effort has to be engaged in generating and sustaining their interest and commitment. Studies have shown that successful projects pass through three main developments at the recruitment stage; first, the arousal of young people's interest in the project; second, that the project should be responsive to their perceived needs yet not too stifling; third, that the obligations of each party, both youngster and 'animateur' are clearly set forth and understood. Relationships between staff and student, as in school, are highly important and, in this connection, the use of residential facilities increases significantly, the development of good understanding between the two groups. Especially important in combatting de-motivation and apathy is the active involvement of young people in the planning of their own programme and carrying it out. The creation of programmes with this particular feature is, of course, easier in the post school sector. It is more than usually important, however, to give low achievers a taste of success by a careful selection of tasks and work in which they may have the opportunity of succeeding. Only by means such as these may the self-fulfilling prophecy that failure begets failure — the mechanism that in schools stands at the root of de-motivation — be broken.

Finally, it is important to note that some of the problems experienced by young people in transition stem from the belief that the choice and decisions made in school are binding for life. Lack of opportunity to take the relevant qualification in time, lack of outlets in their particular area, all contribute to reinforcing this conviction. Much can be done, however, to obviate the former through the creation of recurrent education facilities linked in with transition programmes, though how precisely this might evolve is a matter for further investigation.

5. Impact of the pilot projects:

Although it is somewhat early to assess the overall contribution of the pilot projects, their impact upon policy development at Member State level would appear significant. Initiatives to disseminate the results, sometimes linked with parallel projects, are developing in several Member States. The creation of national dossiers to give wide appreciation of their findings is already under way. In France, the Ministry of Education set up a working group, including three project directors together with representatives from other branches of the Ministry, to discuss the content and distribution of the national dossier. In West Germany, a questionnaire to ascertain the information needs with regard to the pilot projects' findings, both at Federal and Länder level is being drawn up, and in Italy, a central group to plan and coordinate dissemination was formed out of the interministerial committee in charge of pilot projects. The United Kingdom has created separate dossiers for England and Wales on the one hand and Scotland on the other. Local Education Authorities are also considering the possibility of holding national meetings to discuss the main findings and their implications for wider development. An important part in disseminating the findings of the pilot projects is to be played by EURYDICE, the Community's Education Information Network. A special post to liaise between EURYDICE and the Cologne based research organisation, IFAPLAN has been set up, thus strengthening further the comparative perspective upon policy development in the area of transition from school to working life.

The pilot projects have demonstrated that they are capable of generating a high degree of interest and participation, not merely amongst those immediately concerned with them, but also with ventures in parallel fields not directly involved. In Scotland, for example, links have been forged between the Strathclyde project and the programme entitled 'Education for Industrial Society'. A similar relationship has grown up between the Inner London Education Authority's Bridging Course scheme and the 'Industry Project' sponsored by the Schools' Council, a body concerned with research and development in the area of the curriculum in England. This role has been reinforced further by the publication, four times a year of a Newletter: *European Community Action Programme: Education and Working Life Project News,* published in all the Community languages and with a circulation of around 10,000 copies.

Nor should one forget the transnational impact that projects in one country may have upon similar undertakings in another. Especially noteworthy in this respect was the use of materials on guidance counselling, devised by the Ludwigshaven (West Germany) project, by the pilot scheme taking place in Shannon (Ireland). The same two ventures have also exchanged information about ways of mobilising parents to involve them more closely in school activities — an aspect held to be important in fostering understanding about some of the difficulties accompanying transition from school at a time of economic change.

Study visits:

The Communities efforts in the area of transition are not, however, limited to the pilot projects. As part of the programme, a grants scheme for study visits was introduced in 1977 and lasted four years up to the end of 1981. Its purpose was to enable specialists in vocational education and guidance to update their knowledge in the light of the methods and experiences of their fellows in other Member States, the better to develop policies in this field within their own systems of education.

The scheme was aimed specifically at those concerned with helping young people about to make, or in process of making, the transition from education to employment. More particularly, two groups of guidance specialists were encouraged to apply: first, those actively involved in the field of educational and vocational guidance and, second, teacher trainers with responsibility in this domain. It was thought useful that emphasis be placed on those applications dealing with the linkage between the two sectors of education and employment. The Commission's contribution to this was 100,000 Units of Account in 1977-78, 200,000 in 1979-79 and for the following year was calculated on the basis of a maximum of 1,000 Units per visitor.

Statistical guidelines:

Monitoring of the most recent developments in the area of transition from school to work is, obviously, an important aspect both in the development of appropriate measures to deal with the problems posed as well as assessing the impact of measures implemented. The preparation of statistical guidelines to bring together information on the transition from education to working life is being undertaken by the Statistical Office of the European Communities. Discussions have been held both with the Education and Employment services of the Commission and with the European Centre for the Development of Vocational Training (West Berlin). Draft guidelines have been drawn up for further discussion with the statistical services of Member States. It is not expected, however, that Community level statistics specifically geared to the issue of transition on a compatible basis will appear before 1983.

Conclusion:

The development of the Community pilot projects took place against a background of considerable change. Such change was not limited simply to the area of transition, though the difficulties that growing youth unemployment poses are amongst the most important human dilemmas against which it has to be placed. Events over the past six years have shown that, between education and the employment system a new relationship is emerging. This 'new relationship' can be seen in the growing take-over by the compulsory stage of schooling of the task of preparing young people for working life as part of what has previously been called 'general' education in some countries or 'academic education' in others. But, just as there is a penetration at all stages into the education systems of Member States, of programmes designed to develop basic skills, to act as remedial education, or to 'socialise' young people specifically into the ever growing complexities of the working world, so there has also been a powerful counter-current by which industry and the employment sector have assumed responsibilities of an educational nature. The involvement of employment and industry in the provision of the long term educational and training needs of the least skilled or least qualified school leavers — the penetration of school into industry — is no less significant.

Arguably, the historic distinction between academic and vocational education is less realistic today than it has been before. Nor can we be entirely sure of the consequences for the balance of power between the two that the development of the new information technologies will have. Conceivably, they may bring the two domains of 'general' and 'vocational' education even closer together both as regards content, the skills developed and the young people who embark upon them. This was further underlined by the Ministers of Education during their meeting of June 22nd 1981 when they stressed their undertaking to give all young people an opportunity to become familiar with the working world during their education and basic training.

But the other side of this is clearly demonstrated in the pilot projects — namely, the need, if transition is to be adequately prepared — for the involvement of sources of learning that exist outside the schools, whether in the form of collaboration with firms, individuals with special skills (hitherto less regarded in schools than they ought to have been) or even new locations for learning such as the community. The problem of coordination and cooperation between education authorities and other agencies is not limited simply to the administrative requirements of developing a more flexible and consistent policy in the areas of education, social affairs and economic affairs, though this, as has been suggested, is one of the more pressing requirements in the field of transition. It also extends down to the individual school and means, essentially, that schools ought to recognise their interdependence with their community and with those establishments involved with vocational training later in the career of the individual student.

SOURCES

i. **Primary: internal Commission documents**
'Preparation of young people for working life and for transition from education to work', *Document No. 4/32290/e/76 (EN 52)*, October 8th 1976.
'Communication of Mr Brunner to the Commission', *Document No. SEC (76) 3827*, November 26th 1976.
'Implementation of the Resolution of December 13th 1976: progress report on measures taken at Community level', *Document 5471/80, (EDUC 16)*, March 5th 1980.
'General Report of the Education Committee', *Document 8137/80 (EDUC 30)*, July 7th 1980.
'Note to the Education Committee from the services of the Commission: Programme of pilot projects on transition from education to working life. Progress report on the Central Animation and Evaluation Team', *Document V/645/81 EN*, July 1981.

ii. **Secondary: printed sources, official documents.**
Bulletin des Communautés Européennes, No. 5, May 1979.
Bulletin des Communautés Européennes, No. 6, June 1981.
Interim Report of the Central Animation and Evaluation Team for the programme of pilot projects, Köln, March 1980 IFAPLAN.
Incidence des changements d'ordre démographique sur les systèmes d'éduction dans la Communauté Européenne, Bruxelles, EURYDICE, 1981.
'Statistiques mensuelles du chômage enregistré dans la Communauté', *EUROSTAT Bulletin Mensuel Chômage*, No. 9, 1981.

iii. **Tertiary: pamphlets, articles of a non-official nature.**
Guy Neave, 'Editorial', *Research perspective on the transition from school to1 to work*, Amsterdam/Lisse, Swets & Zeitlinger, 1978.
Guy Neave, 'The changing balance of power in the 16 to 19 age range in Europe', *Comparative Education*, Vol. 16, No. 2, 1980.
Guy Neave, 'Education and history: some thoughts on a fluctuating field', *Paper presented to the British Education Management and Administration Society Annual Conference*, Cardiff, Wales, April 12th 1981.
Newsletter of the European Community Action Programme, No. 5, October 1980.

Chapter Four
Education and Training

Structure:
Introduction
Community instruments of intervention
Development of policy in the area of vocational training
   1. First period 1963-1976
   2. Second period 1976-1980: parallel policies
       — New policy initiatives
       — Development of strategies of alternated work and training
   3. Third period 1980 onwards: policies of convergence
Impact of reorganisation on priorities for vocational training
Conclusion
Notes
SOURCES

Introduction

The improvement of vocational training has long been a part of Community policy. In effect, provision for Member States to collaborate closely in the fields of vocational and in-service training and their related areas was enshrined in Articles 57, 118 and 128 of the Treaty of Rome. Thus Community competence in the field of vocational training is clearly set out and the initiatives that may be taken at this level unambiguously stated which is not the case for those aspects of education outside the vocational domain.

From the first, vocational training was seen as an immediate element in the encouragement of the mobility of labour across the Community. It is then scarcely surprising that the earliest move towards the development of a common Community policy in this area, was taken in April 1963. This took the form of a Council decision which laid down some general principles for the setting up of a common policy for vocational training. Amongst the ten key clauses contained in this document was the statement that every person should receive adequate training with due regard to freedom of choice of occupation, place or training and place of work. Of particular importance in view of the subsequent development of Community activity in this area, was Principle 2. The objective of a common vocational training policy, it noted, was to bring about conditions that would guarantee adequate training for all and, further, that vocational training was itself to be broadened and based firmly on general education. The overall purpose of such a policy was twofold: first, to encourage the all-round (*harmonieux*) development of the individual; second, to keep abreast of technical innovations, the development of new methods of production and changes in both the social and economic spheres. Amongst other matters touched upon was the need to improve the basic and in-service training of instructors and the need to establish a general coordinated series of measures to balance the supply and demand for suitably qualified labour. Despite wide ranging change in national economies and society since they were first enunciated, these principles retain their validity, even today.

A second step was taken in December of the same year. This set up an Advisory Committee for Vocational Training the remit of which was to present a reasoned opinion on questions of general importance in the field of vocational training either on its own initiative or at the request of the Commission. Composed of 2 representatives of government, 2 from the employers' side and a further 2 from employees' organisations from each Member State, the Advisory Committee meets at least twice a year. Its mandate is renewed every two years. The creation of this tripartite body has been of considerable importance which is reflected in the establishment of comparable bodies at Member State level.

Community instruments of intervention:

The European Community also disposes of other instruments of intervention in the field of vocational training. Amongst them are the Regional Development Fund, the Fund for the Guidance of European Agriculture both of which may be used to contribute in different ways to the retraining of young people moving out of declining sectors in industry or agriculture. In addition, there is the European Social Fund which may also be used to encourage young workers to become better qualified as well as being more mobile both geographically and occupationally.

The European Social Fund, set up in 1958 by the Treaty of Rome, has undergone various revisions since then. In 1971, it was reformed so as to bring it closer to the evolving requirements of the labour market. Essentially, this involved the extension of its remit to cover those young people who were either out of work, unqualified for existing job vacancies, or alternatively qualified only for jobs no-one wanted. It has tended to concentrate on occupational training. A further change was introduced following the Council Decision of July 23rd 1975 which provided for the Fund to grant assistance to '... *facilitate the employment and the geographical and professional mobility of young people under 25 who are unemployed or seeking employment'*. However, with the spiralling demand placed on its resources, particularly after 1976 when the problem of youth unemployment assumed serious proportions in the Community, the Fund was forced to limit its intervention to certain priority activities lest applications for assistance outstripped its resources. In 1976, the main emphasis *inter alia* lay on the development of innovative programmes, the introduction of new approaches, methods and training structures to ease the transition from school to work. The following year, the priority centred on vocational preparation and assistance for pre-employment schemes for disadvantaged youngsters. A secondary emphasis was placed on supplementary provision for skilled training facilities. In 1978, further guidelines, issued for the management of the Fund, attached special significance to assisting the development of vocational preparation schemes for young people living in regions with above average youth unemployment. Between 1975 and 1977 alone, the Social Fund laid out some 279,000,000 European Units of Account to assist vocational training measures for the young and, in 1978, some one million young people in the Community received vocational preparation with the help of the Fund. Like the Advisory Committee on vocational training, the Committee for the European Social Fund is made up of a tripartite representation of employers, unions and government officials from all Member States.

Development of policy in the area of vocational training:

The development of policy in the field of vocational training may be said to fall into three broad phases, the first of which runs from 1963 until 1976, the second from 1976 to 1980 and the third from 1981 to the present. These periods mark less major turning points in thinking about the role and purpose of vocational training, though obviously this is important, so much as administrative changes in the services responsible for this field and its relationship with others, principally the Education service, which have corresponding and parallel commitments. During the first period spanning the 13 years from 1963 to 1976, the remit for vocational training fell under the ambit of Directorate General V (Social Affairs). If the main burden of activities at Community level tended to concentrate upon the area of vocational guidance, the result of which was the adoption by the Council on July 26th 1971 of a series of general guidelines for furture development of a programme in this area at Community level, effective action was relatively limited. There were a number of reasons to account for such a situation. First, the view of Member States at that time was that vocational training did not have a high priority in the area of public intervention policies. Second, the legal basis for action by the Commission was more implied than specific. And finally, both staff and financial resources inside the Commission were limited. Nor should one forget the emphasis laid upon vocational guidance in drawing up the initial Community Action Programme for the vocational rehabilitation of handicapped persons in July 1974. But difficulties in setting up a coherent strategy were considerable, not least because in most Member States ministerial responsibility for vocational guidance and training tends to be dispersed across different Ministries — Education, Labour, Agriculture, Manufacturing Industries, and Transport and Service Industries.

1. First period 1963-1976:

During this first period, policy development towards vocational training tended to follow the traditional dichotomy between general and vocational education that most education systems subscribed to at that time. It also tended to draw its main inspiration from what may be seen as economic considerations which derived in the main from the notion of Europe primarily seen as a trading community. The Recommendation of the Commission to Member States for the development of vocational guidance, passed in July 1976, falls fully within this framework. Vocational guidance in this context, was conceived as an instrument to complement the removal of obstacles that hitherto prevented the mobility of labour across the Community.

Three developments intervened, however, to bring about a reappraisal of the part that vocational training should play in Community policy. The first of these was the publication in 1971 of general guidelines for a Community Action Programme already mentioned. The second was the Conference of the Heads of State or Government held at Paris in October 1972. The third was the initial move towards setting up a Community Education Programme, the first public announcement of which appeared in 1974 with the publication of the document *Education in the European Community*, otherwise known as the *Janne Report (for this see supra Chapter I, pp.7-8)*. The first noted that changes in the economic, social, technical and educational dimensions of European society required that the question of vocational training be posed in different terms. More specifically, such changes — amongst which were the emergence of multi-national enterprises, the spread of the productive process in particular firms across several countries plus the development of capital-intensive rather than labour-intensive industries – had had the effect of bringing to light the importance of links between education and the economy, on the one hand, and the economy and training on the other. No less significant was the admission that in these fields, the role of both pre-school education (particularly important in the area of job equality for women) and permanent education was primordial. The second involved recasting the context in which Community policy towards vocational training took place. The goal of European union, the Paris meeting pointed out, was not that economic expansion should be an end in itself, but rather a means of improving the quality of life. This redefinition of the long-term purpose of the Community had profound repercussions in the area of vocational training which were apparent in documents appearing in 1975. Not merely did this imply a closer relationship between education and training – a policy that was fully to emerge in 1981 – but also the recognition that both could serve as instruments to provide 'positive discrimination' in favour of various social groups held to be 'disadvantaged'. *Education and training,* the Advisory Committee for Vocational Training noted in 1975, *are ideal instruments to provide for "positive discrimination" in favour of those categories known as "disadvantaged" – including not only migrant workers, but also the mentally and physically handicapped, women and girls, early school leavers and the chronically poor. The Community,* it continued, *is engaged in a number of policies which are aimed directly at improving the situation of all these groups'.*[1]) In other words, from being an ancillary for economic and social change, vocational training assumed, at least theoretically, a more central part as a vehicle of policy in the Community.

This shift had been indicated during preliminary discussions that took place prior to the setting out of an Education Action Programme in 1976. The need to bring education nearer to vocational training was powerfully argued in the Janne Report: *'. . . one of the major tendencies in the revision of the education system in all our countries,* observed this latter, *. . . (is) . . . that there is no longer any good vocational training that does not comprise a sound general training at all levels, and there is no longer any good general training which is not linked with concrete practice, and, in principle, with real work'.*[2]) Thus a notion of polyvalence which extended not only to young people, but also involved adults as well as teachers and instructors in the vocational field began to take shape, following the setting up of general guidelines for vocational guidance in 1971.

A further sense of urgency was added by the oil crisis, the subsequent rise in energy costs and the economic downturn that began in 1973-74. Vocational training and retraining were seen as crucial elements in the development of an

1. 'Advisory Committee for Vocational Training. Meeting of September 11th; working paper for discussion on point 4 of the agenda Vocational training in the European Community' (undated circa July 1975?).
2. 'For a Community policy in Education', *Bulletin of the European Communities (supplement 10/73),* 1973.

Education and Training

overall strategy for economic recovery, an emphasis which was underlined by the Council Resolution of January 21st 1974. This set out broad proposals for a new Community initiative in the form of a Social Action Programme in which the major priorities were the development of full employment and an improvement in working conditions. Though at the time, few thought that the problem of youth unemployment was anything but a temporary and passing phenomenon, the conviction was rapidly acquired not merely that adequate vocational training stood as the key to reducing unemployment amongst the young, but also that it formed an essential item in any strategy designed to enhance the status of any particular group in society by its ability either to reinforce or to diminish inequality. Clearly, the place occupied by vocational training began to shift in the thinking of the Community from being associated predominantly with policies of industrial training to a rather wide context of both social and employment policy across the Community.

Crucial to this reinterpretation of the role of vocational training was the setting up of a Joint Working Party at the end of March 1975 by Directorate General V, responsible for Social Affairs, and Directorate General XII, responsible for Research, Science and Education. Its brief was to explore various possibilities of a closer working relationship between the two services, education and vocational training, with a view to strengthening the linkage between education and training systems. The Working Party met three times during that year. In the course of its discussions, the principle was recognised that vocational guidance should be a lifetime concern and not be confined to a single point in the career of individuals, usually at the beginning of working life. What was less clear, however, was the basis on which the two services should work together. Agreement on the need to develop new education programmes and structures, particularly for those young people who had left or who were on the point of leaving full-time education, was one thing. The question of the basis on which this agreement could be worked out was another. From the standpoint of Directorate General V the most appropriate areas for linkage between the two services within the framework of the Education Action Programme, then under discussion inside the Commission, involved pupil and teacher exchange, and measures designed to increase the mobility of those concerned with vocational and career guidance within the education system.

In part, this reflected the growing concern about the effect of youth unemployment and the belief that further emphasis on vocational guidance would prove the most useful immediate measure to palliate it. Already in the course of 1975, several information courses on this topic had been held for experts at Member State level, the first taking place in Copenhagen on October 22-24th, the second in London in December and a third in Dublin in May the following year. Such a preoccupation equally reflected the disquiet inside the Standing Committee on Employment within the Council where the issue had been raised in June 1975.

2. *Second period 1976-1981: parallel policies:*

Thus, if the rise of youth unemployment and the recognition that many young people entered unskilled occupations on leaving school both served as a catalyst to Community thinking, the interpretation as to the remedies available continued to show considerable diversity between the two services. The policy of Directorate General V tended to focus on specific aspects such as the effectiveness of apprenticeship schemes in Member States, to emphasise the place of guidance in both education and training systems in assisting those moving from full-time education to full-time employment and to commission reports on developments in the vocational guidance systems of Member States. The Education Services equally recognised the lack of vocational education and training as being of decisive importance in that less well qualified school leavers tended also to be those less motivated for vocational training. But, operating 'upstream', the Education Services espoused a more 'systems-based approach' which laid stress on the desirability of educational planning and developments in the labour market to be more attuned to each other than had been the case in the past. *'This,* a report noted, *is true for general education and even more so for vocational education'.*[3] It also argued strongly for the integration of vocational training into the whole education system.

Thus the period from 1976 to 1981 in the development of vocational training policy was one during which two parallel, though largely complementary strategies continued to run side by side. The first, operated by Directorate General V, continued to lay importance on the traditional interpretation of vocational training which assigned distinct and independent role to Education on the one hand and Employment policies on the other, whilst extending vocational training programmes to hitherto excluded groups. Typical of this latter was the creation of a specific category of intervention under the terms of the Social Fund for vocational training programmes for women in December 1977. A further example of this process was the Recommendation on Vocational Preparation issued in July of the same year. Designed as a measure to combat rising youth unemployment, its purpose was twofold: primarily, to make vocational preparation available to young people between the end of compulsory school attendance and the age of 25 in cases where they were either unemployed or threatened with unemployment and where they had no other opportunity for vocational training; second, to ensure that such young persons had a satisfactory transition from school to work by providing them with the minimum skills and knowledge necessary for working life. The second strategy operated by Directorate General XII sought less to develop and extend established practices than to question their essential validity, and more especially in the case of those underpinning accepted relationships between school and work. In this perspective, it was argued, first, that the prime concern ought to be the conception and implementation of preventive rather than palliative measures which implied a

3. 'Preparation of young people for working life and for transition from education to work', *Document R/32290/e/76 (EDUC 52),* October 8th 1976.

long-term strategy pursued across a broad spectrum of the various Commission's services bearing on the linkage between education and work; and second, that greater attention ought to be paid to the different patterns by which vocational training was organised in various Member States. Vocational training, it was pointed out, cannot respond quickly to the changing requirements of the labour market, particularly in those countries where it was organised in full-time educational establishments. In circumstances such as these, the lack of opportunity to combine training with practical work experience added to the difficulties of those with educational qualifications of a general nature to complete vocational training within their employment, meant, in the view of Directorate General XII, that many 15 to 19-year-olds emerging from full-time education faced particular problems in finding a first job. By contrast, occupational insertion in those countries where training took place in firms, seemed, at first, to be less fraught. But for those without apprenticeship places or training contracts, the main difficulty seemed to be in holding down a job. In other words, the quantitative problems of moving from school form to factory involved not merely the nature of vocational training itself, but also its place in the broader structures of the education system as a whole. Attempts to find solutions to these difficulties 'upstream' from the end of compulsory schooling, were the main objectives of the programme of pilot projects described in Chapter III. Accordingly, attention will be paid to those activities undertaken 'downstream' in the area of vocational training.

New policy initiatives:
Central to the development of new initiatives in the area of vocational training was the establishment of the European Centre for the Development of Vocational Training in West Berlin in 1975. The importance of this establishment lay in two areas: first, it increased the research capacity in the field of vocational training and other issues related to it — a consideration not without significance when one bears in mind that the limited success of the first two action programmes of 1965 and 1971 in the vocational field had been attributed to this shortcoming; second, it provided a focus for exploring various possibilities for action in the light of the latest developments, and thus constituted an important instrument for the analysis of policy options that could be reviewed in the light both of developing further initiatives and assessing those already under way.

To underpin the renewed importance of vocational training and guidance in Community employment and social policies, the Commission set up a working party to reinterpret the principles originally drawn up in 1963 in the light of changes that, subsequently, had taken place in the economy. The working party reported to the Advisory Committee on Vocational Training on May 24th 1977. Whilst acknowledging the continued validity of the 10 principles, it suggested that a common policy for vocational training should involve the following objectives:

- to assist those responsible for improving and developing vocational training systems in Member States;
- to facilitate the solving of problems in the transition from school to a job;
- to encourage the development of continuous training;
- to promote the development of vocational guidance and training in the light of the Community objective of equal opportunity;
- to promove the development of vocational training for migrant workers;
- to improve information concerning job qualification;
- to expand Community technical assistance to developing countries as regards vocational training;
- to extend vocational training to the handicapped.

The submission of these guidelines was closely followed by a Recommendation issued in July 1977 which called upon Member States to extend vocational *preparation* to young people who were unemployed or who faced the threat of future unemployment. Vocational preparation by contrast with vocational training is defined as 'those activities that aim to assure for young people a satisfactory transition from school to work by providing them with the minimum skills and knowledge necessary for working life'. This Recommendation, which received the support of the Advisory Committee on Vocational Training, the Economic and Social Committee and the European Parliament, marked an important stage in the thinking about the relationship between education and training. Though it recognised the desirability of extending into compulsory education the groundwork on which vocational training would be based, it did not take fully into account the implications that arose from the differences in structure and organisation in vocational training systems based on full-time further education and those where training was based mainly in particular firms. Nevertheless, the Recommendation represented an important development in that it foresaw, implicitly, the eventual emergence of an intermediary stage prior to fully fledged vocational training and the end of compulsory education, a system that gradually emerged as youth unemployment spiralled.

By 1978, estimates reckoned that some 30 percent of young people in employment faced difficulty in maintaining their jobs through lack of adequate vocational training and that a further 75 percent of those out of work stood to benefit by such a measure. In all, it was thought that across the European Community some 5,700,000 youngsters were in need of vocational preparation. Of these, some 1,200,000 were out of work and 4,500,000 currently employed. Since just over 1,000,000 young people in 1978 received vocational preparation, the gap between the aims of the Recommendation and its achievement remained considerable.

However, if the Recommendation did touch upon such fundamental matters as the necessary minimal level of training, the contents of such programmes and the recognition of the certificates awarded to those following them, it still made the assumption that such actions were transitional, just as the phenomenon of youth unemployment was held to be of a similar nature.

By 1978, it became apparent that this assumption could no longer be made. Far more significant, it could not be assumed that policies designed to extend a traditional model of vocational training were either suited or adequate for the task. Thus, a basic question which arose was whether the training system itself ought not to be adjusted to the changing situation. The fact that many young people aged 18 or 19 and over who, having undergone vocational training, faced unemployment and little prospects for the future, suggested that the time was ripe to review the adaptability of the training system itself. Amongst the arguments put forward in favour of this course were first that, as at present constituted, vocational training did not offer any long term openings for employment; second, that in consequence it might, in certain circumstances, actually increase the peripheral labour market rather than assist in providing stable employment for youngsters in the central labour market; third, that it did not easily match up with the growing trend amongst young people to move in and out of employment, which implied that the distinction between employment and unemployment was rather less rigid than had hitherto been assumed to be the case; and fourth, that in times of prolonged recession, vocational training in its historic form, might well increase the relative disadvantage of those in rural or inner city areas. Studies into the job-mobility of the young unemployed showed that around half had been out of work for less than three months and that in the Community as a whole, 24 percent of 16 to 17-year-olds and 51 percent of 17 to 18-year-olds left school without pursuing any further education or training.

Development of strategies or alternated work and training:

The vehicle through which a wide-ranging reappraisal of the structure, means and purpose of vocational training and of its relationship with the education system took place, was the concept of alternated work and training, expressed in French by the word *alternance*. Briefly, this concept may be described as one linking practice training obtained by the exercise of a vocational activity at the place of work with theoretical training obtained in a training service, organisation or establishment, in essence, the combination of work and training. The starting point of this new perspective was the notion that work experience is itself a valuable instrument to learning. Its major assumption was that such practical learning did not end at school, or begin only in vocational training programmes *stricto sensu*. Rather, based on the idea known as 'experiential learning', the concept of *alternance* hung on the conviction that the transition from school to work involved a quantitatively different type of learning, combining knowledge acquired on-the-job with opportunities for further education and training throughout an individual's working life.

Initial thinking in this area may be traced back to October 1978, when the Commission's services suggested three options for future policy development to the Advisory Committee on Vocational Training. The first of these was the *alternance* model, the second, the clarification of the status of young persons and the third the concept of a 'right' to training for all young people. The Advisory Committee retained the first option for particular attention, and asked the Commission to put forward more specific proposals. The request received further support in March 1979. The European Council demanded that the Council of Ministers of Employment and Social Affairs study *alternance* as one of the measures that should contribute to improving the employment situation and also consider 'concrete action' in this context. The issue was broached by the Ministers of Employment and Social Affairs at their meeting in May 1979 as part of an overall policy aimed at sharing the available volume of work more evenly. The previous month, the Commission's services had presented a detailed proposal to the Advisory Committee which made specific suggestions for a linked system of work and initial training for young people. This was seen as taking place between the end of compulsory education and the age of 18 and included points on such matters as the design and content of the training component, its organisation and finance.

Originally, it had been envisaged that the implementation of the *alternance* model should be carried out through a Directive, binding on all Member States. Partly to relaunch a Community wide-discussion on the organisation and objectives of vocational training, partly also to ensure greater flexibility in drawing up a future development project in this area, a Resolution was substituted. This was adopted by the Council of the European Communities on December 18th 1979.

When it passed the Resolution, the Council noted that the application of *alternance* was particularly appropriate, first, for young people undergoing apprenticeships or post-educational training courses; second, those seeking jobs who were eligible for special training measures designed to integrate them into the labour market and, third, young workers without adequate vocational training. Member States, it pointed out, should be encouraged to establish effective links between training and on-the-job experience and such links should involve the establishment of coordinated programmes and structures between the various bodies responsible. Amongst the other guidelines contained in the Resolution was the need to lay down a training base sufficiently broad to meet the demands of technological developments and future changes in occupational structure and, particularly important, that both the level of competence achieved in, and the content of, such courses should facilitate access to further vocational or general training. Finally, Member States were exhorted to ensure that linked work and training fell into line with full-time training, possibly by sharing the same diplomas. The purpose of this latter was to facilitate subsequent transfers between different branches of training. Also envisaged was an examination of the conditions under which the European Social Fund might be associated with action undertaken by Member States. One possibility was seen as a series of small-scale experiments to develop *alternance* models.

To launch discussion in a wider forum, following this Resolution, two measures were undertaken initially. The first was a conference called by the Commission and held in Berlin in June 1980 at the European Centre for the Development of Vocational Training. Its purpose was to define the various target groups which should be involved in the first instance with the new form of

Education and Training

training, the various methods that might be employed and to review ways of implementing the two-year action programme thus initiated. The second was the establishment of a working group within the Commission's Advisory Committee on Vocational training. This was established in May 1980 with a remit to lend support to the new programme and composed of one representative from each Member State. Later, the European Centre for the Development of Vocational Training was called upon to make a survey of existing provision for *alternance* training in the countries of the Community.

The long term significance of *alternance* training lay not merely in the promise of imparting a new flexibility to training systems — a consideration of particular relevance if such systems were adequately to cope with both industrial and macro-economic change on the one hand and the demands of the individual on the other — but also in bringing nearer to one another policies of development in education and in training that hitherto had run along parallel lines. From April 1980 onwards, discussions on the long term implication of *alternance* began to reflect a convergence of ideas between the Commission's Education services and those responsible for Vocational Training. The impetus behind this did not, however, spring solely from the issues posed by *alternance.* It was also inspired by the recognition of the potential and actual impact of the new information technologies (*for this see Chapter VIII*). Already in March 1980, discussions within the Consultative Committee for Vocational Training on the question posed for community vocational training policy by technological change recognised the importance of paying attention both to continuing education and, no less significantly, to the content of both primary and secondary education. Thus the thesis long maintained by the Education services within the context of transition from school to work — namely, the necessity for an integrated approach to general education, vocational training and permanent training — assumed a new weight.

3. Third period 1980 onwards: policies of convergence:

From an administrative and organisational standpoint, the policy of an integrated approach to education and training received its final confirmation with the reorganisation of the Commission's services in January 1981. It is nonetheless evident that the groundwork had been laid firmly the year before. Particularly important in this regard was the step marked by the so-called 'June Mandate' which resulted from the meeting of the Ministers of Education in June 1980. The vocational relevance of language teaching to both young people and adults, the role of the universities and of teacher training policies together with the necessity of coming to grips with the wide-ranging implications of the new technologies were outlined at that meeting by Commissioner Guido Brunner (*for this see Chapter VII, pp. infra*). The view that education must come out of its isolation and play a recognised role in the shaping of social and employment policy was elaborated further at a meeting of the Consultative Committee for Vocational Training in July 1980. Following the June Mandate, the Commission looked afresh at what actions might be taken at Community level, the likely development in the area of education, and vocational training during the 1980s and the ways in which the latter might be developed in the light of the former. For its part, the Advisory Committee for Vocational Training, as a result of discussions with the Standing Committee on Employment in July 1980, asked the Commission's services to examine and make proposals on the specific role vocational training might play as a result of the changes expected from the impact of the new information technologies. It also called for a review of the possible options that might arise from an integrated approach to education and vocational training. This latter task was given to a British expert, Dr Ron Johnson, whose report *Vocational Training in the 1980s* was discussed initially at the meeting of February 13th 1981.

Just as the Commission's services in charge of vocational training began to review the context in which future developments might be located, so too a similar exercise took place inside those responsible for education. Whilst on the one hand, it was admitted that acting independently, neither education nor training systems could do little directly to help Member States overcome their employment problems, nevertheless, the Education Committee was of the opinion they could and ought to contribute to the search for longer-term solutions. Irrespective of the economic situation, the Education Committee pointed out, education had the explicit responsibility to begin the preparation of young people for working life within the context of general education and before the end of compulsory schooling.

Looked at from this perspective, the challenge facing education in its relationship with work could no longer be confined to the question of transition from school to work. Rather the priority appeared to demand a major overhaul of both education and training systems first, in the light of new demands and new relationships in society at large and, second, in the light of the need to provide educational opportunities for adults throughout their working life. Reviewing various policy options, the Education Committee recognised that the two outstanding areas of priority were:

— the preparation of young people for working life;
— the development of continuing education and training.

As regards the former, the Commission foresaw the eventual development of integrated patterns of upper secondary and post-secondary education which would combine general education, and contain elements of vocational training plus work experience. Equally desirable would be a modification to systems of assessment and certification to ease the passage of individuals across various parts of education and training. Such a development pointed up the need to pool those resources, both financial and staffing, at present spread across different authorities, as a means of making use of alternative facilities out of school for learning. As regards the latter, one aspect of special relevance involved the transfer of that experience gained in *temporary* youth unemployment measures to adult age groups as a whole, particularly those combining further education and training with work.

Education and Training

At a time of accelerated industrial change resulting from the growing application of the new information technologies to all walks of life, it was felt to be a matter of high significance that a second chance be given to adults to acquire basic general and vocational skills.

Measures should also include provision for continuing education aimed at assisting older people, prematurely retired or made redundant. The Council was invited to select priority themes for future development.

The drawing up of integrated policies in which both education and training played a strategic part in the social and economic development of Europe was underlined both in the Johnson Report and the Report presented by a German expert, Arndt Sorge, on *Micro-electronics and vocational education and training*, submitted in June 1981. Symbolic of this new development – and paralleled by similar moves in various Member States – was the inclusion of Education under a new single directorate with responsibility for education, vocational training and youth policy which brought together elements previously held separate in Directorate General V (Social Affairs) and Directorate General XII (Education, Science and Research policy). This took place in the earlier part of 1981.

A further move in the development of the twin themes of education and training was made at the Ministers of Education meeting in June 1981. The Ministers expressed their commitment to the principle of inter-ministerial cooperation and in particular to developing a concerted approach to continuing education and training at a Community level. The previous month, the meeting of the Social Affairs Ministers and the Standing Committee on Employment, which dealt with the Community's new employment strategy, also noted that vocational training, re-training, continuing education, guidance and counselling all constituted important elements in it.

Impact of reorganisation on priorities for vocational training:

How then, has the reorganisation of the Commission's services impinged upon voational training policies at Community level? During the previous period from 1976 to 1980, vocational training was conceived as a measure designed to combat youth unemployment. By contrast it is now looked upon as a dependent dimension which can only be developed within the bounds fixed by political, social and economic policies and more especially within the framework of a Community level strategy designed, first, to master inflation and, second, to improve employment. Another crucial reappraisal has been to see vocational training as a developmental instrument not only in training for new jobs but at the same time in creating them. This reflects a major shift from a policy which, in the words of the Commissioner for Social Affairs, was excessively oriented towards vocational training.

In place of a policy that, in the past, tended to proceed by fits and starts, a strategy is being put in place which involves an overall and coherent linkage between compulsory education on one side and vocational training on the other, with special stress on the need for those young people to obtain suitable and relevant qualifications. This involves five main points:

- strengthening the general level of education during compulsory schooling;
- the development of initial and complementary training grounded upon a broad range of related occupations (*famille de métiers*);
- the development of new options for continuing education of a general character throughout an individual's working life;
- the organisation of the contents of such training, whether initial or in-service, upon a base of modular units in keeping with the model of *alternance;*
- a corresponding reinforcement of guidance and vocational guidance services to provide greater effectiveness to undertakings in the field of vocational training.

A further departure from the previous programme is the notion that vocational training should not be limited to those under 19 years of age but should cover young people under the age of 25. If, in the first instance, the new strategy is to be directed towards the unemployed and the young unemployed in particular, it is also aimed at young migrants, children from the inner city, the rural poor, young women, girls and the handicapped. The key to its subsequent execution is obviously the achievement of greater coordination between public authorities and the various 'social partners' — employers' representatives, delegates of trade union interests and government. Such coordination, it is suggested, should touch upon both the curriculum and the training content. It should also serve to draw up a variety of different approaches in keeping with the likely demands of the labour market and the needs of individuals.

This latter is no less an important departure since it is predicated on the concept that planning an integrated strategy in the area of vocational training depends directly on understanding the state of the labour market, as well as changes emerging in the nature of work itself, whether part-time or labour subcontracting. And, furthermore, it tends to take into greater account than before the considerable variation in the training systems of the Member States.

Conclusion:

In essence, the new strategy for vocational training turns about four major points. These are:

- the vocational and social insertion of young people from the time of leaving school up to 25 years of age;
- the strengthening of a policy for continuous training throughout working life;
- the search for a broader approach to vocational qualifications and their adjustment to changes introduced by the new information technologies;
- the development of policy and practice in the field of training which is better coordinated between the different interested parties — public authorities, local communities (*collectivités locales*) and social partners.

The emergence of an integrated approach to vocational training is a very real innovation in the policy of education in the Community. On the one hand, it bids fair to break down the historic dichotomy between general education pursued in school and full-time and vocational training, carried out either in firms or in establishments and agencies kept apart from what are conceived as 'true' educational institutions. On the other, it contains the potential for a realignment of the structures, content and purpose of a broadly-based system of education in keeping with the economic, social and individual requirements of the latter part of the 20th century. The condition of its success, however, depends on the willingness to carry out at local level a similar revision in the relationship between the various services engaged in administering school-based instruction and those managing out-of-school training and education. *'In short'*, as a recent Commission paper noted, *'the ability to change individuals by training depends fundamentally on the ability of the local authority concerned actively to enter into a process of transformation which is simultaneously economic, industrial, social and cultural'*[4]

---

4. 'La formation professionnelle pour les années 1980: une analyse et des propositions d'action communautaire. Une analyse de réflexion pour une Communication de la Commission au Conseil', *Document V3576/82*, April 19th 1982.

SOURCES

i. Primary: internal Commission documents

'The Commission's role in the development of vocational guidance in the Member States of the Community: a report by the Joint Working Party established by the Directorate General for Social Affairs and for Research, Science and Education', *Document XII/423/75e,* June 1975 (typewritten).

'Advisory Committee for Vocational Training. Meeting of September 11th; working paper for discussion on point 4 of the agenda, Vocational training in the European Community' (undated circa July 1975?).

'Preparation of young people for working life and for transition from education to work', *Document R/32290/e/76 (EDUC 52),* October 8th 1976.

'Activities of Directorate General V in the field of vocational training', *Document V/858/77,* July 6th 1977.

'Activities of Directorate General V in the field of vocational training July 1977 to May 1979', *Document V/535/79,* May 28th 1979.

'Minutes of the meeting of the Consultative Committee for Vocational Training April 26-27th 1979', May 29th 1979.

'Advisory Committee on Vocational Training: meeting of October 25-26th 1979', *Document V/125/80 EN,* February 7th 1980.

'Linking work and training for young persons in the Community: Communication from the Commission to the Council', *Document COM (79) 578 FINAL,* October 29th 1979.

'Implementation by the Member States of the Commission's recommendations on vocational preparation', *Document V/20/80-3EN,* February 12th 1980.

Consultative Committee for Vocational Training: meeting of March 18-19th 1980, April 10th 1980.

Consultative Committee for Vocational Training: meeting of July 2nd to 3rd 1980', *Document V/581/80-E,* July 25th 1980.

'Procès-verbal de la réunion des 12 et 13 février 1981 au Comité consultatif pour la formation professionnelle', *Document V/219/81 FR,* February 24th 1981.

'Outcomes of the proceedings of the Education Committee, April 23rd-24th 1981', *Document 6502/81 (EDUC 14),* April 29th 1981.

'Micro-electronics and vocational education and training', *Document V/780/81,* June 1981 *(Sorge Report).*

Speech by Commissioner I. Richard to the Advisory Committee on Vocational Training, July 16th 1981.

'La formation professionnelle pour les années 1980: une analyse et des propositions d'action communautaire. Un analyse de réflexion pour une Communication de la Commission au Conseil', *Document V/3576/82,* April 19th 1982.

Unpublished documents presented to the Commission:

The material and social standing of young people during transition from school to work: summary of the results of a CEDEFOP Conference held in Berlin in November 11-12th 1980, West Berlin, CEDEFOP, 1981.

Vocational training in the 1980s: a report by Ron Johnson for the Commission of the European Communities, May 15th 1981 (xerox).

ii. Secondary: printed sources, official documents.

'Council decision of April 2nd 1963 laying down the general principles for implementing a common vocational training policy', *Document 63/266/EEC, Official Journal,* April 20th 1963.

'Statuts du Comité consultatif pour la formation professionnelle', *Decision 633/688 CEE, Official Journal No. 190,* December 30th 1963.

'Recommandations de la Commission du 18 juillet aux Etats Membres tendant à développer l'orientation professionnelle', *Document 66/484/CEE, Official Journal No. 2815/66*, August 24th 1966.

'Orientations générales pour l'élaboration d'un programme d'activités au niveau communautaire en matière de formation professionnelle (retenus par le Conseil lors de sa 162ème session du 26 juillet 1971), *Official Journal No. C.81/5*, August 12th 1971.

Exposé sur les activités d'orientation professionnelle et des services de main-d'oeuvre des Etats Membres de la Communauté, Luxembourg, Commission of the European Communities, 1971.

'For a Community policy in Education', *Bulletin of the European Communities (supplement 10/73)*, 1973.

'Education in the European Community', *Bulletin of the European Communities (supplement)*, No. 3, 1974.

Regulation setting up the European Centre for the Development of Vocational training (Berlin) in *Official Journal No. L.39/1*, February 13th 1975.

Exposé sur les activités d'orientation professionnelle dans la Communauté, Luxembourg, Commission of the European Communities, 1975.

L'orientation et la formation professionnelle des travailleurs féminins (Paris seminar November 24-28th 1975), Brussells, Commission of the European Communities, 1976.

Official Journal No. L. 337, December 27th 1977.

Official Journal No. C.1, January 3rd 1980, pp.80-1.

iii. Tertiary, pamphlets, articles of a non-official nature.

Felix Kempf, 'Auf dem Wege zur einer gemeinsamen europäischen Politik auf dem Gebiet der Berufsbildung', *Gewerkschaftliche Bildungspolitik* 1/1982.

Guy Neave, 'Education and industry: some thoughts on a fluctuating field', *Paper delivered to the British Educational Management and Administrative Society*, Cardiff, (Wales) April 12th 1981.

'Social policy: European Commission guidelines and priorities', *Europe* No. 3209, September 18th 1981, p.12.

Chapter Five
Cooperation in Higher Education

Structure:
Introduction
Changes in the pattern of student mobility
Development of a Community policy
Admissions policy
The academic recognition of diplomas
Joint Programmes of Study
Short Study Visits
Information policy
European University Institute (Florence)
Cooperation outside the framework of the Education Action Programme
Scientific Research
Forecasting and Assessment in the field of Science and Technology (FAST)
Impact of the Community on teaching in higher education
Conclusion
SOURCES

Introduction

Europe is the object of many myths, some of which have been forgotten, others of which persist. Yet there is a third category — myths which are in the process of resurrection. Amongst the latter, none is more appealing than the vision of the scholar gypsy, wandering at will across the frontiers of Europe, stopping now and then, as the fancy takes him, at the various seats of learning that cross his path. It is an endearing conceit, perhaps the last vestige of romantic imagination in an age which prides itself on its hard-headedness and practical nature. Whether such figures existed in any great numbers is beside the point, though the largest contingent of wandering scholars hailed not from medieval times and still less from Europe. Rather, they were products of the late 19th century and came from the United States of America — engineers, historians and educators in the main. Still, the figure of the footloose student occupies an important place in the speeches of public personages and in the eschatology of Europe-in-being. For who knows whether this picture of the past might not be a profile of the future and the principle of mobility of labour be applied to the Republic of Letters?

At present, student mobility is as limited today as it was in medieval times. Across Europe of the Ten the academic year 1980-1 saw some 4,550,000 young people studying at various institutions of higher education — universities, teacher training establishments and establishments for higher professional and vocational training. A mere 21,000 or five students in a thousand were enrolled in courses at establishments outside their home country. By all events, the percentage 0.51 is low. Observers close to the Commission consider that a reasonable level of inter-state student mobility ought to be between five and ten percent of all those enrolled in higher education. A number of explanations have been put forward to account for this apparent lack of enthusiasm. It may, in fact, reflect a lack of information about the possibilities available. But it also underlines the large number of obstacles in the way of foreign study. Amongst them are differing entry qualifications and different structures of courses quite apart from variations in what is understood by one country as a given discipline and its nominal counterpart elsewhere. Furthermore, some countries operate a policy of restrictive entry to certain fields — Medicine being the most notorious. Then there are the variations in the fees demanded and in the patterns of student finance. Finally, as if such barriers were not enough, comes the question of whether studies undertaken abroad and the diploma crowning such efforts, will in fact be recognised as comparable with those awarded at home. Such are the obstacles that deter student mobility and such are the pitfalls that stand in the way of closer collaboration between institutions of higher education across the Community.

It is, perhaps not without reason that certain commentators in the field of mobility studies see students as an underprivileged body when compared to the various professional groups in the Community for whom the freedom of movement is a matter not just of right, but a fact.

This situation may well be made worse by the current economic climate – causing students to be rather more cautious in committing themselves to spending time abroad and thereby prolonging their overall duration of studies – and their entry into competition for the diminishing number of available jobs. This, together with more subtle and less obvious motivational factors, all play their part. Yet, these barriers, whether institutional, administrative, economic or motivational, all stand in marked contrast with the conviction, widely shared in all areas of the academic community, that universities – and other forms of higher education by implication – are international by definition, purpose and vocation. They are corporations for the dissemination of knowledge, and knowledge itself knows no frontiers.

Changes in the pattern of student mobility:
Yet, despite the small number of students studying abroad in the Community, significant changes are taking place. In the past, the predominant pattern of student mobility has been based on 'the free circulation' of students. More recently, however, there has been a move amongst several Member States towards what has been termed 'organised mobility', based in particular on structured forms of inter-institutional cooperation. Examples of this development will be discussed later in this chapter. Some 15 of them, as we shall see, may be directly attributed to the Community's efforts to develop such cooperation further.

The development of a Community policy:
Community action in the area of cooperation in higher education has therefore sought to remedy the situation pointed out at the start of this present chapter, i.e. by improving the quality and availability of information on opportunities for cooperation, by taking steps to remove the obstacles currently hindering such cooperation and by introducing a small measure of direct support to facilitate its growth. The basis of this policy was in the first instance the Resolution of the Council of Ministers on June 6th 1974. Three priority areas for action were outlined. They were:

– increased cooperation between universities and other institutions of higher education;
– improved possibilities for academic recognition of diplomas and periods of study;
– encouragement of the freedom of movement and mobility of teachers, research workers and students.

These points were subject to further elaboration in the Resolution of February 9th 1976 which laid out the Education Action Programme previously referred to. The measures to promote cooperation in higher education are contained in section IV, paragraphs 13 to 16 of the Programme. In effect, they amounted to a two pronged strategy. The first, representing the policy objectives, involved measures carried out at Community level, and consisted of four main elements.

These were, first, the establishment of links between institutions of higher education (and organisations representing them) and Community Institutions; second, the development of links between individual institutions of higher education across the different Member States; third, the setting up of a framework to exchange ideas and information on topics of common interest upon which would grow up a solid basis for educational cooperation in the Community; and finally, the strengthening of intra-Community links between the various organisations representative of higher education.

The second prong to Community strategy which may be regarded as an instrument for achieving the goals set out in the first, involved the promotion of free movement of teachers, researchers and students through the progressive removal of obstacles − academic or administrative − that stood in the way of such mobility. Such measures, it should be stressed, were in no manner of means intended to infringe the autonomy of individual institutions. This latter point was, and is still today, of particular importance not just as a matter of principle, but also in its implications for such matters as the issue of the recognition of academic diplomas. It has indeed been a characteristic of the first decade of Community policy in the field of higher education cooperation that this policy has been clearly oriented towards enhancing the opportunities for mutual *cooperation* between highly diverse systems rather than seeking to *harmonise* such systems from the centre. Probably the clearest expression of this policy approach in operational terms is the Community's scheme for the development of Joint Study Programmes, of which more will be said below.

Admissions policy:

In seeking to foster student mobility across the Community, the Commission had before it several examples of earlier attempts in this direction, notably the various Council of Europe convictions on recognition (cf. infra) and the report prepared for the same body by J. Capelle on the mobility of postgraduate students.

As an initial exploration of the extent to which student mobility between Community countries had developed over the years prior to 1975, a study was commissioned from a French expert, M. Jean-Claude Masclet. This was published in 1975 by the then Institute of Education of the European Cultural Foundation, with the title *Intra-European mobility of undergraduate students*. The Education Action Programme made provision for further discussion to take place on the issue of a common policy for admission to higher education of students from other Member States. This took place at Bonn (Federal Republic of Germany) in September 1977, against a background of growing constraint. In some countries, limitations were being placed on the number of students admitted to certain disciplines − particularly Medicine, Pharmacy and Engineering. In others, governments sought to persuade students to opt for short course higher education. A third development, particularly damaging in the intra-Community context, was the introduction of differential fees for overseas and foreign students, a policy introduced by Belgium, Ireland and the United Kingdom. The growth of such obstacles, over and above those already existing in such matters as admission and the recognition of diplomas, served to underline the need for a new initiative by the Commission.

This took the form of an increased budget for those schemes designed to foster inter-institutional links on a bi- or multi-lateral basis, namely the Joint Study Programme and the Short Study Visits Schemes. The immediate result of the Bonn conference on the issue of a common policy for admission to higher education of students from other Member States, held in September 1977, was a document prepared by the Commission. It analysed the problems posed by differences in current practice in the Member States and put forward certain solutions for dealing with the question of admissions. In February 1978, it was despatched for consultation to all Member States. In the light of their reactions, the Commission presented its proposals to the Council in September 1978. In essence, this put forward the idea that a common approach to the admission of foreign students to institutions of education in the Community should rest upon three principles. These were:

- that national policies should reflect the objectives of the Education Action Programme, namely, to increase the intra-Community mobility of students and to eliminate obstacles to this movement;
- that such policies should be based on Member States' recognition of their interdependence and mutual responsibilities in the context of admission of students from other Community countries;
- that individuals should be admitted to institutions in the host country on a basis no less favourable than the host country's own students, and according to academic criteria no stricter than those prevailing in their own country.

These principles were noted by the Council and the Ministers of Education meeting in Council on June 27th 1980. The Ministers recognised, however, that responsibility in the area of admissions policy did not always come under the ambit of central government. In some instances, it was a matter of either collective or individual responsibility of the institutions of higher education themselves. The main points agreed upon as providing the framework for a common admissions policy are set out below:

- where a policy of numerical limitation (viz. *numerus clausus, numerus programmaticus*) on admissions exists in any Member State, a reasonable number of places will be made available for students from other Community countries;
- students from other Member States will be excluded from numerical limitation provisions in the host country, except where these apply nationally, when their period of study abroad is a component part of an overall course of study to be completed at their home institution;

- proposals will be formulated at Community level (. . .) to facilitate and extend the transferability within the Community of credits for periods of study abroad;
- applicants from other Member States will, at most, be required to meet the non academic requirements applicable to home students;
- academic conditions for admission to a full course will normally be based on the possession by applicants of qualifications sufficient for them to be eligible for admission to a higher education institution in their own country and recognised as being equivalent in the host country;
- in the case of students spending part of their course in another Member State, great importance will be attached to the recognition by the competent authority or institution in their own country of the period of study abroad as part of the student's course leading to the home country's qualifications;
- Member state authorities awarding maintenance grants to students should continue to pay them for study periods in another Member State provided that the study periods concerned are recognised by the home institution as part of the full course of studies for which the grant was awarded;
- the degree of language proficiency required to attend courses of study in host-country institutions will be related to the needs of the courses of study chosen. Evidence of such proficiency will be provided and assessed before the commencement of the courses;
- to enable students where necessary to improve their language proficiency in the host country before commencing their course, an analysis will be made at Community level of the provisions for incoming students of facilities in all Member States for intensive study of the language of the host country, and the need for improved facilities;
- discussions will be organised at Community level with representatives of the competent authorities in each Member State and of institutions of higher education with a view to drawing up a common list of the basic information and documentation required from all applicants from other Member States;
- information will be collected at Community level on each Member State's arrangements for receiving and advising foreign students and regular meetings will be held between representatives of those responsible for such arrangements at which experience can be exchanged and problems identified.

To propose outlines for a common admissions policy in higher education is one thing, for them to form part of an active policy is another. In 1979, certain objections were raised by Denmark about the legal basis for such Community level action. It was argued by the Danish representatives at the Committee of Permanent Representatives to the Commission that in fact no legal basis existed for such a policy. Since no agreement has been reached within the Committee of Permanent Representatives on this issue, Community level developments have remained in abeyance pending a solution. It is, however, worthwhile noting that certain governments have, in the meantime, acted on their own initiative. Britain, for example abolished at least formally the differential in fees between home students and those coming from other EEC countries.

The academic recognition of diplomas:

It will be recalled that already during the 1950s, three major inter-governmental conventions on recognition matters had been passed under the aegis of the Council of Europe. The first, passed on December 11th 1953, dealt with the Equivalence of Diplomas leading to admission to universities. The second convention, passed on December 15th 1956, dealt with the equivalence of periods of university study across the 21 States, members of the Council of Europe, while the third passed on December 14th 1959, constituted a European Convention on the Academic recognition of university qualifications. It stipulated that, where the State is competent in matters of equivalence of university qualifications, the signators *'shall grant recognition to university qualifications conferred by a university situated in the territory of another Contracting Party'* (article 3.1).

Many of the provisions arising from these agreements have yet to be put into practice. Nevertheless, they do provide a useful framework within which the discussion on developing further the admission of students from other Member States of the Community might take place. In addition, there has since been passed the Unesco convention on the recognition of studies and of diplomas in higher education in countries of the European region, promulgated in December 1979. This latter provides for the recognition of university entrance qualifications to permit the holders to pursue studies in higher education establishments in the Member countries, though subject to the availability of places and to fulfilling of any linguistic requirements demanded.

Given this tradition of a search for multilateral, inter-governmental solutions to the recognition problem, and the concurrent negotiations between the Federal Republic of Germany and France, Belgium and the Netherlands respectively on the adoption of bilateral arrangements of various kinds, it is not surprising that when these problems were first addressed by the Community, the Resolution of the Council of Ministers of Education of June 6th 1974 called for the setting up of a system of academic equivalences. Subsequent developments, however, have shown that such a Community level policy did not have sufficient flexibility and, on the contrary, appeared too static an approach. During the early debates which took place between this Resolution and the appearance of the Education Action Programme in February 1976, a more pragmatic approach in dealing with the issue of recognising academic diplomas evolved. The original idea of drawing up a scale of equivalence for all higher education qualifications across the Community, was modified. Rather than seeking to develop a policy from above, it was reckoned to be more realistic in the short term, to develop a policy of close and sustained links between individual institutions, thus initiating a policy that built up from below. It was felt that such exchanges on an inter-institutional basis would be more suitable as a means progressively to remove those barriers that stood in the way of a mutual recognition of diplomas than attempting an overall solution at Community level from the outset.

In the same way, it was thought more judicious to place emphasis on 'recognition' rather than 'equivalence'. This had a number of advantages: first, the mutual recognition of diplomas, certificates and other evidence of formal qualifications sought a solution not at national level, so much as at the level of individual institutions; second, it was more expeditious and, finally, it placed initiative at the level of the grass roots, leaving free rein for individual initiative from beneath. It involved, in short, a policy of 'organic development' from below rather than the model contained in both the Council of Europe and the Unesco conventions which imply a legislative action from above.

Furthermore, the approach thus adopted enabled account to be taken of differences which exist between Member States when it comes to the validation of courses. Thus in some EC countries, the State itself acts as a major validating body. This is the case, for example, in France, Italy and the Federal Republic. In others, validation is the responsibility of semi-public bodies. This situation pertains for the non-university sector of higher education in Britain and Ireland. The Council for National Academic Awards and the National Council for Educational Awards have this function in the two countries respectively. By contrast, individual universities in the United Kingdom for example, act as chartered corporations awarding their own degrees. Since the value of a particular course depends on the type of diplomas or degree to which it leads, the question of admissions is then intimately tied up with solving the problem of recognising such diplomas across the Community.

The Community's approach was influenced by the publication in 1979 of a report by a British expert, Edwin Cox, which surveyed existing arrangements in the field and made several suggestions for future guidelines. Student mobility, it argued, would be enhanced by two innovations: first, by the introduction of a system of 'transfer credits' not only *within* Member States, but also *between* them Students moving from one institution to another ought, it suggested, to be credited for work undertaken previously. Second, the academic recognition of diplomas was more likely to succeed if based on either individual institutions or on individual departments within them, than the inter-governmental arrangements common hitherto.

In order to ascertain how far recognition, not least between individual institutions of higher education, either on a bilateral or a multilateral basis had developed, the Commission undertook an information exercise in 1980, in conjunction with the European Centre for the Development of Vocational Training, Berlin. Though not confined exclusively to higher education, the purpose of this exercise was *inter alia* to assemble details on existing mutually agreed equivalences, mutual agreements or 'treaties' between different institutions of higher education in the Member States and to assess how far these had adopted the directives relating to the mutual recognition of qualifications for the liberal professions.

Attention was also paid to any cross validation arrangements in force, for example, the recognition by the English Council for National Academic Awards of certain courses under the Community's Joint Study Programme Scheme or other similar arrangements. (Cross validation involves the recognition by the validating authority of one Member State of those elements of study spent in another institution as part of the integral course in the first.)

The main obstacles to the recognition of diplomas across the Community, the report concluded, did not lie so much at the level of post-graduate study or research. Here the question of selection for admission is relatively clear-cut. It is carried out on the basis of the individual's previous qualifications and their suitability for the field in which he wishes to study further. Rather, the major difficulties are to be found at undergraduate level. Amongst them are such questions as credits being given for those periods spent abroad which do not form part of a required course at the home institution. There are also obstacles in the way of students wishing to follow a programme that is shorter than the full length course up to diploma level. In certain countries, there are in addition, legal problems. For example, national legislation does not always allow establishments of higher education to give recognition to periods of study abroad.

Despite these problems, Community strategy in the area of recognition sets particular store by the development of part-course mobility. It is seen as a first step towards the drawing up of a Community wide network of institutions which recognise each other's diplomas. Further backing for this gradual, step by step approach, was given by the Ministers of Education, at their meeting on June 22nd 1981. The meeting called for the further development of bi-lateral agreements between Member States as a means, in the longer term, of reaching Community wide network agreements. It also emphasised the importance of basing this on existing bi-lateral or multi-lateral agreements reached at the level of individual institutions of higher education.

It is clear from an analysis of the relevant documents that the move towards academic recognition of diplomas across the Community involves three separate stages. The first involves the initiative of individual institutions, the second, the establishment of bi-lateral agreements between Member States and the possible third, the logical outcome of the first two, the arrival at Community level agreement in this field.

However, the crucial element, allowing the move from the first to the second is the dissemination of adequate information to institutions contemplating such a venture, and appropriate Community level structures are being established for this purpose. Nevertheless, the question remains how far the policy of academic recognition of diplomas through what has been termed *'an organic development from beneath'* has, in fact begun to yield results. A recent analysis of the arrangements reached between institutions collaborating within the framework of the Joint Study Programmes scheme is especially interesting. It shows that four different types of academic recognition arrangements are emerging. The first involves those programmes amounting to a complete course of study in which coordination between the participating institutions covers all aspects of such matters as content, structure and administration. Qualifications from all participating establishments are awarded. Examples of this are to be found, for instance, in the four year joint programme in European business administration launched by the Middlesex Polytechnic (UK), the *Ecole Supérieure de Commerce et d'Administration des Entreprises* (France) and the *Fachhochschule Reutlingen* (Federal Republic of Germany). A subvariant of this pattern is to be found in the programme linking the University of Kent (UK) with the *Université de Paris XI* (France) in the field of law. Students sit a fully validated degree course in their home institutions and, later, go abroad either to take a further degree course or a part of one.

In certain instances, for example, in France, the UK and Germany, recognition of such courses requires approval not only from all the participating institutions but also from externally validating bodies such as the central state administration in France, the various *Länder* authorities in Germany or the Council for National Academic Awards in the UK. Yet, experience suggests that despite the initial planning difficulties dual degree programmes of this type enjoy considerable popularity amongst students. So, too, do other forms of dual degree courses, though not necessarily validated in this manner.

A second version of recognition of diplomas involves an award of a qualification from the student's home institution together with an additional certificate awarded by all participating institutions. The latter attests the succesful completion of a partial course, mutually agreed upon by the participating establishments. Typical of this type of arrangements in the tripartite linkage between the *Universität Karlsruhe* (Federel Republic of Germany), the University of Essex (United Kingdom) and the *Ecole Supérieure d'Ingénieurs en Electrotechnique et Electronique* in Paris.

A third version involves the award of a certificate or diploma specifically devised to meet the purposes of the particular Study Programme. This may bear a completely new title — the case of the one year further degree level programme associating the *Fachhochschule für Wirtschaft,* Pforzheim (Germany), the Polytechnics of Leeds and the South Bank (London) and the *ESCAE (Ecole Supérieure de Commerce et d'Administration des Entreprises)* of Dijon (France) in business studies. It may constitute a joint award whose title is already accepted and validated by both all institutions, as with the European Diploma in Environmental Science which is a two-year further degree programme run jointly by the *Fondation Universitaire Luxembourgeoise* in Arlon (Belgium), the *Institut Européen d'Ecologie* (in Metz (France), the University of Metz, the Universities of Trier, Kaiserslautern and Saarbrucken (Germany) and the *Centre Universitaire* (Luxembourg).

The final pattern is, perhaps, less innovative, though no less effective. Students spend part of their course, recognised as an integral part of their home institution study programme, at another establishment in another Member State. This model, long associated with Modern Language degrees, has now been extended to such fields as medicine, economics, engineering, social science, business studies and history. It may apply either to first or to further degrees and involves periods as short as a few weeks or as long as an academic year.

The exact nature of these developments and an assessment of how many institutions outside the Joint Study Programme Scheme have undertaken similar exercises, remains, as yet, unclear. Nevertheless, it does suggest that the policy of leaving the running to individual institutions, acting at grass roots level, is meeting with a suitable and enthusiastic response in the area of recognition of academic diplomas. There is, as the Council of Ministers of Education meeting on May 24th 1982 pointed out, sufficient common ground between Member States to enable further progress to be made in the field of recognition in both the short and the medium terms. In the short term, the Ministers noted, existing arrangements and links which have proven of practical value, should be consolidated. In the medium term a number of avenues for development were open. Amongst those suggested by the Education Committee were:

— that encouragement should be given within the framework of bi-lateral agreements for the inclusion of measures to promote mutual recogniton of academic qualifications and periods of study;
— that Member States should encourage students in higher education to study in another Member State where such study is part of a structured course leading to a recognised qualification;
— that competent authorities in the Member States should adopt a favourable attitude towards qualifications obtained in other Member States that are not already recognised;
— that the Commission should assist in the provision of information about academic qualifications awarded in other Member States as a means of helping students decide whether to study in another Member State.

In order to further these developments, it was also suggested that every two years Member States draw up a report on the evolution of bi- or multi-lateral agreements between universities and other establishments of higher education in the field of recognition of academic diplomas. Equally, it was noted that both Member States and the Commission should consolidate on the experience of the Joint Study Programme Scheme to foster agreements at institutional level in different countries

Joint Programmes of Study:

The Joint Programmes of Study Scheme, to which reference has already been made on a number of occasions above, has clearly assumed a role of increasing significance, both as an instrument for student — and in some cases, staff — mobility and as a foundation stone in the Commission's medium-term policy of setting up a network of institutions of higher education that recognise each other's awards.

The purpose of the Scheme which was set up following the Resolution of February 9th 1976, is to assist in the development of trans-national courses to be planned and carried out jointly by two or more higher education institutions in different Member States. In order to be eligible for a Commission award, the cooperating institutions must have as their aim the establishment of arrangements whereby

- a) students are to spend a recognised or integrated part of their course in at least one of the partner institutions in another Member State, and/or
- b) parts of a course in each institution are to be taught by staff members from at least one institution from another Member State, and/or
- c) courses or parts of courses are to be jointly produced for introduction into the teaching programmes at all the participating institutions, even where no staff or student mobility is involved.

In several instances, the programmes concerned incorporate a work placement period (*stage*) linked to the theoretical instruction provided, though this is not the primary purpose of the Scheme.

Essentially, the objective of the Joint Programme of Study is to 'prime the pump', to start off the organisation and planning of projects, the maintenance of which subsequently becomes the responsibility of the institutions concerned. Though, at first, some suggestions were made that this programme ought to be limited to post-graduate students only, this was eventually felt to be too restrictive, and indeed in recent years, around two thirds of the programmes supported have involved studies at first degree level.

Grants of up to 4,000 European Units of Account are given per project, with an upper limit of no more than 10,000 EUA if the project is renewed. In selecting amongst applications, which have grown from 67 in 1977 to 240 in 1982, the Commission adopts a basically meritocratic approach, preferring on the whole to redress any perceived imbalances as regards such matters as distribution between the Member States, subject area types of institute and the mode of cooperation proposed, by increasing the dissemination of information about the scheme to the sectors concerned, rather than setting up quotas. This has proved particularly successful in the case of the natural sciences and that of Italy, which especially in the early days of the Scheme's operation, displayed a low level of participation.

In the seven years of the Joint Study Programme Scheme's existence, 467 grants have been awarded, involving 269 joint programmes, bringing together three or four institutions in some cases and in two, seven collaborating institutions. To date, some 450 establishments have been involved in the Scheme. An analysis of the type of subject areas and level of study in successful applications shows that, as regards the former, political and social sciences and economics tend to predominate, though there is a notable spread amongst other disciplines such as languages and linguistics, engineering, architecture and urban studies, business studies, law, geography, medicine and dentistry and teacher education.

Originally, the Commission set aside 100,000 EUA annually for this Scheme, a sum which was increased to 300,000 EUA in the academic year 1978-79, partly as a recognition of the fact that the Scheme had begun to 'take off', partly too, in order to encourage applications from under-represented countries.

What are the type of ventures that have received subsidy? What has their purpose been? To illustrate this, four programmes have been chosen from those successful in the academic year 1981-82. The University of Amsterdam and the London School of Economics are jointly developing a one-year introduction to the study of anthropology, based on the theme of immigrant minorities, their history, an analysis of migration flows, comparison of national policies within a comparative context. This is to be introduced as a 3rd year option in ethnic studies in both institutions. In addition, there is to be an element of both staff and student mobility between the two establishments. The problems of planning and planning systems in three small countries of the European Community is the subject of a joint course under development by University College, Dublin (Ireland) in conjunction with the *Arkitektskolen* of Aarhus (Denmark) and the Edinburgh College of Art (Scotland). The course involves staff being exchanged and students spending a minimum of three months as part of the course in each of the three participating institutions. Four universities — University College, Cardiff (Wales), the Catholic University of Leuven (Belgium), the Free University of Berlin (Federal Republic of Germany) and the Catholic University of Nijmegen (Netherlands) — are collaborating on a teaching programme at further degree level, dealing with European Social Security Law. Staff from each institute are exchanged for the purpose of this course and contribute to its teaching in each of the individual establishments. A 9-month, fully integrated diploma course at post-graduate/post-experience level in Shipping Management has brought together Plymouth Polytechnic (England) with the Nautical College *Noorder Haaks* at Den Helder (Netherlands). The course is divided into two phases. The first is identical and provided at both institutions. The second phase differs according to the specialisation and expertise of each institution. Students may choose to continue their programme at either of the two participating establishments.

How successful has the Joint Study Programme Scheme been in meeting its objectives? Some indication emerged from the conference of project directors held. in 1979 at Edinburgh (Scotland). Of the Programmes supported by the Commission in 1976-77 and 1977-78 some 2/3 were already, or on the point of becoming, operational. A further indicator may be seen in the fact that the relative under-representation of programmes involving the natural sciences has corrected itself over the past three years. No less significant from the point of view of the main overall objective of the Scheme, i.e. to foster intra- Community mobility, is that over half the programmes supported up to and including the year 1980-81 were 'student mobility programmes' in which students spent a recognised and integrated part of their course in one partner institution. In this way, as we have seen in a preceding section of this chapter, Joint Study Programmes have begun to make an important contribution to the solution of problems in the area of the recognition of diplomas, between individual institutions. Suffice it to repeat here that the grass roots initiatives of participating establishments of higher education within the framework of the Joint Study Programme Scheme stand as a significant advance in this delicate area.

Furthermore a survey into the Scheme's development in 1980 showed that not only was there a high degree of continuity but that the employment prospects of undergraduates taking part were enhanced. In addition, an important amount of 'academic spin off' often results. Enduring associations between staff, links between library facilities and the development of jointly-run research projects, are amongst the substantial 'by-products' to emerge from the Scheme.

Finally, it should be noted that, though parallel schemes exist, for instance the Integrated Study Abroad Scheme administered by the *Deutscher Akademischer Austauschdienst,* the Joint Study Programme Scheme is the only one to provide substantial support — both financial as well as informational — for higher education institutions in all Ten Member States which wish to cooperate closely in the development of teaching courses with partner institutions elsewhere in the Community. The Commission is assisted in the administration of the Scheme by the Brussels based Office for Cooperation in Education of the European Institute of Education and Social Policy (Paris/Brussels).

Short Study Visits:

The second of the Commission's vehicles for cooperation between establishments of higher education in the Member States is the Short Study Visits Scheme. First introduced in the 1977-78 academic year, again pursuant to the Action Programme in the field of education of 9.2.1976, the Scheme is principally intended to enable individual lecturers, researchers and administrative staff to study particular aspects of the organisation and administration of different systems of higher education and institutions within the Community. The study of the organisation as well as teaching and research methods employed elsewhere is one of its main objectives. It is not intended to provide individuals with the means of pursuing their personal research and the scheme is not limited to academic institutions since members of national bodies involved in access and admission to higher education are also eligible. Grants, up to a maximum of 1,500 European Currency Units, and for visits of no more than four weeks' duration are made. The budget for this heading amounts currently to some 135,000 ECU.

A recent development, designed to impart new flexibility to both the Short Study Visits and the Joint Study Programme Schemes has been the separation of those Short Study Visits whose purpose is to explore the possibility of developing into Joint Study Programmes later from those devoted to an analysis of specific aspect of higher education systems or policies in other Member States. The former type will henceforth be referred to as Joint Study Programme Preparatory Visits and will come under the Joint Study Programme Scheme which will thus in future consist of two types of grant: those for preliminary visits and those for full development of inter-institutional cooperation.

Over the six years of its operation, applications have grown from 176 in 1977 to over 750 in 1982. 341 teachers, researchers and administrators took part in the scheme during its first four years, and in 1980-81, 131 awards were made. It is a feature of this scheme that from year to year, it sets out certain priority groups whose applications will be subject to particular attention. In 1978-79, for instance, special interest was attached to applications from academic staff with responsibilities in the area of career advice to students, who were responsible for student admission or who were involved in organising departments of modern languages. The following year saw a shift in interest towards staff involved in planning the training programmes for administrative personnel. In 1981, priority was placed upon applications from academic or administrative staff responsible for the admission of foreign students and in 1982 the interaction between higher education and industry was one of the priority themes.

A recent evaluation of this scheme shows that just under half of all visits have so far been concerned with organising some aspect of teaching and research and about one quarter with preparing Joint Programmes, though there are indications that this latter proportion is tending to rise significantly of late. The largest single area of interest has been in teaching methods or materials, this accounting for some 31 percent of all visits. As with the Joint Study Programme, there is a tendency for certain countries to be over represented. Over the three year period from 1977-78 to 1979-80, participants from the Federal Republic of Germany and the United Kingdom accounted for just over half the programmes undertaken. Italy received one seventh of all awards.

The importance of the Short Study Visits lies not just in the value of the information obtained and disseminated or the personal contacts made during them. In many instances, they also serve as the first step towards a more substantial form of cooperation that may, later, be based on the Joint Programme of Study model.

The dissemination aspect of the Short Study Visits is held to be especially important. The build up of documentary output resulting from this scheme and the extension of its use to other groups or organisations in higher education will allow the experience of those involved earlier to be used to the maximum advantage of all. As in the case of the parallel scheme for the development of Joint Study Programmes, the Office for Cooperation in Education assists the Commission in the management of the Short Study Visits Scheme of Grants.

Information policy:

For both the Joint Programmes of Study and the Short Study Visits, the dissemination of information is a crucial factor in their success, and considerable attention has been devoted of late to the development of this activity. A series of national information seminars has been held in a number of Member States and a newsletter (entitled 'Delta') initiated (first issue October 1982). Subject-oriented information dossiers and seminars serve to facilitate an exchange of information between grant-holders and to promote the initiation of additional cooperative ventures in the fields concerned, based on the experience of those already involved.

Though neither the Joint Study Programme nor the Short Study Visits Schemes are entirely based on *student* mobility, it is nevertheless clear that the availability of relevant information is essential in the mobility of students. 1977 saw the publication of the first edition of the Commission's *Handbook for Students* in all the official languages, setting out details of the organisation, admission, registration and language requirements of higher education in each of the Member States. In addition, information on financial assistance and scholarships, entry and residence regulations is given as well as lists of addresses and a survey of the courses available in institutions of higher education. The latest edition, published in 1981, ran to 54,000 copies, including for the first time, a Greek language version. The Council of Europe Student Handbook, follows the same format and, as a complementary publication, covers ten countries not included in the Commission's version.

The Commission is currently examining the possibility of supplementing this first student-oriented manual, by the publication of a *Teachers' Handbook*, designed to alert academic staff to the possibilities of researching or teaching abroad. The publication of a *Directory of Higher Education Institutions in the European Community*, currently being prepared at the Commission's request by the Office for Cooperation in Education (European Institute of Education and Social Policy), Brussels, will also be of invaluable assistance as a reference work for all those seeking to establish cooperation with partners at institutions of higher education elsewhere in the Community.

Cooperation in higher education has been reinforced further with the establishment, following the decision of the Education Committee in January 1978, of an information network on education in the European Community. Known as EURYDICE, it became operational in the autumn of 1980. It is based on a series of national units in the Member States with a central unit in Brussels. Conditions of access and admissions policy in higher education form one of its fields of responsibility.

A further proposal for giving added impetus to disseminating information was raised in the Education Committee in April 1981. Amongst the initiatives outlined by the Committee was the support of a network of National Academic Equivalence Information Units in Member States, first set up by the Council of Europe. Their remit will be to collect and convey authoritative information on academic qualifications to students, their parents, advisers, teachers and prospective employers. In some states, such a system is already operational. Close association of the EURYDICE Central Unit with a central body involved in this activity is thought to be particularly appropriate. It would ensure the most efficient use of the Education Information Network's facilities.

European University Institute (Florence):

A further perspective on cooperation in higher education is provided by the European University Institute at Florence. Inaugurated in October 1976, it is an example of the belief that the construction of a United Europe remains incomplete without an intellectual body of this sort. The Institute, jointly financed by contributions from the Member States, has four postgraduate departments — History and Civilisation, Economics, Law and Political and Social Sciences. Currently, it has some 110 graduate students, spread over three years. There are, in addition, some 100 administrative and teaching staff. The European Institute is a degree-awarding body. Students may take Doctorates of the European University Institute in any one of the four fields mentioned above. Amongst research work carried out under its auspices have been dissertation of mixed economies, the history of European unification and the macro-sociology of welfare states.

The budget, functions and guidelines for the European Institute are the responsibility of a High Council, made up of representatives of the Contracting States. A representative of the Community participates in meetings of this body, though without a vote. Research and teaching are matters falling under the responsibility of the Academic Council which also decides on the appointment of academic staff and the admission of research students. The Institute has links with the College of Europe at Brugge (Belgium) which in turn enjoys a close relationship with the various Community institutions.

Cooperation outside the framework of the Education Action Programme:

Cooperation in higher education is not limited to actions laid down within the framework of the Education Action Programme. Others, particularly those carried within the framework of the Lomé Convention, come under the responsibility of the Directorate General for Development. Some 50 training programmes, worth around 100,000,000 European Units of Account, come under this heading. They provide scholarships for students from African, Caribbean and Pacific countries either to study in their own lands or in institutions of higher education within the EEC Member States as well as provision for instructors, trainers, seminars and the furnishing of teaching materials. Up to 1979, some 4,300 scholarships had been awarded, of which 950 were for study in countries of the Community.

The terms of the new Lomé Convention provide for collaboration between institutions of higher education, training and research in the Community and their equivalents in the African, Caribbean and Pacific countries. Included in this are both institutional links and the exchange of staff. Colloquia are organised by the Commission either in Brussels or in the universities of Community countries on topics of interest to scholarship holders from the ACP countries.

Scientific research:

Though neither the Joint Study Programme nor the Short Study Schemes are intended to assist the personal academic research of individuals, the Commission does sponsor such work on condition that it falls into one of the scientific fields included in a Community research programme. Until 1973, this was limited to the area of nuclear research. Now, however, it has been extended to cover such fields as non-nuclear energy, the environment, raw materials, new information technologies and many others.

Research carried out under Community auspices falls into two categories — direct research which takes place in the Joint Research Centres sited in Belgium, Germany, Italy and the Netherlands, and indirect research which takes place in national research establishments and universities. The bursaries scheme is flexible, being open to all levels of scientists and engineers from post-graduate to academic staff as well as industrially based scientists. Bursaries may be tenable for as little as a few weeks or more than a year. Holders may work during this period either in a Community research establishment or in a national institution.

Forecasting and Assessment in the field of Science and Technology (FAST):

A further initiative with obvious implications for education and vocational training was the setting up of a research and development programme dealing with Forecasting and Assessment in the field of Science and Technology (FAST). This followed a decision taken by the Council of Ministers in July 1978. FAST is located inside Directorate General XII. Its purpose is to help define long-term objectives in the research and development field and thus to contribute to the emergence of a consistent policy in this area for the Community. FAST was set up on an experimental basis for a five-year period from 1979 to 1984. Its role is to highlight those possibilities, problems and potential conflicts that are liable to affect the long-term development of the Community and to outline alternative research and development options to meet them.

FAST operates around three main themes: work and employment, which reviews changes over the coming decade; the development of an information-based society over the next twenty years and, finally, the evolution of what is termed a 'bio-society' over a thirty year perspective. The latter involves such matters as the impact of bio-technology, genetical manipulation and the generation of energy from biological sources.

With a core staff of some six members, FAST has carried out reviews of such issues as the second and third order effects of micro-electronics and social support for technological change. It works in conjunction with specialised research groups both in higher education or acting on a self-supporting basis. The main preoccupation of FAST is to explore and review the future relationships between science, technology and society. Its reports are taken into account when formulating policy programmes in such areas as the educational and vocational training implications of micro-electronics, the development of an information-based society and those aspects of education policy that touch upon the future patterns of qualification and skill needs in the labour force.

Impact of the Community on teaching in higher education:

Though most noteworthy in the area of student mobility and in collaboration between institutions of higher education, the impact of the Community in higher education is also significant in such areas as guidance and counselling in higher education, quite apart from its effects on the development of new lines of study, teaching and research. Amongst the latter are law, agriculture, international relations and, last but not least, management studies. Already in 1977, the Commission requested the European Foundation for Management Education to draw up an overall review of the state of management studies across the Community. The report, published in 1978, included a series of national profiles and made suggestions about initiatives that might in future be developed on a Community-wide basis.

The growth in European Studies in institutes of higher education has always been a commitment of the Commission and access to the major sources of information about Community activities is seen as an important element in their furtherance. Particularly important in this connection is the role of the European Documentation Centres. At present there are some 380, established in universities and other centres of higher education. They provide a depository of all official Community publications and legislation. In addition, the Commission helps in disseminating knowledge about work in progress both at the doctoral and post-doctoral level, publishing from time to time a Register of University theses and work completed in areas related to Community policies. A newsletter, *European University News,* giving information about conferences, bibliographies, reviews, courses and other areas of current interest is published under the auspices of the Commission. A further encouragement is provided in the form of occasional grants to institutions of higher education setting up programmes relevant to European integration. Usually amounting to between 2,000 and 4,000 European Currency Units, these subventions are made on the initiative of individual Members of the Commission.

Conclusion:

The purpose of Community policy in the area of cooperation in higher education is, ultimately, to remove the various obstacles, legal, administrative or practical that currently hold up the freedom of movement for students, teachers and researchers in the Community. In essence, this policy is based on three elements: first, the securing of the full implementation of existing conventions and agreements, whether multilateral or bi-lateral, involving the mutual recognition of diplomas and other forms of academic qualifications; second, the improvement in the flow of information on these matters between Member States particularly on such items as courses and qualifications; and third, the full use of that experience gathered from the Joint Programmes of Study Scheme between institutions of higher education of the different Member States. Obviously, this is a long term process. However, there exists sufficient common ground between the Member States for further progress to be made in this area, both in the immediate and in the longer term.

Yet, it should be noted that in this area of activity, the Commission has not espoused what might be termed a 'directive strategy' such as may be seen in the policies dealing with migrants and their families. This respect for academic autonomy has had a profound influence on the 'policy style' of the Communities in this sector. Thus the main — if not the essential — characteristic to emerge from this cooperation is that it is firmly grounded on a 'facilitating approach'. The Commission has placed at the disposal of institutions of higher education, university and non-university alike, facilities for exchanging information, for programmes of joint study and for short study visits. It is currently engaged in strengthening these provisions. Nevertheless, the initiative to make use of them remains entirely in the hands of the individual establishment and its academic or administrative staff. It is then, encouraging to note the willingness of higher education to take them up. It gives a new underpinning to the commitment, as much historical as international, that such institutions have always had to the world of learning.

SOURCES:

i. **Primary: internal Commission documents**
'Education Committee: draft reports on Points IV, V and VI of the Action Programme',*Document No. 910/75 (EN 91)*, July 22nd 1975.
'Communication from the Commission to the Council', *Document COM (78) 468 FINAL*, September 22nd 1978.
'The development of links between organisations representing higher education institutions', *Document No. 2995/79 (EDUC 5)*, March 1979.
'Community grants in the field of higher education', *Document No. XII/1459/80 EN*, June 5th 1980.
'Outcome of the proceedings of the Council and the Ministers of Education meeting within the Council on June 27th 1980', *Document No. 8137/80 (EDUC 3)*, July 7th 1980.
'International recognition of diplomas', *Document No. 12143/80 (EDUC. 52)*, December 2nd 1980.
'Community grants in the field of higher education', *Document No. XII/1070/80 EN*, January 1st 1981.
'The recognition of academic diplomas', *Document No. 4824/81 (EDUC 3)*, February 18th 1981.
'Communication from the Commission to the Council: academic recognition of diplomas and of periods of study', *Document No. (81) 186. FINAL*, April 29th 1981.
'Academic recognition of diplomas and periods of study', *Document No. 6845/81 (EDUC 19)*, May 13th 1981.
'714ème session du Conseil et des Ministres de l'Education réunis au sein du Conseil, Luxembourg, le 22 juin 1981', *Communication à la presse, Document No. 7627/81*, June 1981.
'The European Communities' activities in the field of higher education. *Draft document by the education services of the Commission to the European Parliament's Committee on Youth, Culture, Education, Information and Sport (internal)*, September 15th 1981.
'Note to the members of the Education Committee. Annex II 'Academic recognition of diplomas and periods of study', *Secretariat General of the Council*, March 31st 1982.
Speech by Commissioner Ivor Richard, 'The academic recognition of diplomas and periods of study' at the *Council of Education Ministers May 24th 1982 (xerox)*, April 30th 1982.
'Academic recognition of diplomas and periods of study', *Outcome of Proceedings of the Council and Ministers for Education meeting with the Council Document No. 7276/82 (EDUC 38)*, May 27th 1982.

Unpublished documents presented to the Commission:
Grants from the Commission of the European Communities for the development of Joint Programmes of Study between institutions of higher education in EEC Member States; evaluation report 1978-79, Brussels, Institute of Education of the European Cultural Foundation, 1979.

Conference on Joint Study Programmes in higher education within the European Community: final report, Brussels, Institute of Education of the European Cultural Foundation, 1979, (xerox).
Grants for support for short study visits by teaching, administrative and researchers from higher education institutes, The Hague, Netherlands' Universities' Foundation for International Cooperation, 1980, (xerox).
John Padley, *Short Study Visit Scheme of the Commission of the European Communities*, Liverpool (England), The University, August 1981, (typewritten).
Joint Study Programme of the European Community: an information note, Brussels, Institute of Education of the European Cultural Foundation, October 1981, (xerox).
'Academic recognition: a summary of experience of the Commission's scheme for the development of joint programmes of study', *Information for Directorate General V*, Brussels, Institute of Education of the European Cultural Foundation, October 13th 1981.
Short Study Visits scheme: report to the selection panel for 1981-82, Brussels, Institute of Education of the European Cultural Foundation, October 1981, (typewritten).
'Higher education cooperation in the European Community: Further development of the Joint Study Programmes and Short Study Visits schemes', *Note to the Education Committee from the Services of the Commission*, Brussels, September 1982.

ii. Secondary: printed sources, official documents
Official Journal No. C.98, August 20th 1974, p.2.
Jean-Claude Masclet, *Intra-European mobility of undergraduate students*, Paris, Institute of Education of the European Cultural Foundation, 1975.
Edwin H. Cox, *Academic recognition of diplomas in the European Community: present state and prospects*, Brussels, Commission of the European Communities, 1979. Education series No. 10.
Alan Smith, *Joint Programmes of Study. An instrument for European cooperation in higher education*, Brussels, Commission of the European Communities; Collection Studies, 1979. Education series No. 7.
FAST: sub programme work and employment: research activities, Brussels, Commission of the European Communities, 1980.
FAST: activités en cours, *Document No. EUR 7102*, Brussels, Direction Générale de la recherche, science et éducation, 1980.
Education and training 1970/71-1977/78, Luxembourg, Statistical Office of the European Communities, 1980, p.181.
'Education et formation', *Bulletin Statistique 2/82*, Luxembourg, October 1982, Office statistique de la Communauté Européenne.
Alan Smith, Jean-Pierre Jarousse & Christine Woesler de Panafieu, 'Foreign student flows and policies in an international perspective'. *The overseas student question. Studies for a policy*. Ed. Peter Williams, London, Heinemann, Educational Books for the Overseas Student Trust, 1981.

iii. Tertiary: pamphlets, articles of a non official nature
Guy Neave, On wolves and crises, 'Review of new trends, in European higher education', *Paedagogica Europaea*, vol. XIII, No. 1, 1978, pp.18-26.
Guy Neave, 'Foreign student mobility in France', in Barbara B. Burn (ed.), *Higher education reform: implications for foreign students*, New York, International Institute for Educational Exchange, 1978.

Alan Smith, 'From "Europhoria" to pragmatism: towards a new start for higher education cooperation in Europe?' *European Journal of Education,* vol. 15, No. 1, 1980, p.78.

Alan Smith, 'Diversified structures and a structure for diversity: some recent trends and developments in engineering education cooperation in the European Community', *European Journal of Engineering Education* 6 (1981), pp.221-234.

Jean-Claude Eeckhout, 'The European University of Florence: history and future prospects', *Cahiers Européens 4/81,* October 1981, p.44.

Guy Neave & Martine Herlant, 'Communing with the Europe', *Times Higher Education Supplement,* March 12th 1982.

Alan Smith, 'Bright future for cooperation', *Times Higher Educational Supplement,* September 17th 1982.

Chapter Six
Equality of Educational Opportunity

Structure:
Introduction
Equality of opportunity and education activities in the Community
Community action in the area of pre-primary education
Equality of opportunity of girls
A new impetus
Recurrent education
Conclusion

Notes

SOURCES

Introduction:
There are few terms more subject to debate and disagreement than 'equality of educational opportunity' notwithstanding the fact that it has been a watchword for both social and educational policy throughout the post war period. Some writers have identified three different strands within this *omnium gatherum* which correspond to three main political ideologies — the Conservative, the Liberal and the Radical. Others have placed less emphasis on the political ideology — though this can never entirely be dismissed and have stressed, rather, the educational and social models that emerge from it. Though an apparently monolithic term, equality of educational opportunity covers a wide range of beliefs about the nature and educability of the individual, just as it also covers major differences in the way those holding any particular interpretation believe the education system ought to function. Furthermore, it is not a concept that remains constant over time. Circumstances change and with them the views that mould society, with the result that what appeared as a radical interpretation of equality at one moment of history may, with the passage of time and reform, assume a conservative overtone. Thus, if we are to grasp the notion of equality of opportunity as it emerges in the education activities of the Community, it is useful to take a brief look at the three main elements the slogan contains.

In its earliest form, equality of opportunity may be traced back to the French Revolution of 1789 and to the meritocratic concept of 'la carrière ouverte aux talents': that careers in public service should be open to ability and talent rather than to birth and inherited wealth. In the context of the post war period, this same driving force has come to denote the right of 'able' young people to enjoy access to the highest levels of education irrespective of income or social origins. The role of the education system was, formally to identify talent, usually at the junction between primary and secondary education, and to concentrate upon such individuals the full resources that education could provide. Though seen as a radical measure even in the immediate post war reconstruction of Europe's education, it has come under increasing challenge on grounds both psychological and sociological. Early selection at 11 years of age, it was argued, did not afford sufficient time for real ability to emerge particularly amongst children from manual and low income homes.

The main challenge to the meritocratic or Conservative notion of equality of opportunity came from what some writers have identified as a 'Liberal concept' of the same. If the full reserves of talent could not be effectively identified by early allocation practices, supporters of the Liberal interpretation argued, then it was logical to extend secondary education to encompass the whole school population, without distinction between those later destined for vocational, technical or academic training. Furthermore, some measure of compensatory or remedial provision ought to be made to offset disadvantage or handicap resulting from unfavourable home environment. Such a definition, translated into policy, brought about widespread reorganisation in the structure of secondary education systems and in the internal organisation of the school. In countries such as Britain, France, Denmark and in the three other Scandinavian lands, it gave rise to the establishment of all in, comprehensive schools.

The third interpretation of equality of opportunity — called 'radical' by some, 'individual' by others, takes the compensatory element of the Liberal definition further. It argues that if equality consists in equality of outcomes, then the right of access to educational provision, whether directly of a compensatory nature or not, should be available to the individual throughout his or her lifetime. Access to education is not confined only to secondary schooling. Rather, post secondary education should be open to all who feel they may benefit from it. Thus, the notion of *'education permanente'* or recurrent education is, today, closely associated with the radical concept of equality of educational opportunity. It may be seen in various forms of distance teaching, in the Open University systems in Great Britain, Germany, the Netherlands and Spain, in the 22 *Centres de Télé- enseignement universitaire* in France and in the Swedish legislation known by the acronym of 25/4. This latter provides places in Swedish higher education for those aged 25 and over with at least 4 years work experience.

There is, of course, no reason why one part of a nation's educational provision should not endorse a different interpretation of educational opportunity from that upheld elsewhere in the system. It is, for instance, perfectly possible to have one sector of secondary education devoted to a meritocratic interpretation coexisting with another founded upon the Liberal interpretation. Such a situation exists in the Federal Republic of Germany where a small 'comprehensive' system lives cheek by jowl with the traditional 'Gymnasium'.

Equality of opportunity and education activities in the Community

Though an examination of the developing activities of the Community in the area of education shows an increasing resolve to achieve 'equality of opportunity', it is by no means clear in which of the commonly accepted interpretations of the term its policy is to be ranged. Certainly, the significance of attaining such equality was explicitly mentioned in the Resolution of the Council of Ministers in February 1976. But it was mainly a nominal reference to the general idea and left its more precise interpretation open to subsequent elaboration. Indeed, a close analysis of that Resolution suggests that the Ministers deliberately limited themselves to what might be called a minimal interpretation which rested essentially upon the notion of 'access' to different forms and levels of education. 'Free access' to all forms of education, the Ministers agreed, was an essential aim of the education policies for all Member States. The Education Action Programme brought several areas of future activity under the heading of vehicles for achieving equality of opportunity: the preparation of young people for working life, provision within the framework of in-service training (*formation continue*). But this was no more than a recognition of a situation which already existed de jure in all Member States, for few indeed still operated a system of either fee charging for entry to public secondary schools and none denied the right of access to secondary education. The real question remained untackled namely on what conditions should access itself be regulated. But since this would have meant penetrating into areas of Member State policies, it remained unspecified.

There is, however, some indication — though slight — that in certain areas, the Ministers did grope towards a dilute version of the 'liberal' interpretation of equality of educational opportunity. The Resolution noted that if all children and those from underprivileged groups in particular, were to benefit from access to secondary education, attention ought to be paid to the way nursery education linked in with primary schools. Here again, though underprivileged groups were mentioned — a nod in the direction of some form of compensatory strategy — such compensatory approaches were to be deduced rather than explicitly stated. A similar caution is also visible in the general heading devoted to the organisation of compulsory secondary and vocational education. Here the Resolution made a certain obeissance towards the vocabulary of the 'liberal' definition of equality without going further. The organisation of these two sectors should be such that all children might have 'the opportunity to develop their full potential', a statement that none could dispute since no education system, irrespective of form, structures or practice, could in reason see its task as anything less than that goal.

It was on this politically appealing but intellectually fragile base that initiatives were to be taken within the framework of the Community Education Action Programme. Precisely what areas were to be pursued with reference to equality of educational opportunity were given further substance at the Ministers' meeting of December 13th 1976. A number of Community level initiatives were drawn up to be developed over the period up to December 31st 1980. Three groups in particular were mentioned. These were young migrants, those facing specific difficulties — defined as the young mentally and physically handicapped and, finally, actions intended to promote equal educational opportunities for girls — groups for whom compensatory action could legitimately be claimed as a matter both of policy and principle without necessarily infringing the right of Member States to determine each of his own measures by which such a goal could be attained.

The mention of girls as one of the target groups on which Community Action should focus was particularly significant since it linked in with previous action undertaken in another area of Commission interest. Seen from this viewpoint, the Education Action Programme stands, to some extent, as a complementary underpinning to developments that had taken place earlier. Already in 1974, the Council of Ministers' Resolution setting up a Social Action Programme, placed considerable importance on achieving equality between men and women in employment, training and conditions of work. Such action derived from Article 119 of the Treaty of Rome which dealt with the question of equal pay between the sexes. To this was added the concept of 'positive action' in these fields, following the promulgation of Directive 76/207 and more specifically Article 2 (iv) in 1976. The Social Action Programme noted, in those sections that dealt with the children of immigrants, that measures designed to bring about equal pay for equal work could in the long run only be effective if backed up by further action in the educational domain. Clearly, thinking within the Commission ran strongly in favour of compensatory strategies in the field of education but, at the same time, left sufficient manoeuvre to develop them later by referring to the general principle of equality of opportunity.

Other chapters of this study are devoted to Community policy as it touched upon the children of migrants, young people moving from school to work and the handicapped. Here, the main focus will be upon the development of Community policy in the field of pre-school education and the education of girls.

Community action in the area of pre-primary education:

The development of pre-primary education has been a concern of growing significance throughout the seventies. In terms of enrolment rates the period between 1970 and 1978 revealed three main tendencies: first, those Member States where major growth took place: Denmark (+21.9 percent to 1980); Greece (+52.8 percent), Germany (+36.7 percent); second, those Member States where moderate though substantial increases in the enrolment of pre-primary pupils are to be seen: Italy (+19.4 percent), France (+17.2 percent), the United Kingdom (+8.2 percent) and Ireland (+7.9 percent); third, those Member States where enrolment at this level has undergone contraction: the Netherlands (-5 percent), Luxembourg (-8.8 percent) and Belgium (-11.4 percent).

A number of factors contributed to this development: the drive of middle class parents to ensure a good education for their children and also to prevent them grade repeating in the early stages of primary education; the belief, endorsed by public authorities, that pre-primary education could provide an important vehicle for compensatory education for disadvantaged groups, following the model provided by the American Headstart programme developed in the late 1960s; the conviction that there was considerable benefit to be had by all children from enhanced provision at the pre-primary level and, finally, the need to provide more facilities to meet additional demand following an increase in the tendency for women to continue their careers.

Amongst the prime concerns of the Community in this area was the examination of the assumption that early childhood education was capable of compensating for certain types of disadvantage, cultural minorities and the handicapped, those in declining urban areas, children living in sparsely populated regions. The task, at Community level, was to identify certain priority areas and to suggest what type of contribution would ensure equality of access and equality of opportunity in this sector.

As a first step in this undertaking, the Commission asked Mrs Madeleine Goutard, a French *Inspectrice départementale,* to undertake an analysis of the issues current in this area across the Member States of the Community. The report, prepared during 1977-78 was published in 1980, and entitled *Pre-school education in the European Community.* It concentrated on the educational needs of the age group 3-6 years, explored the links between pre-school education, family structures and the tendency, which appears to be growing in some Member States, to make this stage of education to all intents and purposes indistinguishable from primary education. It argued strongly in favour of maintaining the autonomy of the nursery school and against too much integration with primary education. Autonomy, the report suggested, was a prior condition both for opening up the pre-primary school to the local community and for the coordination of services to meet the whole range of needs appropriate to young children.

The Goutard Report served as the principal background document at a European seminar, held at Sèvres (France) in May 1979 under the auspices of the French Ministry of Education in cooperation with the Commission of the European Community. The Sèvres meeting made a number of recommendations including a programme of studies and action research. It also called for a reliable information service on latest developments in the area of pre-school education as well as exchanges of both teachers and administrators to underpin this.

One of the main conclusions to emerge from this meeting was the desirability of involving parents as well as other adults in the local community, in educational projects at this level together with their children. This prompted the Commission to undertake in 1979 a survey of the various forms of parental participation in the different education system of the Member States. The task was entrusted to a Scottish expert, Mr Alastair McBeth of Glasgow University Department of Education. Presented in October 1981, the report was entitled *The Child Between: a report on school-family relations in the countries of the European Community.* This is the first major study to be undertaken on this theme by the Commission. It was followed up by a European conference of parents' organisations held in Luxembourg in 1983. This too is a first time event in the framework of the Commission's educational activities and was organised in co-operation with the Luxembourg Ministry of Education.

In developing priority areas for action in the pre-school sector, the Community has been in close touch with other programmes in this field undertaken by the major international organisations like the Council of Europe and the Centre for Educational Research and Innovation (CERI) of the Paris-based Organisation for Economic Cooperation and Development, both of which have done substantial work in this field. The Commission also presented papers to the 12th session of the Standing Conference of European Ministers of Education held at Lisbon in June 1981.

Though, at the moment, it has not proved possible to implement the Resolution of the Ministers of Education of February 9th 1976, and to set up a distinct Action Programme on pre-school education, the Commission is currently examining this dossier with a view to future developments. Three options are under consideration. The first is to continue to see pre-school education as an adjunct or dependent element in one of the other areas of the Action Programme such as those dealing with the children of migrants or the handicapped. In other words, that specific themes such as disadvantage will be maintained and their scope limited to the field of education alone. The second option also maintains the emphasis on the educational aspects of pre-school education, but suggests that it may be extended to other target groups in a systematic manner. Amongst these would be families in sparsely populated areas, or in areas of inner city decline, gypsies and travellers. Though it would take into account such matters as the impact of demographic decline and the need to coordinate services bearing on the requirements of the pre-school population, such aspects would be considered simply from the standpoint of their effects upon the school. A third option, drawing on the conclusions of the Council of Europe seminar on Preschool education at Strasbourg in December 1979 and the report of the Centre for Educational Research and Innovation, *Early Childhood Education,* published in 1980, points to a rather wider approach. This extends the perspective from the relatively narrow confines of the school and includes all sectors of social policy involved in caring for infants and young children. In this latter option, the educational aspect is but one in a broad ranging series of interconnected services underpinning the concept of 'care' for young infants, a notion initially launched by the Council of Europe.

Equal opportunity for girls:

One of the most important shifts inside education policy during the mid-seventies has been the expansion in the number of separate interests or 'priority groups' whose performance inside national education systems has, increasingly, come to be seen as a gauge of success or inadequacy of those same systems of education. The importance of the education of girls is, in this context, a major development with wide-ranging repercussions at all levels of the education system and especially in the area of the curriculum.

Within the Community context, the theme of equal educational opportunities for girls must be placed in the wider perspective of Community action intended to promote equality of treatment between men and women workers. In the first instance, Community policy concentrated on achieving equality of pay and equal treatment in such matters as access to employment, vocational training, promotion and working conditions. This was reinforced by various forms of 'positive action' in particular fields outlined in Article 2 of the Directive No. 76/207 of 1979. Very early on, it was realised that a programme for equality for women required not merely sustained action over a long period, but that measures introduced in the area of employment or vocational training could, at best, only partially compensate for those more deeply embedded inequalities whose origins lay in the earlier school and family experience of girls. The inequalities affecting the future career chances of women are usually to be found in the formative years prior to their entry to working life. Thus the whole question of treatment is intimately linked with equality of opportunity both for boys and girls at the upstream stage, that is, in the realm of education and vocational training.

This point emerged in the course of a seminar organised by the Commission in November 1975 at Paris which brought together experts in the area of guidance and vocational training for women workers. It noted the need for non-discriminatory guidance in education as well as the desirability of opening up a wider range of future choice of career both for boys and girls. Earlier this year a

Equality of Educational Opportunity

Commission document laid down the basic premises by linking equality of opportunity in employment with equal opportunity in training. *'This'*, the document stated, *'in practice involves comparable general education for both sexes with comparable educationcal and vocational guidance and equal opportunity in access to initial and advanced vocational training and retraining'.*[1]

In order to clarify the major difficulties as a preliminary to presenting specific action to ensure equal educational opportunities for girls, the Commission invited Dr Eileen Byrne, a British consultant, to draw up a report dealing with the situation in Member States. Her report was presented in 1978 and published the following year with the title *Equality of education and Training for girls (10-18 years)*, having in the meantime provided the substance of a Communication laid before the Council in October 1978.

The report summarised the main aspects and dimensions involved in the education and training for girls at secondary level — that is the period covering the age range 10 to 18 years. Its purpose was to identify specific areas where joint action could be undertaken at Community level, taking into account similar work in the area of educational provision for girls carried out by other international bodies such as the Council of Europe, the OECD, the International Labour Office, Unesco and the Nordic Council.

Secondary education, the report pointed out, constitutes an important stage in the emergence of some of the more perennial obstacles to the achievement of equality of opportunity for girls. First, because at this point in the individual's life, a career choice had often to be made between different types of school — academic, technical or vocational — and secondly, because many systems introduced the principle of single-sex schools thus separating boys' education from that received by girls. All the evidence reviewed pointed to a considerable degree of under-achievement by girls. They tend to have a lower participation rate in vocational and technical education, not to mention in upper secondary education generally. If girls tend to opt for general education, their choice is more likely to fall in with the shorter courses. Alternatively, they leave before completing long-course secondary education. However, though recruitment to higher education tends to be lower for girls than for boys, the trend over the past seven years has been for a marked improvement in the participation rate for girls in this area of the education system. This is not to deny the fact that there are still disciplines, particularly in science and engineering, where the participation of girls is abysmally low.

The Byrne report argued that the introduction of co-education would go partway to removing certain barriers to equality of opportunity, principally by providing equal access to all types of curricular provision as well as improving social education through the presence of teachers of both sexes. Other obstacles thought detrimental to the motivation of pupils were the system of lock-step yearly promotion and its attendant problem of grade repeating for those not

---

1. 'Equality of treatment between men and women workers', *Document COM (75) 36*, February 12th 1975.

reaching the required standard, as well as early specialisation. *'The deferment of specialisation'* the report pointed out, *'and the establishment of a compulsory and balanced central curriculum up to the minimum school-leaving age to which options can be added, can make a considerable contribution to offering girls (and boys) a better foundation for later choice of third level education or training for employment'.*[2]

No less important was the interpretation given to the notion of equality of opportunity. The Community concept, the Byrne report noted, was that equal means the same — a principle stated both in the Action Programme itself and also in the legislation dealing with vocational training for work. The question this begs, however, is whether 'the same' is to be defined as similarity of provision or whether it is to be seen in terms of the level of qualifications attained at the end of secondary education.

The burden of policy operated inside the education system, the report suggested, was to remove the influence of those 'passive factors' such as social class, status, intelligence and place of residence leaving legislation to act upon the 'active factors' of discrimination found in legislative, administrative or structural barriers outside the school system. However, the removal of structural obstacles inside the school such as different options reserved for boys and others for girls ought to be underpinned by more sensitive action in those areas involving what might be termed 'girls' self-perception'. Amongst the most significant of these is sex stereotyping, often reinforced through schoolbooks and further reinforced by present practices in the field of counselling and vocational guidance. As the report pointed out, *'Education must be offered to each child in accordance with his or her actual — not assumed — personal gifts and needs; not on any other pre-conceived normative basis and not on grounds of sex. We no longer deliberately prescribe a different education for children of different social class simply because they are deemed to be aristocrats, middle class or in the poorer sectors of society. Similarly, there can be no parallel justifications for consciously prescribing a different curriculum for pupils because they are boys or girls'.*[3]

This report also formed part of the Commission's contribution to the Standing Conference of European Ministers of Education held in June 1979 at the Hague, when the main topic of discussion was the education and training of girls and young women.

However, as the development in the economies of Member States has revealed over the past few years, equality of opportunity inside the education system, together with a gradual change in attitude towards the education of girls, is neither automatically nor inevitably accompanied by similar developments in the place of work. Unemployment on the one hand and reductions in government expenditure on the other, particularly in the area of *crèche* and pre-primary

---

2. 'Education Action Programme at Community level: equal opportunities in education and training for girls', *Document COM (78) 499 FINAL*, October 3rd 1978.
3. Eileen Byrne, *ibid.*

Equality of Educational Opportunity

provision, have not made matters any easier. If anything, the transition from school to work is more difficult for girls than for young men especially since the range of occupations for which the former apply tend still to be relatively narrow.

Positive action has been taken by the European Social Fund, first in the context of its pilot projects and more recently by the setting up of a special intervention in the form of vocational training programmes for women. It is perhaps too early to assess the full impact of the pilot projects, the aim of which was to train women for non-traditional occupations. Yet, it would seem that attempts to revise those models that induce girls not to choose training in technical subjects, still have a long way to go.

The main agency dealing with vocational training policies throughout the Community is the European Centre for the Development of Vocational Training, set up on February 10th 1975. In September 1977, CEDEFOP held a seminar in Berlin on the topic 'equal opportunities and vocational training', the main theme being the opportunities in this field for women. A three-phase action programme emerged from this meeting:

— the identification of recent innovations in guidance and training undertaken in Member States;
— the promotion in firms of training policies designed to improve career opportunities for women and to increase their chances of access to available jobs;
— to contribute towards changes in attitudes by making information more widely available on those initiatives outlined previously.

The first element of this programme was carried out in 1978. The task of picking out innovative training programmes was entrusted by Member States to a national team. The reports resulting from this exercise were made available in 1979. The third element has been implemented with the thrice-yearly publication by CEDEFOP of the journal *Vocational Education* which, since 1980 has been published in all community languages.

A new impetus:

Despite certain difficulties in the specifically *educational* dimension of equality of opportunity for girls, a new impetus to this policy was imparted by the *ad hoc* committee on women's rights in the European Parliament. The Committee, which took into account the conclusions of the conference held at Manchester in May 1980 and organised by the Commission in conjunction with the United Kingdom Equal Opportunities Commission, called upon the Community institutions to intensify their activity in this area. The European Parliament's Resolution of February 11th 1981, on the position of women in the European Community, added weight to the drawing up of a new proposal for the promotion of equal opportunities for women.

Since December 1980, the Commission has brought together a Liaison Group for Equal Opportunities to advise it in this field. Further calls for a new initiative in this area were made by the Youth Forum of the European Communities. The programme, which was adopted on December 9th 1981, covers a wide range of activities and interventions, some of which fall into the education field *stricto sensu*. Amongst them are measures intended to reinforce positive steps to improve equal opportunity in education, particularly the training of vocational guidance counsellors and instructors to make them aware of the need for opening up career choices for both boys and girls; new measures to integrate women in those areas likely to be affected by the new technologies — which implies a more open-ended attitude towards the type of jobs deemed appropriate for girls — and also plans to make girls, their families and their schools more aware of the type of jobs available to them. The Commission, through the European Social Fund and in liaison with the European Centre for the Development of Vocational Training (CEDEFOP), will place further emphasis on the comparative evaluation of innovatory action in this area. And, in addition, the Commission is to support measures taken in Member States by establishing an experimental network of equal opportunities advisers to complement the activities of the European Social Fund and those of CEDEFOP. Its purpose will be to foster the development of integrated national programmes of education and training in keeping with the priorities mentioned earlier.

Recurrent education:

In the past, the notion of equality of opportunity has usually been confined to school-based education. This meant, in effect, that those generations no longer of school-age were liable to find themselves deprived of the opportunities their children now enjoy. This concept is changing and, in the 'Radical' interpretation of the term, is extended to providing a 'second chance' for adults. Whatever the word chosen, whether 'permanent', 'recurrent' or 'continuing' education, the extension of facilities for learning basic skills, survival skills or those associated with changes in the structure of the labour force, is becoming daily a greater necessity.

In the first place demographic change in Western Europe means, broadly speaking, an ageing society and an ageing labour force, though Ireland and Greece are exceptions to this general rule. From an utilitarian point of view, to limit education and training solely to the younger generation may therefore be ill-advised. In the second place, Western Europe is going through a major restructuring of its industry, as well as a reappraisal of the place occupied by work, leisure or non-employed times in the lives of its citizens. In the third place, only now is it realised how many adults are lacking in such elementary skills as reading or writing. Current estimates place the number of illiterates in the Community as a whole to be some 10-15 million. However, with the exception of a few urbanised countries, such as the United Kingdom and the Netherlands, the problem of adult illiteracy remains unrecognised in many Member States. The development on a larger scale of recurrent education, not merely as an instrument for alleviating such disadvantage, but also as a means of bringing closer together tasks that have hitherto largely been separated between general education on the one hand and vocational training in the other in the context of full-time schooling, is thus a significant challenge. The new perspectives presented by such a form of adult education was the topic of a seminar held at Berlin in October 1980 by CEDEFOP under the auspices of the Commission.

Concern with continuing education reflects a shift in emphasis in Community policies from a concentration on structural readaptation to a concern for their social implications both at local and at individual level. It also reflects, to some degree, an intersectorial approach to planning which cuts across previously impermeable boundaries, the best example of which is the introduction of the new information technologies. New information technologies, it is argued, will require a basic understanding of their workings at all levels of society and among all age-groups. Such a massive need for education and training for the younger generation, and for re-education and retraining amongst the older, underlines not merely the importance of continuing education, but also the need for new forms of induction that cut across the historic divide that distinguished education from training. The implications of this redefinition and the possibilities offered by continuing education are under active consideration by the Commission.

Conclusion:

Equality of opportunity stands as one of the constant features of Community activity both in education and in training. Formally it involves equality of *access* to education but, as this chapter has pointed out, action carried out by the Community, whether in relation to the education of girls, the children of migrants or the transition from school to work, also involves a high degree of 'remedial' or 'compensatory' education. Action at pre-school level is regarded as fundamental not merely to allow disadvantaged children the opportunity to overcome some of the more outstanding handicaps of their environment, but also, from a more long-term perspective, to underpin those broader changes in society that impinge upon the emancipation of women and the establishment of more open career opportunities for girls. In short, policies for equality of *educational* opportunity are seen as interlocking and complementary to activities for equality of opportunity in other areas of the social system, in the factory, office and in access to employment or leisure. Changes in one area have repercussions on the other. In most policies that have equality of educational opportunity as their goal, their effects upon the non-educational areas are usually assumed. In Community policy the linkage is explicit and an integral part of its overall development.

Even so, it is apparent, that the subsequent development of actions undertaken at Community level has given a rather more precise interpretation to the notion of equality of educational opportunity than that first laid down in the Ministers' meeting of February 1976. The growing importance attached to 'compensatory strategies', largely the result of studies commissioned from outside experts, has given substance to what at first appeared to be a mere hortatory statement. Education activities in the fields examined in this Chapter reveal a deliberate move to what might be termed a halfway house between the 'liberal' interpretation and the 'radical' view of equality of educational opportunity. It is significant, however, that the clearest examples of this process of policy elaboration are to be seen on the margins of official education systems — at the preschool level on the one hand and in the semi official informal systems of adult education and training on the other. By relating developments in the non-educational field to their down stream consequences for the school, Community level activities are in effect obeying a political rationale. This rationale springs from the fact that Community activities in the vocational training system and working life have a clear mandate contained in the founding Treaties. It also springs from the fact that the issues posed by equality of *educational* opportunity and equality of opportunity in working life are to a high degree influenced by the nature of the link points between the formal system of schooling, the informal system of adult education and training and working life. It is then, logical for Community level action, designed to foster equality of opportunity, to focus on what some have seen as the traditional areas of administrative segmentation — those areas where the responsibility exercised by Ministries of Education passes over to oversight exercised by Ministers of Labour and Employment.

SOURCES:
i. Primary: internal Commission documents
'Equality of treatment between men and women workers', *Document COM (75) 36*, February 12th 1975.
'Mise en oeuvre du programme d'action au niveau communautaire', *Document SEC (76) 216*, January 21st 1976.
'Education Committee: unrevised translation note', *Document 1109/75 (EN 105)*, October 6th 1976.
L'Education dans la Communauté Européenne: rapport d'activités préparé par les services de la Commission', *Document XIT/429/77 F*, 1977.
'Education Action Programme at Community level: equal opportunities in education and training for girls', *Document COM (78) 499 FINAL*, October 3rd 1978.
'Pre-school education in the European Community from 1980 onwards', *Document XII/259/81*, February 19th 1981.
'New Community programme on the production of equal opportunities for women 1982-1985', *Document COM (81) 758 FINAL*, December 9th 1981.

Unpublished documents presented to the Commission:
Eileen Byrne, *Equality of education and training in the second level of education and training in the second level of education (age range 10-18 years)*, Brussels, July 1978 (mimeo).
Equal opportunities and vocational training: a seminar report, West Berlin, CEDEFOP, 1977.
New perspectives on continuing education and training in an enlarged European Community, West Berlin, CEDEFOP, 1980 (mimeo).
Séminaire du Forum de la Jeunesse Européenne à Lange (République Fédérale d'Allemagne), November 16-17th 1981, Annex IV.

ii. Secondary: printed sources, official documents
'Resolution of the Council and of the Ministers of Education meeting within the

Council of February 9th 1976 comprising an action programme in the field of education', *Official Journal,* February 19th 1976, para. VI, point 20.
'Resolution of the Council and of the Ministers of Education . . . of December 13th 1976',
Impact of demographic change on the education systems in the European Community, Brussels, EURYDICE, 1981.

iii. Tertiary: pamphlets, articles of a non-official nature
G.H. Bantock, *The parochialism of the present: contemporary issues in education,* London, Routledge & Kegan Paul, 1981.
Ignace Hecquet, Christine Verniers and Ladislav Cerych, *Recent student flows in higher education,* Paris, Institute of Education of the European Cultural Foundation, 1976.
L. Cerych & S. Colton, 'Summarising recent student flows', Review of New Trends in European Higher Education, *European Journal of Education,* vol. 15, No. 1, 1980.
Sam Crooks, 'Open learning and non traditional study', Review of New Trends in European Higher Education, *Paedagogica Europaea,* vol. XIII, No. 1, 1978.
Torsten Husen, *Talent, Equality and Meritocracy,* The Hague, Martinus Nijhoff, 1974.
Guy Neave, *Nouveaux modèles d'enseignement supérieur et égalité des chances: perspectives européennes,* Brussels, European Commission, 1978, Education series, No. 6.
Guy Neave, 'Research on equality of opportunity', in M. Dino Carelli & R.G. Morris (eds.), *Equality of opportunity: values in education for tomorrow,* Amsterdam/Lisse, Swets & Zeitlinger, 1979.
Guy Neave, 'Recent trends in education policy in Western Europe', in Colin Brock, Patricia Broadfoot & Witold Tulasiewicz (eds.), *Politics and educational change,* London, Croom Helm, 1981.
Ulrich Teichler, Dirk Hartung & Reinhard Nuthmann, *Higher Education and the needs of society,* Windsor, NFER, 1980.

Chapter Seven
The European Dimension in Education

Structure:
Introduction
Community activities before 1976
New definition of the European dimension
Teaching about Europe
Pupil mobility and pupil exchange
Teaching of foreign languages
European schools and schools of an international nature
Teacher education and the mobility of teachers
Conclusion

Notes

SOURCES

Introduction:

Amongst the prime tasks the state assumed when it took over responsibility for the financing and running of public education, was the initiation of its citizen's children into the rights and duties of citizenship. Though the precise nature of these obligations may vary from country to country as too the methods of presenting them, it has long been held that one of the main functions of schooling is to create a sense of national awareness and a sense of belonging to a national community – whether defined by common history, a shared language or languages or determined by geographical proximity.

Today, this task is infinitely more complex. There is, for instance, wide disagreement over whether the school, rather than political organisations, should be responsible for this activity. There is also considerable fear – amongst certain quarters at least, that what may start as an introduction to citizens' rights may end up as outright ideological indoctrination. These are not the only pressures, however. The notion of what constitutes the legitimate community is itself under question. For some, the community ought to be defined along linguistic grounds, a phenomenon that has led to the division of Belgium into two clear linguistic areas – one French speaking, the other Dutch speaking, each with their own separate education administrations. Similar impulses can be seen in the Breton and Basque speaking areas of France. In the Netherlands, considerable support has been given by the government to the Frisian-speaking minority whilst the Danish authorities have upheld a policy of liberalism vis a vis the Faroese and Greenlandic cultures and languages. This process of redefining the political community below the level of the nation state has been portrayed as the 'renationalisation' of Europe.

At the same time, the nation-state – and its education system by extension – faces another challenge, this time from above rather than below. Such a challenge comes in the form of the growing economic interdependence that characterises all highly developed industrial nations. And, no less important is the relocation of power, whether financial, commercial or political, beyond the bounds of the nation-state. The fact that the annual revenue of IBM is greater than the national budget of Belgium may stand as a striking-even though exceptional-illustration of this tendency. In certain fields, interdependency has received further expression underlined by military alliance – for instance the North Atlantic Treaty Organisation, cultural coordination through the Council of Europe and most recent of all, its elected political expression in the form of the European Parliament. All of these organisations, each in their different spheres, may be seen as various stages in the emergence of bodies whose functions lie between and sometimes, above the individual states composing them. The question such a development poses is whether schools should extend the responsibility they had for transmitting the rights and duties of future citizens of the

119

national community to embrace those that come from being future members of an international community.

To many people, the issue is often erroneously posed in terms of 'Teaching about Europe in the schools'. It is a muddled notion for the simple reason that whether historians, economists or geographers, any teacher who did not include the teaching of the history, economy or geography of Europe to his or her students would be guilty of gross professional incompetence. The fact is that such subjects have always included a European dimension as part of their relative disciplines. What they have not done is to include the notion of educating for 'European citizenship' as an integral part of their programme. And, secondly, the teaching of these subjects has often been coloured by a high degree of ethnocentricity. It has, after all, been a constant source of wonderment to young French-speakers, visiting London for the first time, that the capital's most famous places are named after notorious defeats: Trafalgar Square, Waterloo Station or, further afield, Blenheim Palace!

Arguments put forward by those in favour of 'Europe in the schools' are many. First, they point out that the teaching of such subjects should be adjusted to emphasise the unity of Europe rather than its past history of national rivalries. Second, is the argument that to create a consciousness of what Europe is demands the creation of a new version of 'European history' — a point not without its significance given the role of history in forging national unity through the syllabus of public education throughout Europe these hundred years past. Third is the argument that in many Member States, the age of majority and thus of voting has been reduced to 18 from 21 years of age. This, it has been pointed out, places an added responsibility on the school, particularly since young voters now have the opportunity directly to elect representatives to the European Parliament. Without a suitable understanding of the workings of the political system at this level, few young people will be interested in shaping a Community which, after all, they will inherit.

Arguments against this are, of course, no less strongly held. First of all, the definition of Europe itself is by no means agreed upon, still less, its future political structure. Should it be a unitary body with the nations as subordinated units? Should it be a union of states with a federal government on the lines similar to those found in the United States of America? Or should it be a confederation of states on the Gaullist model, an emanation from the basic authority and sovereignty residual in the nation-state itself? The fact that none of these issues have yet been agreed upon means, at least to those opposed to this venture, that teaching about Europe is not an educative exercise so much as a camouflaged form of propaganda, since that which is taught in schools should reflect a widely held agreement in society at large. And, in certain countries that agreement, insofar as it involves Europe of the Ten, does not exist. In short, the problems of teaching about citizenship are no less fraught by the pressures of 'renationalisation' from below than they are by the pressures of 'de-nationalisation' from above.

Community activities before 1976:

From the earliest days of the Community, considerable importance has been attached to the opportunity for young people to gain direct understanding and experience of developments in other Member States and also of the Community itself. Community activities in this area prior to 1976, when a new stage of co-operation in education was reached, tended to revolve around the provision of information and the provision of materials for teaching. The latter were intended to furnish up-to-date information about the purpose, development, institutions and activities of the Community, either for direct use by the pupils themselves or by teachers. Indeed, the teaching profession was, relatively early on, seen as a prime target to which such information should be directed.

The development of these activities was considerably furthered by the creation in 1959 of the Kreyssig Fund, set up on the initiative of Mr Gerhard Kreyssig, Member of the European Parliament for the Federal Republic of Germany. The proceeds of this fund are set aside for the purpose of '... *advancing the education of young people in a European spirit'.*

At the present time, the Kreyssig Fund is jointly administered at two levels by Directorates General X (Information) and V (Employment, Social Affairs and Education). The first of these levels is centralised and based in Brussels, while the second is decentralised and operated from out of the Commission's national information offices in the Member States. The funding of school-based projects at Community level is carried out centrally by Directorate General V, while that of projects based on youth organisations is centrally administered by Directorate General X. The total budget of this undertaking is in the region of 1,400,000 European Units of Account and, since 1976, has been voted directly by the European Parliament. Amongst those organisations receiving support for school based projects are the European Association of Teachers, teacher-training establishments, curriculum research units and resource centres producing teaching material. Similar work carried out by youth organisations or bodies involved in adult education is subsidised by the Kreyssig Fund through Directorate General X.

In addition, however, the Fund is responsible for the costs of the European School Television Committee's meetings. It also bears responsibility for the Commission's contribution to the production costs of programmes jointly sponsored by the Television Committee and the Fund. The finance for the 'European Documentation' pamphlets originally came from the same source. These pamphlets which run to between eight to ten issues a year provide the most up-to-date information on particular Community problems and, issues of policy developments.

Though the Kreyssig Fund is one of the longest established instruments for the development of a European perspective on schools information policy, two other initiatives took place before the passing of the Ministerial Resolution of February 1976. The first of these was the educational dimension of the European Communities action programme for the Environment. The declaration of the Council of the European Communities and of the representatives of the governments of the Member States meeting in Council on November 2nd 1973 noted that *'children and adolescents must be made aware of the problems of the environment when attending primary and secondary school....'*.[1]

The task of developing materials and evaluating the standing of environmental education (particularly for the 9-14 age-group) was entrusted to the Curriculum Development Unit of Trinity College, Dublin. A survey carried out in 1975-76 showed that the emergence of similar trends in environmental education in the Member States was most noticeable at primary school level, where it was seen as a natural extension of the curriculum and could serve as an integrating principle for the entire curriculum. A number of factors militated in favour of concentrating on the primary school level: first, because considerable difficulty was foreseen in maintaining an integrated approach at secondary level due in part to subject orientation and in part to the difficulty of inserting it into existing examination structures; second, because primary education was less subject to the need to subordinate the curriculum to public examinations and, third, because subject boundaries in primary education tend to be more flexible, thereby permitting a more rapid introduction of the new environmental perspective into the curriculum.

The environmental education programme was extended by a Resolution adopted in 1977 by the Council of the Community. It called for the establishment of a network of pilot primary schools to exchange information on the experience to be derived from the integrated approach. This was set up in February 1977 under the sponsorship of the Environmental and Consumer Protection Service of the Commission, now Directorate General XI. A permanent advisory committee was also set up, with representatives from the Ministries of Education of Member States, to supervise the undertaking. A coordinating team was established in the Curriculum Development Unit at Trinity College, Dublin. In all, some 13 schools were involved in the project which, for the reasons mentioned above, limited itself in the first instance to the 9-11 age range. Subsequent development work will extend the presentation of materials to include pupils up to the age of 14. A number of seminars were held, in Dublin in June 1977 to discuss the concept of environmental education and to define more precisely the role of the school network. Two further seminars were held during July 1978 in Hertfordshire (England) and at Rovereto (Italy) in late April 1979. The former discussed the type of materials produced in the participating schools and the latter dealt with the development of teaching resources on environmental education of relevance to schools within the Community.

The second initiative, which had a European perspective and an educational content, involved the development of consumer education in schools. In April 1975, the Council of Ministers adopted a preliminary programme for consumer

---

1. 'Declaration of the Council of the European Communities and of the representatives of the Governments of the Member States meeting in the Council of November 22nd 1974 on the programme of action of the European Communities on the Environment', *Document No. SEC (74) 70014,* January 30th 1974, title II Chapter 6B (Projects).

information and protection policy. Amongst the priority measures to be undertaken in this area, the need to develop teaching materials for schools and for the training of teachers was noted. 1975 and 1977 constituted a preliminary period during which various approaches and issues involved in consumer education were discussed. In December 1977 a seminar was held in London. It stressed the need for consumer education to be introduced as soon as possible into the school curriculum. The following year, the Commission drew up a work-schedule and with it a network of 20 schools to test, develop and evaluate teaching materials. Aimed at developing courses for 10-12-year-olds, the purpose of this programme was to draw up models for consumer education to be carried out in stages over a period of several years. Its objectives were two-fold: first, to enable young people to become discriminating consumers, capable of making an informed choice of both goods and services; second, to develop an attitude towards consumption that was both critical and responsible, aware of the growing problems of the environment, of energy wastage and the exploitation of natural resources. A working party on the training of teachers in consumer education was also set up. Its remit included guidelines to define consumer education, the topics that ought to be included, indications about the choice of teaching material, and various practical and theoretical aids for teaching it. It is proposed that, in the near future, a draft resolution be submitted to the Council to encourage Member States to promote consumer education in schools. Ultimate responsibility for school based consumer education lies with Directorate General V.

New definition of the European dimension:

The impetus to set up undertakings in the area of school teaching materials production in both environmental and consumer education took place in the context of the Community acting as an economic entity. And, though this developed into a *de facto* area of cooperation, the initiatives were largely pursued in parallel to the Commission's education services. In 1976, however, following the adoption by the Ministers of Education of an Education Action Programme, a new definition was given to the European dimension in education, and reflected the view of the Community as a cultural, social and political entity. Thus, the Ministers of Education agreed to *'give a European dimension to the experience of pupils and teachers in primary and secondary schools in the Community'*.[2] It was also agreed that *'Member States will promote and organise (inter alia) educational activities with a European content'*. At Community level, cooperation in this area was to develop in the light of the experience and activities of Member States. This was to be of considerable importance in view of certain misgivings which emerged later over the ticklish question of Community competence in some areas included in the European dimension.

The European dimension is, in effect, made up of several elements. They may be summarised under six heads:

2. 'Resolution of the Council and of the Ministers of Education meeting within the Council, December 13th 1976', *Official Journal*, December 20th 1976, para. IV, Section 5.

- teaching about Europe;
- pupil mobility and pupil exchange;
- the European school record card;
- language teaching;
- schools of an international nature;
- teacher mobility and teacher training.

Thus, the European dimension in education consisted of a series of interlocking and mutually supporting actions in which the fortune of some depended to some degree upon the success of others.

Teaching about Europe:

Prior to presenting a series of concrete proposals for a Community-level action programme in this field, the Commission, in 1977, invited Member States to submit reports on the latest developments and trends in teaching about Europe in the various national education systems. The general conclusion of these reports was presented by the Commission to the Council in June 1978 in a document entitled *Educational activities with a European content: the study of the European Community in schools.*

All Member States set aside an important part of the school timetable for the study of Europe. There are, nevertheless considerable variations between the different countries, both as regards the amount of time allocated and the particular subject framework into which this is inserted. In some, the study of Europe takes place within the general context of geography; in others, of history, economics or civics. The majority of studies in school appear to be based on contemporary Europe which naturally includes the Institutions of the Economic Community. But, in its general report, the Commission suggested that little attempt has been made to bring these diverse themes and disciplinary approaches to bear upon a coherent study of Europe. The situation was made no easier, it was felt, by the relative lack of suitable materials for those wishing to teach this subject.

To remedy the situation, the Commission proposed that priority be given to the development of the European dimension with particular reference to the European Community, arguing that *'a basic understanding of the Community is necessary on the part of its citizens if it is to succeed in building a "closer union among European peoples" to which all its Member States are committed'.*[3] Additional support for this proposal came from the European Parliament which, on November 16 1978, adopted a Resolution stating that it was of the opinion *'. . . that the citizens of a community with a directly-elected parliamentary assembly need to be better informed about the European Community and that*

---

3. 'Activités pédagogiques à dimension européenne: l'étude de la Communauté Européenne à l'école, Communication de la Commission au Conseil', *Document No. COM (78) 241 FINAL,* June 18th 1978.

Community Studies should therefore form an integral part of the teaching programmes in all schools'.

In outlining its programme proposal the Commission suggested that it be divided into two phases, the first of which would concentrate on development of the subject for school students up to the age of 18, with a second phase taking place later for those above this age.

Despite — or rather because of — its importance to the future relationship between Member States and the Community, the issue of teaching about the Community in schools became a matter of high controversy. It is not appropriate in this account to delve into the finer nuances and details of this disagreement, save only where it had direct consequences upon the development of Community education policy. Broadly speaking the issue at stake was whether the Community was entitled to take initiatives in areas unspecified by the Treaty of Rome or whether, in such instances, it ought to confine itself to playing a complementary and supporting role in activities initiated by Member States. Behind this lay a question of a more subtle though no less important nature, namely, whether the powers transferred by Member States to the Community as an economic entity could implicitly be extended when such an entity became increasingly regarded as having a cultural and social dimension. This disagreement involved not merely the proposed programme for teaching about Europe in schools, but also the drawing up of a Community policy on the teaching of foreign languages.

The immediate effect on the creation of an operational definition for a European dimension in schools was twofold: in the first place, the Council decided to suspend work at Community level on both items from the beginning of 1980; secondly, a new interpretation was put upon the place of the European dimension in schools in an effort to find a way through the impasse. Teaching about Europe, it was suggested, should be complementary to existing subjects and be governed by the concerns of individual Member States and the needs of individual schools and teachers. It was not to be introduced as a new subject into the already established curriculum. Despite the fact that at the meeting of Ministers of Education on June 27th 1980 it did not prove possible to draw up credits for this heading, some progress was made towards defining those areas that might lend themselves to implementation at Community level at some future date. Four main areas were seen as being potentially fruitful:

1. support for the development of joint activities between teacher training institutions and the arrangement of study visits for the training, administrative and advisory personnel concerned;
2. support for short study visits for teachers working in this field;
3. support to provide the necessary materials for teachers through
   - the preparation and circulation of materials concerned with the European Community;
   - the development of teaching materials adapted to school curricula linked

with a series of exploratory studies and experiments to define ways of supporting the efforts of Member States;
4. the promotion of an exchange of information and experience through
   - the organisation of seminars of experts, teachers and teacher trainers;
   - the publication in the languages of the Community of such seminars and reports and other relevant studies;
   - an examination of ways enabling existing organisations to cooperate in meeting the needs of teachers.

A careful analysis of these areas suggests that, if agreement should be reached later on the topic of teaching about Europe in schools, the Community's role will emphasise the supportive activities to initiatives taken at the base inside Member States.

This does not mean to say that all activity in this area has ceased. What it does mean, however, is that initiatives tend to have passed to projects that are largely independent of the Community, carried out by non-governmental organisations or private associations, such as, for instance, the Centre for European Education in Bonn. Equally significant is the cooperation between the European Community and the Council for Cultural Cooperation of the Council of Europe. The foundation stone of this cooperation was laid in December 1979 when the Commission cooperated with the Council of Europe by holding a conference at Braunschweig (FRG) devoted to 'Teaching about Europe since 1945'.

Pupil mobility and pupil exchange:
Understanding Europe by means of the school curriculum is one thing, though no less important for all that. Direct experience is another. Put together, they provide a powerful and mutually reinforcing incentive not merely to learn more, but also to appreciate the myriad differences, cultural, social, historical and psychological that spring from direct contact with other countries and peoples. This tradition has, of course, long been enjoyed intermittently by certain privileged sections of European society since the early 18th century. The 'Grand Tour', well known to certain aristocratic families during that period, is an example of the value of such a type of educational experience.

The advantage of extending this type of experience to the usual child was recognised by the December 1976 Action Programme. It stated that *'In order to enable the greatest number of students to learn the languages of the Community . . . Member States . . . will encourage exchanges by pupils or groups of pupils'.* Moreover, this dimension was explicitly seen by the Ministers of Education as both reinforcing and underpinning the European dimension in schools. *'In order to give a European dimension to the experience of teachers and pupils in primary and secondary schools in the Community'*, the Resolution continued, *Member States will promote and organise . . . the development of the national information and advisory services to promote the mobility and interchange of pupils and teachers within the Community . . . Cooperation in these areas at*

*Community level will develop in the light of the activities and experience of Member States'.*4

During 1977, the Commission received reports on the situation of pupil exchange systems in various Member States from their respective Minister of Education and, in October of that year, brought together experts, both regional and national, at Venice. The conference discussed a report presented by a Danish expert, Mrs Bente Aarup, which dealt with existing facilities for both pupil and teacher exchange in the Community. Together with the conference proceedings, this report was published in 1979 under the title *Pupil exchange in the European Community*. As a result of this, the Commission put forward a scheme of support for existing provision for exchanges on both an individual and group basis. It consisted of four main points: first, to enable Member States to overcome two major difficulties, namely, the inability of poorer families to pay and the geographical disadvantage suffered by peripheral regions; second, to organise holiday activities, in the form either of conferences or field studies based on one particular language, for senior pupils in secondary education from all Member States; third, the launching of pilot projects to explore the needs of handicapped pupils participating in exchanges, as well as the possibility of extending the scheme to students in technical and vocational education; and finally, to investigate the problems involved in exchanges with those Member States whose language was not widely used. A report based on the experience of those pupil mobility schemes already developed was presented in November 1981. Entitled *Case Studies in Pupil Mobility*, it was prepared by an Italian expert, Roberto Ruffino of the *Istituto Intercultura,* Rome.

Experience from those countries that have already organised substantial pupil exchanges suggests that a crucial factor in the success of such ventures is the presence of well-provided specialist units at national level to advise on preparation and planning. Therefore, the Commission proposed that those Member States which do not, as yet, have such facilities, should set them up as soon as possible. To help in this development, the Commission also proposed to organise regular meetings of all the Directors of such units as a means of building upon experience in other Member States, as well as creating further contacts between those organisations involved in such an enterprise.

Though pupil visits and exchanges may, obviously, be seen as a means of improving the individual's language ability, the Education Committee decided in 1978 that the two issues should not be treated together. In part, this decision was taken because the issue of language teaching was itself under dispute, some Member States arguing that it did not come within the frame of reference of the Treaty of Rome. Amongst the priorities reviewed in the Commission's planning exercises were group visits and exchanges for pupils aged 11 to 16 in both general or technical education and, secondly, a series of study conferences or

---

4. 'Resolution of the Council and of the Ministers of Education meeting within the Council, December 13th 1976', *Official Journal,* December 20th 1976, para. IV, Sections 5, 17, 19.

field study programmes for students aged between 16 and 19 in general education. These holiday activities, it was proposed, should be so organised as to involve pupils from several countries. Further exploration of this issue has continued, following the Resolution adopted by the European Parliament on March 12th 1981 after the presentation of the Report by Mrs Pruvot on Youth Activities the previous month. An expert meeting held in December 1981 reviewed the various possibilities of moving beyond the traditional concept of 'pupil exchange' towards the setting up of a 'Youth Exchange System' within the Community.

Exchanges, however, are only a temporary aspect of mobility in the life of a young person, even though, later, such experience may enable the individual to be more mobile in his or her working life. There remains, nonetheless, the question of those pupils who, following moves by their families from one Member State to another, are obliged to transfer from one education system to another. For a number of years now, the Council of Europe has been committed to developing an International Pupil Record Card, designed to provide information about the performance and achievement of such students, and to assist in their placement and transition in their new educational context. The Commission, in collaboration with the Council of Europe, is supporting a three-year evaluation of this scheme, the work programme for which was elaborated in the course of a national experts' meeting in January 1979. The evaluation period lasted until 1982.

Teaching of foreign languages:

One of the first priorities to be identified as crucial to the future of the European Community as a cultural entity is the teaching of foreign languages. The 1976 Education Action Programme set three objectives for Member States in this area: first, all pupils should have the opportunity to learn at least one other Community language; second, as a matter of general principle, all teachers of foreign languages ought to spend a period in the country where the language they teach is spoken; and, third, attention should be paid to non-traditional methods in both language-teaching and learning, particularly with a view to meet the vocational requirements of adults.

As a first step towards developing this policy, a colloquium of government experts involved with language teaching in primary and secondary education was held in December 1976. Its purpose was to single out those policy trends and issues that might be developed at Community level. Further discussions were held in the course of 1977, and revolved around such questions as the exchange of foreign language assistants and language teacher training. Preliminary work undertaken during this period included a joint study, sponsored by the Commission, into the feasibility of setting up a Community-wide information service on language teaching. Two bodies, the Paris-based *Centre d'Information et de Recherche sur l'Enseignement et l'Emploi des Langues (CIREEL)* and the Centre for Information on Language Teaching and Research, London were given this task, the aim of which was to ascertain how far such a network might provide speedy information on the latest developments in this area in Member States.

This report was considered by the Education Committee as part of a rather more wide-ranging proposal to establish an education information network in the Community. This network, its remit and workings are described in greater detail in Chapter XI. One of its responsibilities is, however, information on language teaching.

A further step in this field was taken with the presentation of a communication by the Commission to the Council on June 4th 1978. It outlined the basis for a Community Plan for continuous opportunities for language learning from primary school through to higher and adult education. Amongst the proposals included were an initial three-year programme (1980-83) for the exchange of future language teachers, which would involve an annual figure of 10,000 assistants a year across the Community as a whole; an agreement for the setting up of a community scheme for the *long-term* interchange of language teachers for periods of between 3 to 5 years which, it was suggested, might take place from 1980; and the proposal for a series of pilot projects to assess the most effective methods of early language teaching in primary school.

The belief that a Community Action Programme in this area might infringe national prerogatives, however, required a rather more accommodating and flexible approach to this question. After examining the Commission's proposals throughout 1979, the Education Committee proposed, as a way out of the impasse, that certain Community initiatives be regarded as subordinate to those taken within the framework of Member States. More particularly, the context of foreign language teaching underwent a subtle shift with more emphasis upon the vocational aspect — which falls fully in the Treaty area — rather than the purely school-based dimension which, some claim, does not. This shift is reflected in the four headings which the Ministers of Education, meeting in June 1980, agreed in principle should be the main areas of future effort. They were:

- the teaching of foreign languages to young people from a vocational point of view;
- the teaching of language to adults for vocational purposes;
- the initial training of foreign language teachers and the use of foreign language assistants, particularly in the context of vocational training for young people and adults;
- the continuing training of foreign language teachers, particularly in the context of vocational training for young people and adults.

This change of *context* did not, however, involve a change of *content,* as a closer examination of these four headings reveals. Amongst the various proposals included under the first were the following items:

- to review the scope of extending opportunities for acquiring a working knowledge of at least one Community language in addition to the mother

tongue, as an important aspect of the preparation of young people for adult and working life;
- to review the main strategies followed by Member States to improve the performance of *pupils* (our italics) experiencing difficulties in learning a foreign language, including those showing little motivation, and the organisation of a number of experimental projects to define ways and means that might be developed to meet such difficulties;
- to review means of extending opportunities for students in higher education to combine foreign language studies with the pursuit of their discipline as an integral part of their degree programme.

Amongst the elements to be included in the teaching of foreign languages to adults for vocational purposes was a report, the remit of which was to cover the following four aspects:
- the possibility for greater collaboration between the education and employment sectors in identifying and providing for foreign language requirements in different sectors and levels of employment;
- the special linguistic needs of young workers with a view to improving the value of exchange programmes organised for them;
- the degree of collaboration required for the development and presentation of teaching methods and materials, including the use of the mass meda;
- the supply and training of foreign language teachers for adults particularly within the context of continuing general and vocational education programmes.

Under the heading that dealt with the initial training of foreign language teachers was included the introduction of an experimental scheme (envisaged for the period 1981-83) in order to assist the efforts of Member States in improving the initial training of foreign-language teachers by providing for appropriate experience abroad. In keeping with the reorientation of context, particular emphasis was to be placed on providing further opportunities for language learning in vocational, technical and higher education. And, as a measure of continuity, it was pointed out that experience gained in developing such exchanges within the context of general education would be harnessed to the innovative and experimental aspects of these institutions. The scheme, building on existing arrangements for the exchange of language assistants would, however, be tailored to meet the following purposes as national circumstances permitted:
- diversification of the type of educational establishments in which future foreign language teachers would be placed, especially those in the vocational, technical and higher education sectors;
- improved provision for the preparation of this group of future teachers and evaluation of their experience as participants in the scheme;
- opening the scheme to participation of foreign language assistants from all Member States.

The European Dimension in Education

Community participation in the financing of this undertaking would be no more than 50 percent of the cost of each project.

In the area of in-service training (the final heading) it was proposed that opportunities should be extended for practising teachers to spend a recognised period of further education and vocational training in another Member State. Two main priorities were designated: first, the exchange of teachers, particularly those involved in vocational training for both young people and adults, for one term abroad; second, ten-day intensive visits for language specialists (including advisers and inspectors) to up-date their knowledge of the latest methods of foreign language teaching for vocational ends.

Though the Ministers of Education agreed in principle to these activities in June 1980, little could be done throughout 1981 to implement them, with the issue of language teaching retaining its controversial nature. Initiatives in the area of such teaching were thus reduced to the limited, if important, field of exchanging information. However, particularly noteworthy in this context was the second colloquium on language and cooperation in Europe held in mid-September 1981 at Urbino (Italy) at the instigation of the *Centre d'Information et de Recherche pour l'Enseignement et l'Emploi des Langues* (Paris) and the Urbino-based Centre for Advanced European Studies.

European schools and schools of an international nature:

The notion of setting up European schools or establishments using several working languages was also part of the Education Action Programme of 1976. This was first, to provide some facility for children from families that were professionally mobile across several countries; secondly, to underpin the concept of 'education with a European dimension' and, finally, to respond to the interest expressed by the European Parliament in extending the principles developed in the network of European schools already in existence.

At present, there are 9 European schools – three in Belgium (Mol, Uccle and Woluwe, the latter two being in the Brussels suburbs), two in the Federal Republic of Germany (Munich and Karlsruhe) and one in Luxembourg, England, the Netherlands and Italy, located respectively at Luxembourg, Culham, Bergen and Varese. They enrol some 10,560 pupils.

The first European school was set up at Luxembourg in April 1957 following the signature of an inter-governmental statute. In 1962, a protocol for the establishment of other European schools, principally for the children of the Commission's personnel was passed, though it also accepted other pupils to a limited extent. A supplementary protocol in 1977 enabled the setting up of a European school in Munich, mainly for the benefit of children of staff in the European Patent Office, and a similar development took place in 1978 at Culham (England) in relation to staff involved in the Joint European Torus – a research project investigating hydrogen fusion as an energy source.

Students in these schools work to a common curriculum, with teachers recruited by each Ministry of Education. Basic subjects are taught in up to six languages with the further possibility in other disciplines for pupils from different language backgrounds to work together. Students are prepared to present themselves for the European Baccalaureat which is recognised as valid for admission to higher education by all Member States.

In 1978 the Commission, as part of its proposals for an Action Programme in language teaching, put forward the proposal for a scheme for European Community Schools. Its purpose was to encourage public sector schools to assume a specific European identity on the grounds that this would extend some of the advantages hitherto enjoyed by children of the international elite, especially in the area of foreign language learning, the promotion of bilingualism, and the evolution in national school systems of a greater awareness of Europe. If, to some extent, the fate of this scheme also hangs upon the outcome of the broader issue of language teaching in general and, as such, is still under deliberation of the Education Committee, the principle of bilingual education has received a powerful boost from another quarter, namely the legislation involving the education of young migrants (see Chapter II).

Limited though the numbers of European schools might be, they constitute nevertheless a certain contradiction in the area of Community education policy. This contradiction emerges from the fact that by setting up special establishments for one group of migrants' children, the Community has not extended this principle to the whole of the migrant population. Community civil servants, though it might be indelicate to say so, are a professional substratum of a migrant population numbering around 12,000,000. By according separate establishments for some 10,560 pupils and endowing them with separate status from those attended by the remaining 1,435,000 in the public schools of Member States, the Commission's stance would appear at odds on the one hand with its general policy for the education of migrants' children and on the other, also closely associated with this same group, the principle of equality of educational opportunity. If the public education of host countries is good enough for their nationals and for the children of immigrants in manual occupations, there can, in equity, be no case to make in support of special facilities for the children of those migrants whose occupation places them in the professions. On the other hand, it may be that a Member State's schools *are* failing to provide the equipment, teaching and academic standards. And, this on its own might be sufficient to justify the creation of separate and special schools. If this is the case, then it would be reasonable for the Commission to argue, again in the name of equity, that similar provision be made for the children of those migrants who, by any act of the imagination one cares to name, *must* possess less cultural and monetary capital than that particular section of the migrant population which already enjoys such rare and special facilities.

It may be argued that the children of functionaries need to maintain contact with the syllabuses, courses and examinations of their home country, on grounds that they may well wish to study there later. But this point can equally be made — if not more so — for the sons and daughters of those whose employ is even more precarious and subject to termination with far less notice. If Europe is to be built on the twin principles of equity and social justice — and none could reasonably believe that it is not so to be — then it can hardly be out of place to point out that the hereditary principle finds little backing in such imperatives. There can, surely, be no such thing as one measure of equality of opportunity for the bulk of the migrant population and a second for a minority. Since most reforms in the education systems of Member States have, over the past twenty years, been driven by the need to remove such anomalies of treatment, it seems surprising that the contrary example should be given by those most closely engaged in building the new Europe.

Teacher education and the mobility of teachers:

If a sympathetic understanding of Europe constitutes both an interest and a challenge to the young, that challenge must, perforce, be presented through the efforts of those who are elder. Hence, to a very great extent, implementation of many facets of the 1976 Education Action Programme depends on the education of the teaching profession, both initial as well as in-service. In order to establish an overview of the current situation in the countries of the Nine, the Commission arranged for a report to be drawn up on this topic. The task was entrusted to Mr Georges Belbenoit, a French expert, in 1977. His report, published in 1979, was entitled *In-service education and training of teachers in the European Community*. Close cooperation was established with the OECD (Paris) which was also at that time analysing teacher education policies. The Commission also acted as co-sponsor together with the Council of Europe and the European Cultural Foundation (Amsterdam) to the Association for Teacher Education in Europe, launched in July 1976 at a conference in Liège (Belgium). In addition, the Commission normally gives practical support to the Association's annual conference. A special working group has been set up by the Association to examine the curriculum of initial training for teachers. In addition, its remit has been to consider further developments in this field since the publication of the Belbenoit Report. The report entitled *In-service Training of Teachers in the European Community* was presented in November 1980. The systematic examination of teacher training policies at various levels of Member State education systems has been continued by ATEE, under contract to the Commission's education services. A report dealing with *Primary teacher education in Member States of the European Community: international perspectives* was completed in August 1981, while *Teacher Education in the context of children of migrant workers* was submitted in December of the previous year, and a further study was presented in the course of 1981 on *'La formation des enseignants et le passage de l'école à la vie active'*.

Another aspect of influencing the way teachers regard Europe was mentioned in the Education Action Programme. It involved the possibility of extending to this profession the principle of mobility of labour implied in the Treaty of Rome, by allowing teachers to work for a time in a Community country other than their own. The various difficulties such as pension rights, the civil servant status of the teaching profession in certain countries, and recognition of seniority in time spent abroad was examined in the course of 1976 and 1977.

Education and the European Community

There remain, nevertheless, a large number of problems outstanding in this area, not least of which is the mutual recognition of qualifications necessary to teach in primary, secondary or technical education. In an attempt to examine this problem more closely, the Commission had asked the Association for Teacher Education in Europe to develop a taxonomy of teachers' qualifications in the Member States.

Conclusion:

The European dimension in education is a highly complex area in the Community's activities which developed over a considerable time. Nevertheless, it remains an extremely sensitive issue and one in which Member States are jealous of their responsibilities, particularly in those aspects that touch directly upon the control over what goes on in schools. Commission activities in this domain were pursued simultaneously across a broad spectrum of interests, a strategy imposed by the need to move quickly, to produce results and that with an economy of effort. Such an approach depended, however, on agreement being reached in certain key fields, one of which was teaching about Europe in schools. This was not forthcoming and as a result, other initiatives amongst which the area of teacher training that followed on logically — fell by the wayside.

In fact, the question of the European dimension in schools posed issues which, though conducted through the dialogue of education, went far beyond this immediate concern. The argument over curricular control is, of course, a matter of special delicacy since it was not mentioned as an area included in the Treaty of Rome. As such, it illustrates very well the narrow margins of negotiation that exist in the education field between the Commission, the Education Committee and the Member States. But behind this *contretemps*, however, are matters of a more fundamental and abiding nature. First of these is the degree of legitimacy that ought to be accorded in the field of education to reinforcing those institutions that bade fair to transform what had hitherto been an Economic Community into a Community with political and cultural dimensions as well. The second which followed from the first, was of high symbolic and concrete importance; how far are Member States willing to yield sovereignty at most, or initiative at least, in those areas which remained outside the Treaty of Rome? And, third, whether it is, in fact, possible to create a Europe beyond the economic domain without so doing?

These issues may be resolved by other means in the future. In the meantime, whatever the efforts to construct a feeling of being a citizen of Europe, they are probably best pursued from beneath rather than seeking to force their emergence from above.

SOURCES:

i. Primary: internal Commission documents

'Declaration of the Council of the European Communities and of the representatives of the Governments of the Member States meeting in the Council of November 22nd 1974 on the programme of action of the European Communities on the Environment', *Document No. SEC (74) 70014*, January 30th 1974, title II, Chapter 6B (Projects).

'Resolution of the Council and of the Ministers of Education meeting within the Council of December 13th 1976', *Official Journal*, December 20th 1976, para. IV, Section 5.

'Activités pédagogiques à dimension européenne: l'étude de la Communauté Européenne à l'école, Communication de la Commission au Conseil', *Document No. COM (78) 241 FINAL*, June 18th 1978.

'Education Action Programme at Community level: the teaching of languages in the Community: Communication of the Commission to the Council', *Document No. COM (78) 222 FINAL*, June 14th 1978.

'Preliminary Community programme for consumer protection and information adopted April 14th 1975, paras. 43-44, in 'Background Memorandum submitted by the Commission', *Document No. ENV/528/79 EN*, (no date 1979).

'Consumer education in schools: outcome of the proceedings of the Education Committee', *Document No. 11287/80 (EDUC 49/CONSOM 57)*, November 19th 1980.

'Outcome of the proceedings of the Council and Ministers of Education meeting within Council: general report of the Education Committee', *Document 8137/80 (EDUC 30)*, July 7th 1980.

'Examen des possibilités d'apporter des modifications aux propositions controversées au Conseil en raison des limites du champ d'application des traités', *Document No. SEC (80) 1773*, November 27th 1980.

'Meeting of the Education Committee January 29-30th 1981', *Document No. 4823/81 (EDUC 2)*, February 13th 1981.

'Some Danish reflections on the use of Article 235 of the Rome Treaty', *Note by Per Lachman, Legal Advisor, Danish Ministry of Foreign Affairs*, (undated, circa June 1981?), (typewritten).

Working Paper for the Expert Meeting 'Youth and educational exchanges in the European Community', November 1981 (mimeo).

Unpublished material submitted to the Commission:

Environmental education in the age group 9-14 years within the Commission (sic) of the European Communities, Dublin, Curriculum Development Unit (mimeo), April 1977.

Henk Oonk, *Europe in the school: interim report until June 1980*, Brussels, Centre for European Education, (undated).

ii. Secondary: official Commission publications

Georges Belbenoit, *In-service education and training of teachers in the European Community*, Brussels, Commission of the European Communities, 1979, Education series.

Bulletin of the European Communities No. 9, September 1981.

iii. Tertiary: pamphlets and articles of a non-official nature.

Guy Neave, 'Accountability and control', *European Journal of Education*, vol. 15, No. 1, 1980.

Chapter Eight
Education and Training for Disabled Children and Young People

Structure:
Introduction
Legal basis of Community policy
Policy development
New concept of integration
Obstacles
New Initiatives
Reassessment of Community policy for the handicapped
Research and development
Commission liaison with handicapped organisations
Conclusion
Notes
SOURCES

Introduction:
1981 marked the International Year of Disabled People, an event intended to bring to people's notice the difficulties faced by this group of persons. It also marked a new stage in the development of the education and training programme launched by the European Community. Early in the previous year, in February 1980, at a meeting in Luxembourg of the National Committees set up to organise the Year of Disabled People, it was announced that the Commission would undertake a new series of initiatives. They would be specifically devoted to the problems of education for the disabled and with the problems associated with the transition from school to work. The new Programme was, in short, to be the Community's contribution to this event.

Information about the number of handicapped people in the Ten is difficult to come by. Much depends on the definitions of handicap. Estimates carried out by the World Health Organisation suggest that this may be as high as one person in ten. Included in this estimate are those suffering from physical, mental or sensory impairment, loss or abnormality of a psychological, physiological or anatomical structure or function. If one accepts these criteria, then it is reasonable to reckon that around 27,000,000 handicapped people live in the countries of the Ten. It has to be born in mind, however, that handicap varies from individual to individual and that whilst for some, such impairment may be stable over time, for others it will grow worse. In short, there is no one single group of 'the disabled'. There are, rather, a large number of different groups and individuals within them whose condition will alter, in varying degrees, with the passage of time.

Legal basis of Community policy:
The Community's new initiative, in fact, built upon a long standing series of actions already developed within the field of social policy and more specifically within the framework of training policy. The Council Resolution of June 27th 1974 laid down the broad lines of the first community action programme in favour of the vocational rehabilitation of the handicapped. In the preamble to this Resolution it was stated that the general aim of Community initiatives for the handicapped should be to enable them to lead a life that is normal, independent and fully integrated with society. The setting up of a Community network of rehabilitation and training centres, and the introduction of a series of pilot projects dealing with the adaptation of buildings for the disabled were two consequences of this Resolution. In addition, substantial support was provided through the European Social Fund, estimated at some 48,000,000 Units of Account in 1978, 61,000,000 in 1979, 71,000,000 in 1980 and 65,500,000 in 1981.

A further dimension was added to the programme for rehabilitating the disabled with the passing of the Resolution of February 9th 1976 by the Council and the Ministers of Education. In paragraph IV 20, the Ministers agreed that:

> 'The achievement of equal opportunity for free access to all forms of education is an essential aim of education policies in all Member States and its importance must be stressed in conjunction with other economic and social policies in order to achieve equality of opportunity in society',

The Commission's view on this, supported by the Education Committee, was that implementation of the Resolution required particular attention be paid to seeking out and identifying various categories of pupils suffering from exceptional disadvantage. The physically and mentally handicapped, obviously, come under this interpretation. Thus the Community's policy vis-à-vis the handicapped assumed a dual function: on the one hand, those aspects concerned with training and rehabilitation which came under the responsibility of Directorate General V (Employment) and, on the other, those concerned with education which were the responsibility of Directorate General XII (Research, Science and Education).

In December 1976, a further refinement to the strategy for education and training of the handicapped youngster was reached within the framework of the programme on transition from education to working life. The Ministers agreed to a series of actions intended to assist, evaluate and develop national policies in this area and, in particular, to provide adequate measures for groups with special problems in the field of transition. Both the mentally and physically handicapped were included (*see Chapter III, supra pp.45*).

It is self evident at a time of rising unemployment and, more specifically, youth unemployment, that the handicapped are amongst one of the most vulnerable groups to be affected. It is no less evident, however, that simply to confine measures on their behalf to the stage of transition between school and working life is to tackle only the end product of an experience that reaches down deeply into the life of the handicapped individual from the pre-school period onwards. There is considerable evidence to support the view that intervention at the transition stage, however useful *per se,* is in fact too late for, by that time, a young person's situation vis-à-vis education and training may be so impaired as to be virtually impossible to rectify.

Policy development:

To understand and, therefore, to anticipate the type of disadvantages that young handicapped people face as they move towards working life and adulthood requires a series of actions located 'upstream' from that point in the individual's school career. Thus, as a preliminary to definining the type of measures that the Community might undertake, it was agreed that both pre-primary and the whole of compulsory education and provision for the young handicapped be reviewed. This task was conferred upon Mr Skov Jorgensen, head of the Special Education Department of the Danish Ministry of Education. His report, on the organisation of special Education in the Community countries was completed in 1978 and entitled *Special Education in the Community: Developments*

and Trends. The analysis contained in the report suggested that nine points of convergence could be identified across the Member States. These appeared to be:
- to relate responsibility for education of the handicapped to ordinary schools and to guarantee special paedagogical guidance and assistance;
- to make educational and psychological guidance and special education available without cost to the family, the financial and administrative responsibility being established by legislation;
- to consider the environmental and servicing aspects essential for meaningful education as an inseparable component of education and hence of the education budget; this includes building, transport and technical aids;
- to provide special teaching assistance at nursery school age as soon as the need is recognised and to make it the responsibility of the school authorities, which in this context cooperate with the school and health services;
- to ensure specialised and further training for staff giving psycho-educational guidance and special education. The training should help to facilitate cross-disciplinary measures;
- to involve parents to an increasing extent in the planning of special paedagogical assistance;
- to provide assistance and guidance to the handicapped after they leave school as part of the education system, with the cooperation of industry;
- to include as part of special education in schools preparation for further training and vocational placement including vocational practice via cooperation in this area with the two sides of industry. In addition, to offer preparation for further education and continued personal development. It should be possible for the adult education system to meet the requirement for special education;
- to ensure that funds are provided for specialised paedagogical research and development work including the production of technical aids.

The Jorgensen report subsequently formed the principal background document for a Conference, held in Rome in December 1978 on the initiative of Senator Pedini, then Minister of Education and chairman of the Committee in the European Parliament which has oversight for Education. Organised by the Italian Ministry of Public Instruction in collaboration with the Commission, the opening session of the Conference was attended by the President of the Italian Republic, by the Mayor of Rome and by the Commissioner in charge of Education, Mr Guido Brunner. In addition, delegations participated from other Member States together with observers from the OECD (Paris), Unesco (Paris), the Council of Europe (Strasbourg) and other international organisations including Rehabilitation International, the European Association for Special Education and the World Confederation of Organisations of the Teaching Profession. The principal topic discussed, amongst others, was the question of integrating the young handicapped into society.

New concept of integration:

Over the four years between 1974 and 1978, the notion of integrating disabled young people into society underwent considerable change. Social integration is, naturally, a major political factor behind the operations aided by the European Social Fund as part of the Community Action Programme for the vocational rehabilitation of handicapped persons. Subsequent study revealed, however, that such operations were often carried out by local authorities and, whilst aimed at specific categories of people, nevertheless were designed to respond to the need of both *social* and *vocational* integration. This approach highlighted not only the problems of the mentally handicapped in addition to those physically disabled, but also suggested that the problems of work and leisure, education and training could be dealt with without necessarily having recourse to specialised means, but rather using those services available to the general public.

The educational implications of this new approach were raised at a meeting in Brussels in April 1979, which the Commission organised for national liaison officials designated by the Member States' Ministries of Education together with a representative of the OECD which was also working in this field. The purpose of the meeting was to draw up recommendations for the next step in the Community's programme.

The discussion threw up one general tendency and identified three specific issues. The growing trend, it noted, was that responsibility for the education of all categories of handicapped youngsters and at all levels of the education system lay with the local authorities. From this it followed that the responsibility for coordinating policy should rest at this level of administration. Turning its attention to the question of integration, the Brussels meeting suggested that the policy of integrating handicapped young people within normal education establishments should be pursued positively. In addition, if successful integration was to be achieved, it was likely that the supporting services — such as guidance, training and placement — associated with such schools would require substantially to be strengthened. However, if the young disabled person was to be supported by the usual facilities available to his or her non-disabled counterparts, the implications for the area of teacher training were considerable. As far as special teaching services were needed, it was suggested that only those with special teaching qualifications should be entrusted with this task, which in turn implied that national education budgets might have to be adjusted accordingly. Furthermore, if handicapped children were to be received into classes with the non-handicapped, then trainee teachers would require special courses within the framework of their initial training to enable them to cope with the new situation. The third and final area of discussion concerned developments in the area of pre-school education. Some attention ought to be paid to this field within the context of the local community and a better grasp of good practice demonstrated by means either of pilot projects or animation exercises. These should be centred on sparsely populated areas, zones of urban depopulation or areas of high immigration in order to give a total picture of the varying conditions of pre-school provision for this group of young people.

Obstacles:

Though the key issues outlined at this meeting were circulated for comment to all interested parties and non-governmental organisations, the task of developing a programme of supporting action appropriate to each key issue made little headway, due in part to disagreement as to the extent to which education fell within the realm of Community competence. Thus, despite calls by the Employment and Social Affairs Committee that Community-level measures in favour of young people and the handicapped, *inter alia,* deserved to be continued, the impetus for development was confined largely within the Commission itself. Throughout the second half of 1979 and the whole of 1980, therefore, attempts to coordinate work amongst the various Commission departments, continued, around three main themes:

– vocational training and occupational training of the handicapped;
– education of handicapped children;
– technical aids that might be used by elderly and handicapped persons.

During this fallow period, development continued into the further implications of positive social integration of the handicapped. In the area of vocational integration, emphasis became increasingly placed on using the normal guidance, training and placement services open to the population at large, as well as special measures. Recommendations along these lines were put to the Council by the Commission in April 1980 and the proposals discussed by Council on June 9th. Momentum was further sustained by the need to prepare a series of actions to take place during the International Year of the Disabled, scheduled for 1981. In this latter context, three actions in the field of education were prepared; the first involved an updating of the Jorgensen report in the light of the eventual membership of Greece, Portugal and Spain to the European Community; the second was a report on the contribution of pre-school education to the development of the handicapped child, to be presented at the 12th Standing Conference of European Ministers of Education, to be held in June 1981 at Lisbon on the theme of 'Education of the 3 to 6-year-old'; and the third, the importance of new technologies in the education of the handicapped. Thus the International Year of the Disabled provided a springboard for the development of a new series of initiatives intended to extend over a substantial period.

New initiatives:

In January 1981, following the collation of the reactions to the consultative paper sent out in March 1980, a second meeting of experts took place to discuss the new draft action programme for the disabled. The theme of linking the new interpretation of the social integration of the disabled to initiatives undertaken at local level formed the main points on which Community strategy rested. In effect, the concept of social integration drew considerable strength from the argument that any measure to reduce the social consequence of disability would also reduce the burden on social services, public assistance and costly forms of institutionally-based care. The general objectives of the new programme, the Commission considered, should lay particular stress upon more imaginative action at local level, and around this consideration a unifying framework for Community action for the next five years should be constructed. No less important a development was the notion that vocational rehabilitation and social integration should be brought closer together, rather than remaining administratively speaking, in separate areas. Indeed, the theme of closer coordination emerged as the *leitmotiv* at another experts' meeting, called at the end of April 1981 at Cologne whose task was to develop further the design of the action programme. '*A Community action strategy for the handicapped,* a document noted, *which intervenes only in respect of training or retraining for employment and only in favour of those handicapped people who have a good chance of entering into open employment is not a policy but a fragment of a policy'.*[1] Whereas earlier, strategy for assisting the disabled set great store on 'upstream' developments, primarily in the area of pre-school and primary education, Community thinking now began to move towards considering the needs of this group within a global and lifetime perspective, thus recognising that the education and vocational needs of the handicapped are not limited to a particular point in time, nor are they similar in nature, but undergo rapid change both in relation to the economic situation and also in relation to the evolving needs of the individual.

The development of the new action programme it was proposed, would revolve around four main points. The first was the proposal to establish a series of locally-based development actions to last four years beginning in 1983. This would consist of a limited number of projects — between 16 and 17 are proposed — chosen to reflect the average distribution within a particular Member State on such items as level of income, employment structure, density of population and '*with an average reputation as far as social integration (of the handicapped) is concerned'.*[2] Their population, it was suggested, should be between 150,000 to 300,000. The second proposal was the establishment, primarily for the benefit of policy-makers in the field, of a European Community data base directed towards this group of people. It would bring together employment, teacher training and other sectors bearing on the condition of the handicapped. Such a data base would draw upon the European Centre for the Development of Vocational Training (West Berlin) and the Community's Education Information Network, EURYDICE. The third proposal which reflected the concern to strengthen what might be termed intersectorial planning at the Community level, an aspect which also underlay the issue of transition from education to working life *(see*

1. 'Foundations and guidelines for a Community Action Programme on the lifelong education and training of handicapped people', *Working Paper,* April 6th 1981.
2. 'The social integration of disabled people: a framework for development of Community action', *Document No. COM (81) 633 FINAL,* October 1981.

Chapter III, supra, pp.53-54), was the need to reinforce cooperation within the presently-existing Community Network of Rehabilitation Centres, particularly in the area of modular training and the training of teachers. Finally, a series of conferences should be launched, the first of which would take place in 1982, to examine the responsibility of local authorities in promoting social integration. This, it was suggested, would form part of the process of setting up the district projects.

Two developments served in particular to sustain this momentum. The first of these was the preoccupation expressed by the European Parliament that the Commission should present a new comprehensive programme of action early in the International Year of the Disabled. Furthermore, on March 11th 1981, the Resolution of the European Parliament containing proposals to facilitate economic, social and vocational integration of the disabled, was adopted by the Assembly. The second was the allocation of education to the portfolio of the Commissioner responsible for employment and social affairs early in 1981. This latter was of particular significance. It brought about a closer relationship between the two aspects: on the one hand, the vocational and training dimension which had grown out of the Resolution of June 1974 and, on the other, the educational dimension which had grown out of the two Resolutions of February and December 1976, under which intervention in favour of the handicapped had evolved. It also ensured that the Commission possessed both the administrative means and the decision-making capacity to bring this about.

Reassessment of Community policy for the handicapped:

The Cologne meeting in April 1981 was held to bring together three experts, including one from IFAPLAN, an independent social research institute, and another from the OECD whose CERI (Centre for Educational Research and Innovation) had recently carried out an evaluation of policies for integrating handicapped adolescents into normal schools. In a preparatory paper, it was argued that Community policy vis-à-vis the disabled had been cast in too narrow a perspective. To meet the fundamental needs of these persons, a broader approach was required, not merely in the range of policy which, it was argued, should be lifelong, but also in the definition of the handicapped themselves. In addition to the normal definitions of mentally or physically handicapped, the Community's understanding of this term was no extended to include those suffering from social or psychological maladjustment as well as the chronically ill or the delicate.

It also set out a proposed structure for the action programme based on one 'core action', three thematic actions and a set of supporting activities. The 'core action', followed closely the model, though not the range or scope, of the 'pilot projects' already developed within the context of measures for the children of migrant workers and the transition from education to working life. It involved the creation of a network of district projects, thus taking up once again the main lines that emerged from the January experts' meeting. The purpose of the 'core action' fell into three headings: first, to study the whole of education and training provision for the handicapped in a given district across all age groups and all categories of handicap. Second, it was intended to support existing services and whilst focussing primarily on education and training, health, social welfare and employment services and especially the way they were 'delivered' to the handicapped of the local community, were to be an aspect of the evaluation. Third, to evaluate the extent to which such services tended towards integration, to report on good practice, to identify obstacles to such a 'holistic' approach. Under the heading 'thematic actions' were included such matters as the development of technological aids for the disabled, teacher training and the question of parental participation as part of the development of local provision as a whole. Teacher training, it was pointed out, not only required imparting new specific skills but the learning of new roles as well as the acceptance of new cooperative relationships, the latter involving a more active and positive attitude towards parental participation and also the attitude of non-handicapped pupils towards their disabled fellows in school. Supporting activities would include the dissemination of information, the development of statistics and statistical indicators, provision for conferences and publications.

Research and development:

The new coordinated Community programme received the approval of the Social Affairs Council at its meeting in Brussels on December 9th 1981. The two part Resolution called upon Member States to continue and intensify their actions to promote the social and economic integration of the handicapped, to facilitate the coordination of various services with remits in this field and to ensure that the handicapped are able to lead a life as independent as possible. At Community level, proposals for developing a series of local-level actions also received backing.

As a result, the Commission has created a Bureau for the Handicapped inside the Directorate for Education, Employment and Social Affairs. The first moves towards setting up a 'coordinating group' have begun. This group will, it is hoped, have the confidence of the disabled themselves, of local authorities, as well as professionals, local employers, trades unions and voluntary associations. The programme of local level 'development actions' will start in 1983 and last for four years. Also part of the 'coordinated programme' is the improvement or, if necessary, the setting up, of information systems intended to provide a suitable flow of data between local authorities and the 17 'project districts'. It will also have the task of enhancing communication at Community level between voluntary organisations and the associations representing the disabled. Current estimates reckon the expenditure on the district programmes for 1983 will be in the order of 425,000 ECUS with a further 1,500,000 ECUS for information projects. By 1986, the handicapped programme will account for an overall budget of 7,154, 125 ECUS.

The European Social Fund, as has been pointed out, provides considerable resources under Article 304, for the vocational training of the handicapped and the possibility of its further extension was discussed at a meeting in Mullhouse

(France) in October 1981. In addition, it is able to finance innovatory schemes and actions for the handicapped in the disadvantaged regions of the Community, including Greenland, the Mezzogiorno (Italy) and Northern Ireland.

In terms of concrete developments and research, however, certain projects associated with the transition from education to working life have been concerned with the particular problem of handicapped school leavers. In Störstrom county, Denmark, a group of socially handicapped students, accompanied by a class teacher, are sent in their final year to a vocational education institute for a period between two to five weeks. The courses they follow are designed to give a foretaste of vocational skills with some related work in basic skills. In the Federal Republic of Germany, another project is taken up with the integration of physically handicapped pupils in the upper secondary section of the *Freiherr vom Stein* Comprehensive school at Lichtenau in Hessen whilst in Bridgend, South Wales (UK) an associated project involves the vocational preparation of backward or mentally retarded young people as well as providing a residential unit for the physically handicapped student. The question of preparing disabled youngsters for adult working life was also the topic of a conference held in October 1981 at Noordwijkerhout (Netherlands) by the Commission together with the European Centre for Work and Society, an independent institute based in Maastricht (Netherlands).

Commission liaison with handicapped organisations:

Research and development, however, require the participation not merely of experts, but also representative organisations and groups to put forward the needs of the handicapped. Though, prior to 1979, some difficulty was experienced in creating a regular dialogue between the associations representing disabled persons and the Commission's departments, due to a lack of a representative framework at European level, this situation has since improved. In 1979, a group of such associations – The European Action for the Disabled (Luxembourg) – emerged. At European level, several international bodies have set up liaison committees including the International League for Societies for the Mentally Handicapped and the International Federation of the Blind. These and other organisations are of particular help in enabling the Commission to deepen its understanding of the needs of handicapped people. In 1980, for example, it asked the Association for Parents of Psychotic Children (Belgium) to prepare, in association with similar organisations in other countries, a report on the type of difficulties faced by these parents and the kind of services they needed. This report dealt with both the training and information of parents, the institutions catering for such children and the kind of assistance required for autistic adults. A further example of the developing links between the Commission and the handicapped is provided by the conference held at Luxembourg on May 25-26th 1981 by the European Committee of the International Federation of the Blind. The Commission supported and participated in this meeting.

Education and the European Community

Conclusion:

The Community action programme for the disabled, which combines both education and training, for young children, adolescents and adults, is important for two reasons. First, because it is a gauge of the extent to which the Community is committed to enhancing the quality of life for one of its least privileged groups. The handicapped in a very large number of cases form part of what is known to social investigators as the 'poverty cycle'. In some instances, this is because of the lack of adequate education or training which places them at a disadvantage on the labour market. In others, because their span of income earning may drastically be foreshortened either by the nature of their handicap or by its subsequent deterioration. In the second place, it is important because it represents what might be called 'the second generation' of Community action and thus is symbolic of the Community's will to move forward. The development at an earlier stage of this programme suffered in no small manner from differences in interpretation in the matter of Community competence. The setting up of an action programme for the education and training of the handicapped is, in fact, far more than a test case.

SOURCES:

i. Primary: internal Commission documents

'Meeting of national experts concerned with the special education of handicapped children', *Document No. XII/246/79*, April 4th 1979.

'Education of the handicapped in the European Community: consultative document prepared by the Commission's education services', *Document No. XII/436/80*, February 1980.

'342eme session du Conseil: Travail et Affaires Sociales, Luxembourg, le 6 juin 1980', *Communication à la presse, Document No. 7723/80 (presse 80)*.

'Note from the education services of the Commission to the Education Committee to be held on July 15th 1980', *Document No. XII/798/80*, July 2nd 1980.

'Foudations and guidelines for a Community Action Programme on the lifelong education and training of handicapped people', *Working Paper*, April 6th 1981.

'Opinion of the Economic and Social Committee on the situation and problems of the handicapped', *Document No. SOC/63 CES 744/81*, July 2nd 1981.

'The social integration of disabled people: a framework for development of Community action', *Document No. COM (81) 633 FINAL*, October 1981.

'Community measures to promote social integration of handicapped people', *Circular Letter, Directorate General V*, (undated).

ii. Secondary: printed and official publications

'Résolution du Conseil du 27 juin 1974 portant éstablissement du premier programme d'action communautaire pour la réadaptation professionnelle des handicapés', *Official Journal No. C80/30*, July 9th 1974, para. 1.

'Resolution on the motion for resolutions concerning the economic, social and vocational integration of disabled people in the European Community with particular reference to the International Year of Disabled Persons', *Official Journal No. C77/27*, April 6th 1981.

Skov Jorgensen, *Special Education in the Community: developments and trends*, Luxembourg, Commission of the European Communities, Education Series No. 11, 1979.

Interim reports of the Central Animation and Evaluation Team for the pilot projects, Cologne, IFAPLAN, March 1980.

iii. Tertiary: pamphlets, articles of a non-official nature

The education of the handicapped adolescent: integration in the school, Paris, OECD, 1981.

Chapter Nine

The Micro Electronic Revolution

Structure:
Introduction
Main dimensions in the educational debate
Origins of Community Policy
Development of Community strategy
Implications for school structures and curriculum balance
Priority Areas
Conclusion
SOURCES

Introduction:

One of the more powerful axioms held by educational planners is that changes in the structure of industry and the economy require new skills and techniques to be developed in the labour force. From this it follows that one purpose of educational planning is to introduce into the education system the means by which this may be accomplished. The link between industrial development, the school and the training system is, historically speaking, an obvious one. The coal and steel revolution of the late 18th and early 19th century in Europe was highly influential in the development of compulsory schooling if only to provide the basic skills of literacy and numeracy necessary for the type of production then in place. The second industrial revolution, often identified with the rise of the electro-chemical industry towards the end of the last century, threw up further skills of a more specialised nature. Education's response to this was the creation of more elaborate vocational systems of training, some of which derived from previous artisan-apprenticeship and craft methods, others of a more innovatory nature. In fine, the second industrial revolution brought about a profound change in vocational training in such countries as Sweden, Germany, the Netherlands and Austria. It removed the creation of industrial skills from a guild or craft model, based on the individual relationship between master and apprentice, and organised them in a systematic and institutional framework, financed in part by employers and in part by public monies. For many people, Western society now stands on the threshold of a third industrial revolution. This potential revolution comes in the shape of the micro chip. Its revolutionary nature stems from the fact that micro electronic instrumentation amounts to nothing less than the application of machine intelligence to the productive process. What the precise consequences of this will be are difficult to forecast, though it is apparent that one outcome, already visible, is the wholesale redundancy of groups, unskilled in the main, who hitherto have been central to the productive process.

Whatever the future holds in store, it is perhaps unwise to rely entirely on a model of educational development moulded by historical determinism. It is one thing to note the links that grew up between vocational training and industrial development. It is another to seek deliberately to reshape them in an effort to accelerate society's adjustment to it. The articulation between industry, education and training which evolved over the course of the first and second industrial revolutions, did so over a long time span. Thus, what we see today as a process of successful adjustment was not merely protracted, but knew many failures and paid a high price in human misery. The issue that the micro-electronics revolution places four-square before educational planners is whether they are able, *rapidly* and *effectively*, to bring about those readjustments in the systems of education and training that the advent of micro-electronics and high technology industry apparently require. The issue is complicated further by the fact that the experience of two decades of reform has shown education systems to be remarkably resistant to rapid change in their internal organisation and working. Legislative intention is one thing, but implementation at the base is an entirely different matter.

Main dimensions in the educational debate:
Amongst the education services of the European Community, the debate over the implications of the new information technologies divided into two distinct phases. During the first, discussion concentrated on the implications for transition and the preparation of young people for working life. In the second, a broader perspective began to emerge. From this latter, four main points were retained. These were:

- the desirability of providing everyone with a general understanding of micro-electronics and computer-related activities and in particular to demonstrate the potential and limitations of such information systems.
- the importance of education's contribution to the use of leisure time, whether as a consequence of reductions in the working week or through the greater availability of spare time through unemployment.
- the necessity of a new form of political education, designed to increase the participation of the individual citizen as a result of his being better informed, through new information technologies, of those decisions that may affect his daily life.
- the risk that social isolation might increase if individuals came to rely overmuch on long distance communications rather than on human contact.

That the repercussions of new information technology extended to such widely different, though inter-related, domains as general education, political socialisation and the social psychological comportment of individuals profoundly influenced the approach of Community action in this area. Though based firmly in the educational domain, it involved a high degree of cross coordination and integration with other services inside the Commission. Such a move towards what might be termed an 'integrated and holistic' approach to the problem is characteristic of what some officials have called the 'second generation' of educational activities.

This is not to say that such a strategy was totally absent before. On the contrary, attempts to coordinate policy across different fields — education, training and working conditions — can also be seen in those parts of the Education Action Programme which dealt with children of migrants or the transition from school to working life. Nevertheless, those measures planned within the framework of the Action Programme on the New Information Technologies placed far greater stress upon integration and coordination than had been the case previously. Furthermore, two other factors intervened to give the Information Technologies Programme a qualitatively different slant from the previous projects undertaken by the Commission's education services. First, it is not aimed at specific target groups — a characteristic that had accompanied all previous undertakings. Rather, its target group was the full range of school students and young people as well as certain specific sub groups such as the handicapped and those deemed in need of recurrent education as a result of industrial restructuring. The second factor, though highly influential upon the type of strategy developed, was perhaps rather more fortuitous. The preliminary moves to defining a Community policy in this area coincided with a reshuffle in the Commision's services. This resulted in the separation of Education from Scientific Research and its transfer to Directorate General V whose responsibility covered the general field of Social Affairs and Employment. In other words, though the Education Services had been thinking in terms that went well beyond the limited confines of education *stricto sensu,* this re-arrangement which took place in January 1981, provided a wider platform from which to launch the new initiatives.

Origins of Community policy:

The impact of the New Information Technologies was first broached at the Heads of State conference held in July 1978 at Bonn. The main purpose of the new technologies was seen primarily in terms of creating new sources of growth and employment and to offset the long term decline in such basic industries as coal, steel, shipbuilding and textiles. At further meetings in Strasbourg, the importance of setting up new information industries based on them was given another boost. Industries such as these, it was thought, would constitute the major source both of economic expansion and of social development.

The following year, on November 29th, the Commission presented a communication to the European Council meeting at Dublin. The document identified certain specific difficulties that might arise with the introduction of the new technologies. It also argued that the type of social and industrial changes which flowed from these new techniques could not be left to develop unaided. Whatever their evolution in the future, it should be in keeping with the overall political and social objectives society had agreed upon. The communication went to enumerate some of the principal benefits that might accrue. Amongst these were prospects for enhanced individual development and expression, new life for small and medium sized firms, new avenues for the underprivileged and in particular for the handicapped, the elderly and the infirm. Various options for future action by Member States were laid out as well as areas involving the three social partners — unions, employers and government. At Community level, three main areas were set out for development and initiative. These were: the impact of the new technologies on employment, on cultural change and on education. For obvious reasons, our attention will be focussed on the latter.

At Community level, the Commission proposed to set up a programme in the key fields of education, training and the dissemination of information as a complementary approach to the proposed activities of Member States concentrating on schools on the one hand and industry on the other. The major objective, it was suggested, would be to raise the average level of technical training and individual initiative in the population at large. This, in turn, required substantial improvements at all levels of education as well as the extension of training on a life-long basis on a scale far beyond existing provision. In setting out the strategy for developing the new information technologies, it was further suggested that the Commission should prepare a Programme of Action for submission to the Council of Education Ministers in the course of 1980 with a view to its adoption in 1981. In the specific field of education, this involved increasing the exchange of information between Member Stats and turn around the following objectives:

- the spread of new technologies into all subject areas and at all levels of the education system;
- the development of methods of teaching and the familiarisation of pupils with these technologies in schools;
- their application to teaching the handicapped;
- their application to techniques of teacher training.

It also put forward that the Consultative Committee for Vocational Training should be consulted on the various aspects of training.

Development of Community strategy:

The development of Community strategy vis-à-vis the new information technologies took place on a broad front, the issue being discussed by the Standing Committee on Employment on February 26th 1980, and by the Advisory Committee on Vocational Training on July 2nd in the same year whilst the Council and Ministers of Education meeting within the Council discussed the broader implications for employment and social policy, and the particular repercussions they would have on education and training at their meetings of June 27th 1980 and June 22nd 1981. This wide-ranging involvement is also reflected in the fact that currently five Directorates are taking part in the exercise. These are Directorate General III (Industry), Directorate General V (Social Policy and Education), Directorate General XII (Research and Development), Directorate General XIII (Innovation and the internal EEC market) and finally, Directorate General XVI (Regional Affairs). There is also some linkage with the Organisation for Economic Cooperation and Development (Paris), this being mainly at desk level between Directorate General V and the Centre for Educational Research and Innovation, since the latter is also embarked on assessing the impact of the new information technologies.

In the first instance, concern focussed on the implications in the area of vocational training and the need to develop a flexible approach to this. This gave added weight to the Resolution passed by the Council on December 18th 1979 which dealt with the problem of linked work and training for young persons. The Resolution also pointed out the need for better links between the training system on the one hand and the education system on the other. Thus, explicitly changes in training to prepare future works at all stages of life for the new technology also pointed to the need to improve basic education as well.

The Micro Electronic Revolution

The recognition that the role of compulsory education was crucial to setting up a strategy designed to prepare for change, as well as to improve articulation between education and training through the development of 'alternance education', emerged clearly in the meetings of the Advisory Committee in the latter half of 1981. At its meeting of September 30th 1981, several Member State delegations urged that at all levels of the education systems, programmes should be redesigned with the purpose of instilling a basic knowledge of technological innovation at the level of compulsory schooling. Likewise, at its November meeting, the chairman of the Permanent Employment Committee noted that the discussion should take a wider view than that at present used to resolve economic and social problems. As the increasingly interlinked effects of micro-technology across employment, working conditions, training, and education became apparent, so the notion that this same innovation could contribute to an integrated approach, bridging the gap between technical education on the one hand and general education on the other, came to the fore.

In the meantime, as a preliminary to moving towards an Action Programme in this area, it was decided that the European Pool of Studies and Analysis should assemble and evaluate recent research as well as the various experiences of micro-technology in the Member States. This analysis is being undertaken in cooperation with the Dublin Foundation for Living and Working conditions, with the European Centre for the Development of Vocational Training (West Berlin), the European Trades Union Institute (Brussels) and the International Labour Office (Geneva).

In the area of the educational applications of the new technology, the Commission has concentrated on consulting the relevant authorities in the Member States and other interests to assist in the development of its proposals for future activities. A number of reports were commissioned into the particular repercussions of micro-technology. One of these, entitled the *New Information Technologies and Education: implications for teacher education,* was presented in July 1981 by a British expert from Manchester Polytechnic, Rhys Gwyn. Other studies, mainly in the area of the impact of micro-computers on the education systems of various Member States, have been put out to the Association for Teacher Education in Europe. Amongst the countries for which reports are currently in progress are Britain, France, Denmark, the Federal Republic of Germany and Ireland. Also as part of the lead-in phase, several meetings were held in the course of 1980 and 1981 both with education experts and representatives of teachers' organisations. Work is also in progress to prepare for a major conference, the purpose of which will be to allow policy-makers in both the education and training systems to exchange experience on this topic with representatives of employers and trades union interests. In addition, EURYDICE, the education information network of the European Communities working in conjunction with the national units of the network in Member States, has begun to assemble information pertaining to the whole field.

Naturally, at the time of writing, the major axes of Community initiatives concerning the educational dimension of new information technologies, are still under discussion. But a few main lines of approach, even though tentative at this stage, may be discerned. In the area of compulsory education, the principal goal to which most proposals tend is the introduction of micro-computers into the mainstream curricula of the school. This strategy is intended to give all students some first-hand experience with these instruments, as well as a real awareness of their capabilities. It will also provide the building blocks for those who, eventually, will go on to more specialised studies or go directly to vocational training. No less important, it is felt, is the contribution that may be made in the area of assisting the handicapped, either as an aid to communication or, more particularly in the paedagogical domain, as a teaching device through which rote learning may be given to those both mentally and physically impaired. Development of a future programme in the field of new technologies is thus a complement to whilst also reinforcing, action undertaken within the context of the social integration of the handicapped. A similar role is also foreseen in relation to opening up opportunities both in the area of technical and vocational education for girls and women. It is, then, complementary to the objective of equality of access to education which forms part of the Resolution of February 9th 1976 on which the first Education Action Programme is based.

Implications for school structures and curriculum balance:
It is difficult to foresee with any precision the exact effects the arrival of micro-technology will have upon the organisation and structure of both the school and its curriculum. However, it does raise, once again, the old question of whether education and training should be directed towards generic or specific skills, the former allowing a relatively rapid adaptation to changes in the economic structure by the individual, and the latter being related to a particular job which may not necessarily provide a life-time's work. The Education Committee in its discussion of options for action in April 1981 looked forward to considerable structural change, first in the area of preparing young people for working life and, second, in the field of education and training. In the case of the former, the Committee foresaw the emergence of integrated patterns of upper secondary and post-secondary education, bringing together both general and vocational education and including work experience. It also anticipated important modifications in the area of assessment and certification the purpose of which would be to facilitate transfers between various parts of the systems of education and training. The Committee also noted the importance of the need to pool those resources at present distributed across different authorities — some responsible for education, others for training — to develop further alternative out-of-school facilities for learning. Thus, the advent of micro-technology in the school curriculum acts as a catalyst for redrawing the map of both education and training, bringing the two areas and their competent authorities into closer coordination.

Equally significant, it is thought, will be the effects on continuing education, providing a second chance for adults to learn basic general and vocational skills, as well as re-equipping them for the openings created by the new information technologies. Here, the Education Committee suggested, it was especially important to build upon the experience gained from *temporary* measures intended originally for young people and to apply it to adult age groups as a whole. The possibility of setting up models of continuing education combining work, further education and training along these lines was regarded as a suitable course in the future.

Priority areas:

The Commission is currently drawing up a series of proposals that may, eventually, emerge in the form of pilot projects or demonstration projects which might form the next stage in the Community initiatives in this area. They will turn around three priority areas. These, at the time of writing, are:

— the training and in-service education of teachers and instructors through the application of the new information technologies;
— the appropriate adaptation of training programmes for young people and, in particular, the young unemployed;
— the needs of specific client groups including women and older workers, and the social integration of the handicapped.

As it reflects current thinking inside the Commission, the programme for execution over the years 1983 to 1984 foresees linking the pilot projects for training young people and in-service teacher education to local-level possibilities for industrial development. The projects are seen as having a dual purpose; first, to improve vocational training programmes — particularly in the area of transition from school to working life; second, to serve as back-up for public information exercises carried out both at national and local level by the mass media to inform the public about the potential of the new technology. Priority will be given in the first instance, to the development of programmes for 16 to 18 year-olds, for those seeking jobs and those with relatively low educational attainment. The geographical location of these projects will be in the most disadvantaged areas of the Community, the choice of location being assisted by the Member States. In the development of the pilot projects, the Commission is taking into account work done by the consultative Committee for Equality of Opportunity for men and women.

Also envisaged as part of the future action programme are a series of demonstration projects, to be set up with the Commission's initiative in association with Member States. These will bring together, it is suggested, both local authorities, representatives of the training system and the social partners (i.e. trades union and employers representatives). In the first phase of the proposed Commmunity Action programme dealing with micro-technology and social change, some 25 to 30 demonstration projects are envisaged.

Especially noteworthy since it demonstrates a different model of action research than that applied, for example, to the transition from education to working life, is the proposal for an accompanying parallel series of projects to run in tandem with the demonstration projects. This will consist in a series of investigations on themes of common interest to both Member States and the various services of the Commission. It will turn around two main themes: first, improvements designed to bring closer into line vocational qualifications with demands for flexible apprenticeship modules and, second, the effect of micro-technology on the conditions of work and work organisation. The former is conceived as a means of integrating the new information technology in the training systems especially in such areas as computing, electronics and 'telematics' and adjusting accordingly the patterns of apprenticeship. From this it is hoped that further pilot projects, dealing with the training of technicians and skilled workers in this field, will emerge at a later stage.

A further innovation is to be seen in certain changes in the financial instruments of the Community. It is proposed, for example, that the demonstration projects be financed out of the European Social Fund.

Conclusion:

Though the Community has yet to establish an Action Programme centred on the social implications of the new information technologies, planning is already far advanced. This planning is, at the same time more complex and involves closer and more sustained cooperation between more sectors of the Commission's services than other projects that earlier grew from the Education Action Programme outlined in December 1976. It also demonstrates very clearly the qualitative change in the strategic approach that has begun to emerge more strongly since the Education services became fully and formally drawn into the ambit of Social Affairs. This change involves a particular stress on what might be termed 'integrated planning' or what others have identified as a 'holistic' approach to educational policy. Far more important is the fact that in moving into the area of micro-technology and social change as expressed in education, training, consumer education, reskilling and all the myriad aspects this implies, the Community is not responding to a problem that has already reached a critical level. Rather, it is developing a strategy before the issues posed by the new technology have reached these proportions. It is this characteristic that sets the development of Community actions vis-à-vis the micro-electronic revolution apart from its previous activities whether they are called transition from school to work or the education of migrant workers' children.

SOURCES:

i. Primary: internal Commission documents

'European society faced with the challenge of new information technologies: a Community response', *Document COM (79), 650 FINAL,* November 26th 1979.

'Employment and the new micro-electronic technology: session of the Standing Committee on Employment, February 26th 1980', *Document COM (80) 16 FINAL,* February 5th 1980.

'Implications for education and the preparation of young people for working life which arise from the progressive introduction of new information technologies in the European Community: Statement by Mr Brunner. Outcome of the proceedings of the Council and Ministers for Education meeting within the Council, June 27th 1980', *Document 8538/80 EDUC 33,* July 10th, 1980.

'Outcome of the proceedings of the Education Committee April 23rd-24th 1981', *Document 6502/81,* April 29th 1981.

'New Information technologies and social change in the area of employment, working conditions, education and vocational training', *Communication from the Commission to the Standing Committee on Employment, Document COM (81) 578 FINAL,* October 12th 1981.

'Nouvelles initiatives communautaires pour la période 1983 à 1987 concernant les nouvelles technologies de l'information et le changement social', *Projet de Communication de la Commission au Conseil (version n⁰ 5)* February 11th 1982, (typewritten).

ii. Tertiary: pamphlets, articles of a non-official nature

Guy Neave, *Patterns of equality: the impact of new structures in European higher education upon equality of educational opportunity,* Windsor, NFER, 1976.

Chapter Ten
Information Policy and Educational Development in the European Community: EURYDICE

Structure:
Introduction
Background to Community information policy
Structures
Priority areas for information and users
Services provided by the information network
Development of the information network
Functioning of EURYDICE
Future areas of development
Relations with International Organisations
Conclusions

Notes

SOURCES

Introduction:
Money, it is said, is the sinew of war, and likewise information for the activities of the decision-maker. If correct within the context of individual countries, this aphorism is no less so when applied to a Community consisting of ten. In education, as in politics, it is often the case that insight into one's own problems can be gained by studying the way other people have dealt with theirs. Though the comparative study of education does not have as long a history as that of politics which may be traced back to Aristotle's examination of the constitutions of the Greek city states, it is nevertheless solidly founded. First developed by Marc Antoine Jullien in 1819, the comparative analysis of education systems as a contribution to policy development continued throughout the 19th century. In Britain, for instance, a close examination of educational practice in both France and Prussia was carried out by Matthew Arnold, who, as pioneer in educational reform and as one of Her Majesty's Inspectors, was well aware of the importance to be had from information culled from abroad.

This exchange of information increased considerably in the post-war period and more particularly from the end of the fifties. Several reasons have been advanced for this. First, there is the phenomenon of economic interdependence between the industrialised countries of the West. This has been touched upon earlier, and gave rise to what some people have called 'the convergence thesis' in comparative education. This thesis says that as the economies of different countries come to resemble one another, so the solutions sought in the educational field will follow a broadly similar path. Second is the fact that from this same period, the effects of the post-war baby boom began to bear down upon the educational provision of different European countries, forcing them to rethink both structures, plant and organisation. Though solutions varied, the overall effect of such pressures brought about change that was broadly comparable across the nations. Universal access to secondary education, the opening of upper secondary school to the overwhelming majority of pupils, the emergence of 'mass higher education' are all examples of this process. And, though the silent social revolution did not lead to an *educational* version of economic interdependence, nevertheless it did place an additional premium on knowing what was going on elsewhere. Third, the use of information between countries to enlighten the education policy of individual States received further legitimacy in the mid Sixties through the activities of various international organisations such as the United Nations' Education Scientific and Cultural Organisation and the Organisation for Economic Cooperation and Development, both located in Paris, the Council of Europe at Strasbourg and, more particularly in the context of Community affairs, with the direct elections to the European Parliament in 1979. Within the European Parliament, the establishment of the Committee on Youth, Culture, Education, Information and Sport may be seen as an important political forum for the discussion of common issues in education, which, by definition, involves both exchange of information and the comparative approach.

Background to information policy:

Within the Commission, the underpinning role of information exchange as an instrument for policy development was recognised by the Resolution of the Council and the Ministers of Education passed on February 9th 1976. *'It is necessary'*, the Resolution noted, *'to increase and improve the circulation of information between those responsible for education and those receiving it at all levels'*. To meet this requirement, it was decided to set up an information network. *'Each Member State'*, the Resolution continued, *'would appoint a national information service on education in the Community'*.[1] The coverage of this instrument was extended to the field of vocational guidance and the preparation for working life, by the Resolution passed at the Ministers' meeting of December 13th 1976.

In the course of 1977, the Education Committee organised two meetings of national experts to outline the various possibilities and to identify the types of service such a network might provide. Seen from a long-term perspective, the purpose of an information network was to underpin the programme of co-operation in education across the Community, to improve the understanding of the ways in which education systems of the Member States function and, finally, to encourage education projects of a collaborative nature to develop across the Community. It also called for the setting up by the Commission's Education services of a Central Unit whose role would be to coordinate and animate the network. The prime task of this network was seen as serving education policy-makers at Community and Member States level and in certain cases, at regional and local levels as well. A complementary role was to provide information to education policy-makers inside the Commission — assisting the Commission to reply to questions raised in the European Parliament and giving information to the Economic and Social Affairs Committee. These latter two services were seen as part of the remit to be covered by the Central Unit which, in addition, would supply details on such matters as current trends and tendencies in the educational development of Member States as well as information on the type of measures they envisaged for the future. In effect, the overriding objectives of the Community's education information network can be summed up under four heads:

— to provide a Community information service both internal and external to the Commission of the European Communities;
— to improve existing mechanisms of information;
— to respond to the requests from national systems of education by a dynamic and continuous flow of information on policies, trends and

---

1. 'Resolution of the Council and of the Ministers of Education meeting within the Council of February 9th 1976 comprising an action programme in the field of education', *Official Journal No. C38/3,* February 19th 1976, para. III, points 8 and 9.

developments in the education systems of individual Member States;
— to provide information on the characteristics and on the structures of, and practices in, the national education systems of the Community.

Structures:

At its meeting of November 21st-23rd 1977, the Education Committee gave its approval to the establishment of an information network. Member States were invited to appoint the heads of National Information Units. At present, each of the Member States of the Community has set up an information unit, though in the case of the Federal Republic of Germany, Belgium, the United Kingdom and France, there are two separate bodies. In the case of Germany these correspond to the Federal Ministry of Education on the one hand and the *Länder* on the other, the latter being constitutionally responsible for education in their areas. In the United Kingdom, one Unit covers England and Wales, with a second based in the Scottish Education Department's Research and Intelligence Unit at Edinburgh, the Scottish education system being legally separate from that of England. In Belgium, both the Dutch and the French-speaking areas of the country are represented by their respective bodies. In France, the two units are functionally rather than either territorially or linguistically distinct, one dealing with higher education, the other with those areas outside higher education. This division, which corresponded to the administrative distinction between the Ministry of National Education and the Ministry for Higher Education prior to May 1981, has been retained, even though the latter administration is now responsible to the Ministry of National Education alone.

The majority of National Information Units are located inside the Ministry of Education though there are three exceptions, Italy, England and Wales and Northern Ireland where units have been set up on a special contract basis. In some countries, National Units form part of the Education Ministry's own information and documentation service. In others the links are less formal. The French units for instance are linked with the *Centre National pour la Documentation Pédagogique (CNDP)* whilst the Scottish Unit has computerised access to other information networks as well. The EURYDICE Units have been active in developing links with other documentation centres within each Member State and at Community level.

The Brussels-based Central Unit of the network was set up for an initial period of working by the Commission in 1979. The administrative framework of the Central Unit was provided by the European Cultural Foundation of Amsterdam (Netherlands) under contract to the Commission. The offices of the Central unit are near to those of the Commission's Education services and its work is closely integrated with this latter. In September 1979, the head of Central Unit took up post and, after a test period of a year, the EURYDICE network became operational in September 1980.

Priority information areas and users:

The group of national experts called together by the Commission to advise ways in which the network might develop, identified four key areas of interest which, in the first instance, would form the main information activities of the network. These were:

– policies and measures to assist young people in their transition from school to working life;
– the teaching of foreign languages;
– the education of the children of migrants and migrant families;
– admission policies to higher education.

To this was added a residual category of 'major policy trends'.

At present, those who may use the network's services are defined by the individual Member States. As a result of discussions that preceded the official opening of the network in September 1980, six user groups were identified. These were:

– national, regional and local governments and administration;
– institutions and organisations related to, or depending on, governments and administration;
– parliamentary bodies;
– institutions and organisations in the education sector;
– professional and private bodies and institutions;
– others.

Some Member States, such as Denmark, the Federal Republic of Germany and the Netherlands, limit those who may use the network to national ministries. Luxembourg, by contrast, extends its definition of user groups to the administration of postal and telegraphic services and the administration of the *Ponts et Chaussées*.

Services provided by the Information Network:

Known by the acronym EURYDICE, the network is designed to provide its users with speedy access to information on education policy both in the Member States of the Community and at Community level. This it does through four particular types of services: first, it provides an analysis of current documentation and compiles overviews, specially prepared, on policy topics at both levels mentioned. Second, it is engaged in setting up a documentary data base to serve as a reference system at both Member State and Community level. This is based on the Central Unit. Access is available to Member States through their particular national units. Third, it provides an abstracting service of important current events through a system of Newsbriefs and 'Services documents' which monitors some 145 educational periodicals per month as well as newspaper articles, speeches and press releases. These are subsequently distributed to national units, key personnel and policymakers at Community level and in the

Information Policy and Educational Development: EURYDICE

Member States. Finally, the network assists the Commission in the joint management of the EUDISED thesaurus (an educational classification and information retrieval scheme initially developed by the Council of Europe) which is now being jointly developed by the Commission and its original creators. Following an exchange of letters between the Commission and the Council of Europe in June and July 1981, this information retrieval language is being developed further. In December 1980, a Danish expert, Mrs Roberta Jensen was asked to set up a Danish language version of EUDISED and a further contract given by Directorate General XIII to a Danish agency, *Datacentralen*, to develop a computerised management programme for the thesaurus. A third contract was put out to improve its structure.

In addition, the network draws up background information and dossiers for seminars organised by the Commission in the field of education and training. Amongst the various tasks in this area which the network has performed has been the compilation of a background dossier for the Education Committee on the 'Impact of demographic change on education systems in the European Community'. It was presented as part of the material for the Council and Ministers of Education meeting on June 22nd 1981. A summary of the main trends presented in this dossier has since been published in all the Community languages. The network has been called upon to provide further information in this field, as well as in the area of the recognition of Diplomas and Short Study Visits, to be carried out in association with the *European Centre for the Development of Vocational Training* (West Berlin). It is also provided in helping disseminate the results of the pilot projects on the transition from school to working life in conjunction with IFAPLAN, the Cologne-based research institute. Statistical information on educational developments and trends in the Communities is provided through the Central Unit drawing on the publications of the Statistical Office of the Community as well as information of a similar nature included in the press releases sent by Member States. Supplementary data is also obtained by National Units making use of their own statistical institutions.

Development of the information network:

Throughout 1978-79, seven meetings took place between the heads of the various national units to organise the network, to coordinate its development, to consolidate links with the Central Information Unit at Brussels and, finally, to decide future planning requirements. The Commission organised a series of information seminars in cooperation with individual Member States. These took place at the Hague on September 7th-8th, 1978, Windsor (England) on March 22nd-23rd, 1979 and in Paris on June 14th-15th, 1979. In addition, the Commission organised a seminar for the heads of national units the topic under discussion being 'The introduction of modern information systems'. The purpose of this was to ensure that methods for handling information throughout the network were compatible. Prior to opening the network to a wider public of policymakers, a test period was introduced to run through and check working procedures. This period, which lasted up to the official opening in September 1980, was especially valuable in that it allowed an evaluation to be made of the types of topic that were of major interest to Member States.

During the test period some 93 questions were processed by EURYDICE. Over half of these were devoted to topics of general policy (55.9 percent). The second most significant topic was the transition from school to work (20 percent of questions asked) followed by admissions policy to higher education (15.1 percent). An analysis of the 308 answers given by the network revealed that 63.3 percent dealt with the area of general policy, 15 percent were in response to questions about admissions to higher education and that 13 percent replied to requests for information on transition from school to work. A further breakdown to see which topics were of concern to particular Member States showed that the French Ministry of Education was highly interested in issues dealing with transition from school to work and also general policy issues, that the Federal Republic asked the most questions in the area of modern language teaching and the admission to higher education and that, amongst the questions put to the network in the area of the education of migrant families and their children, 2/3 came from Italy.

A later analysis of the types of questions included in the heading 'General Policy', based on the period July 1st to September 1982 when some 149 questions were treated by EURYDICE, is particularly interesting. Of the 70 that corresponded to this heading 54 percent dealt with the nature and workings of the education systems in different Member States and with such matters as the length of school day, the way in which vacations were spread out and staggered in different parts of the country, the number of pupils per class, school size, ways of maintaining educational standards and, finally, the structure of, and emphases in, the school curriculum. Considerable help in providing answers to some of these questions was given by the publication in 1981 of an overview of 'Schools systems in the Member States of the European Community'. Commissioned from an English expert, Lionel Elvin, the work appeared late in 1981 and was published by Nelson-National Foundation for Educational Reseach Publishing Co. A brochure brought out by EURYDICE dealing with the school calendar in the Community is under preparation. It will be entitled, 'Compulsory schooling in the Member States of the European Community'.

The volume of information provided by the network has increased rapidly, as can be judged from the fact that between July 1st 1980 and September 1981 it provided some 807 answers compared with 333 in the period up to June 30th 1980. Given the volume of work, the control of information flow, the development of procedures for putting questions either to the Central Unit or to other National Units within the network, the monitoring and production control aspects are highly important. And this, in turn, raises the question 'How does EURYDICE function?'

Functioning of EURYDICE:

All requests for information must proceed through the National Unit of the country where the question originates. The National Unit has the task of verifying whether the user is entitled to access to the network (which is defined according to the particular country concerned) and, further, verifies whether the request falls broadly into the priority themes outlined earlier. In those instances where the question is sent to no more than four National Units, it is forwarded directly to those involved. The Central Unit receives a copy of the request form which enables it to keep track of the general throughput and to monitor the nature of the questions. If, however, more than four information units are involved, the question, after due checking by the national unit, is dispatched to the Brussels Central Unit. The Central Unit acts as a further filter to ensure that the request is clearly understood and, if necessary, redefined in keeping with the various educational contexts of the different systems in Member States. The request is then translated and forwarded to the Units concerned.

Replies are not sent directly to the user, but rather proceed to the Unit from whence they came. A copy of the reply is lodged with the Central Unit, thus enabling it to build up a documentary base and, at the same time, to analyse the reverse information flow. It is reckoned that the time taken to process question into the network is around one month from the date of the request. The processing of replies averages around 50 days.

The mechanism described above involves essentially what might be termed 'passive response' to requests presented to the network. There is, however, a second type of information provision distinguishable from the first in that it involves an 'active' information support service. It disseminates the 'Newsbrief Service' (some 3,000 have been distributed so far), the 'Service Document', the IFAPLAN Newsletter, the CEDEFOP Newsletter and documents from the *European Centre for the Development of Vocational Training* (West Berlin) and other information of a similar nature. In addition, the 'active information policy' circulates and dispatches policy information from both National and Central Units. Also included under this activity is the gathering of material for the National Units of the network which is coordinated from the Central Unit in Brussels for redistribution throughout the whole network. Both the 'Newsbrief' and the 'Service Document' are actions undertaken by the Central Unit acting for the Commission's services. These 'information packages' are sent to National Units for eventual distribution to policy-makers within individual Member States. It is reckoned that the exchange of information in the area of comparative education policies and trends amounts to some 50 percent of the exchanges carried out under this heading.

In addition to its coordinating role in the network as a whole, the Brussels-based Central Unit monitors and analyses the flow of questions and replies through the network. National Units are advised monthly on the stage of processing that questions have reached. In building up the central data base from the 5,000 texts that have passed through the Central Unit in the course of providing information, Central Unit has so far indexed 3,500. Information retrieval, with the exception of the Scottish National Unit is not computer-based. However, within the coming three years, both French National Units intend to automate their data system and similar developments are in progress in the Dutch, Belgian and United Kingdom units. The question of compatibility between these systems of data retrieval was discussed by a working group set up during the meeting of Unit heads on June 29th 1981. It was composed of technical experts from Member States and the heads of the French-speaking Belgian Unit, the French Unit dealing with higher education affairs, the Netherlands and two representatives from the United Kingdom Units. The report of this working group was discussed at the 12th meeting of Heads of Unit held in December 1981. Its main recommendation was to proceed as fast as possible with the task of placing the documentation held in Central Unit on a computerised basis. This question was discussed by the Education Committee at its meeting of December 8th 1981.

In order to maintain a high degree of coordination, to discuss new developments both within and between the different national units, regular meetings are held for heads of Units. These take place in Brussels. Others are held in the Member States. The latter are mainly information seminars and are jointly organised by the Commission and those states involved. The German Units hosted such an occasion at Munich (October 8th-10th 1981) as did the Luxembourg and Italian Units. The meeting arranged by the latter was held at Rome in June 1981. It was attended by Mr Guido Bodrato, Minister of Education and Mr Della Briotta, Secretary of State for Foreign Affairs. The discussion, which covered some of the key issues currently facing policy-makers in Italian education, was published under the title *Il sistema formativo italiano*. The purpose of further seminars in Ireland and Belgium was twofold: first, to familiarise other Units with the documentation systems existing elsewhere and, second, to provide them with a greater appreciation of the differences in structure, practice, administration and procedure of other systems of education.

Future areas of development:
In the initial stages of the network's development, it was decided that EURYDICE should deliberately confine its services to specific user groups and provide information only where it corresponded to the four themes and to the residual category 'Major policy trends'. However, priorities change and fields of interest alter. For the moment, the emergence of new areas of concern can be dealt with through a broader interpretation of what may be included under the category of questions included in the rubric 'Major policy trends'. Nevertheless, it is thought that in future such issues as teacher training policy and questions posed by policy-makers at National level on the conditions of service in the teaching profession ought to figure more prominently in the topics covered by EURYDICE. Questions touching upon the field of Vocational Training can, as a result of the close cooperation between EURYDICE and the European Centre for the Development of Vocational Training, be handled under the heading

'Transition from school to working life'. Likewise, those involving the recognition of Diplomas and Short Study Visits can be accommodated under the rubric 'Conditions of admission to higher education'. There is, then, sufficient flexibility to enable the network to meet new demands without immediately having to redefine the formal priority areas with which it is concerned.

A further issue is raised by the question of whether or not the list of authorised user groups should be extended to administrators in institutions of higher education. Another possible client group might well be administrators and policy-makers involved in school management either at regional or local level as well as the European Teachers Trades' Union Committee.

A third area of future development might involve extending links between the various National Units of the EURYDICE network and other information systems operating both in the Member States and also at Community level. The purpose of so doing would be to improve the type of information available to users of the network and, from a more long-term perspective, to create a more substantial exchange of information between networks specialising in other areas relevant, complementary or ancillary to both education and social policy in its educational ramifications. There are some significant indications to suggest that this is happening in all Member States.

Relations with international organisations:

The principle of linking up with other bases of information has proved to be a substantial part of the development entailed in the Community's Information Network. It also presents advantages in being able to build on undertakings already well-established. Amongst the most significant of these are the documentation thesaurus set up under the aegis of the Committee for Cultural Co-operation of the Council of Europe, known as EUDISED and the thesaurus drawn up by the International Bureau of Education at Geneva (Switzerland). In June 1979, a working party was set up to examine the possibility of joint management of the EUDISED thesaurus in view of its potential for the EURYDICE network. After several meetings in the course of 1979 with both the Council of Europe's Directorate of Education, Culture and Scientific Affairs at Strasbourg, it was decided that both EUDISED and the IBE thesaurus should be used as initial sources. As part of the joint management of the EUDISED thesaurus, the development of new key words based on the four central topics contained in EURYDICE's remit was agreed upon. This was welcomed unanimously both by the Education Committee in the Commission and by the Directorate for Education, Culture and Scientific Affairs in the Council of Europe.

The further development and translation into other language versions of the EUDISED system has been dealt with earlier in this Chapter. It is not the only example of the way in which the Community's Information Network collaborates with international organisations. The exercise involving the analysis of demographic change also profitted from the development of working relationships with Unesco, the Organisation for Economic Cooperation and Development (OECD), the International Labour Office (ILO), and the Council of Europe.

Conclusion:

EURYDICE, the Community's Education Information network has been fully operational for some five years. During that time, it has played a significant role in providing policy-makers in the Member States with information about activities in other Member States as well as emerging trends within the Community as a whole. Within the Commisson, its study on 'The Impact of demographic change on education systems in the Euoprean Community' served as a major background document for the meeting of the Council of Ministers of Education on June 22nd 1982. Its services are also used by the Education Committee of the European Community which in turn acts as the main forum for the national delegations of Member States to discuss educational affairs.

At another level, EURYDICE's role may be seen as complementary and, at the same time, completing that part of the Commission's activities which involve the setting up of cross-national teams of experts to investigate topics such as the transition from school to work, the education of migrants' children and cooperation in higher education. Research without the diffusion of results is almost as nonsensical as development without research. Investment in the one, just as the pay-off for the other is largely dependent on the knowledge so gained being brought to the notice of those who may benefit from it.

The main difference between EURYDICE and other information networks in the field of education is its interactive nature and the fact that it is able to respond to the specific demands and requirements of its client groups. With certain exceptions, it is still unusual for the comparative study of education to be undertaken within the framework of government administration, whether central or local. And, by the same token, it is no less rare for analyses that are both relevant to public policy and up-to-date, to be undertaken within the realm of the pedagogical sciences. By furnishing information on specific topics which governments and administration at all levels themselves define as relevant to their present concerns, EURYDICE may help to extend the comparative analysis of education *policy* as an integral part of that dimension in educational development for which the Community stands.

Information Policy and Educational Development: EURYDICE

SOURCES

i. Primary: internal Commission documents

'Note technique destinée au Comité de l'Education: services d'information concernant l'éducation dans la Communauté Européenne', *Document No. XII/1011/77F*, (undated, 1977).

'Note to the Education Committee: progress report on the Information Network on Education in the European Community', *Document No. CAB 107 79*, (undated), 1979?

'Progress report on EURYDICE, the Education Information Network in the European Community', *Note to the Education Committee from the Services of the Commission*, (undated), circa November 1981.

'Provisions ruling the flow of questions within the EURYDICE network', 1981 EURYDICE Commission's Unit (xerox).

'Rapport d'activités concernant EURYDICE, le réseau d'échanges d'information sur l'éducation dans la Communauté Européenne', *Document No. XII/769/80 EN 55*, July 10th 1980.

Unpublished material submitted to the Commission:

EPIC progress report, Windsor (England) 1981, National Foundation for Educational Research (xerox), Appendix IX, section 4.

ii. Secondary: official Commission publications

'Resolution of the Council and of the Ministers of Education meeting within the Council of February 9th 1976 comprising an action programme in the field of education', *Official Journal No. C38/3*, February 19th 1976, para. III, points 8 and 9.

'Resolution of the Council and of the Ministers of Education meeting within the Council of December 13th 1976 concerning measures . . . to improve the preparation of young people for work . . .', *Official Journal No. C308*, December 30th 1976, para. III, subsection 5.

iii. Tertiary: pamphlets and articles of a non-official nature

The development of secondary education, Paris, OECD, 1969.

The development of higher education 1950-1970, 2 vols., Paris, OECD, 1972.

Guy Neave, *How they fared: the impact of the comprehensive school upon the university*, London, Routledge & Kegan Paul, 1975.

Guy Neave & Henry Cowper, 'Scotland: a less reported system of education', *European Journal of Education*, Vol. 14, No. 1, 1979.

Chapter Eleven
International Relations

Structure:
Introduction
Commission cooperation with international organisations of a governmental nature
   1. Council of Europe
   2. Organisation for Economic Co-operation and Development
   3. United Nations Education, Scientific and Cultural Organisation
International Organisations of a non governmental nature.
Youth forum of the European Communities
Conclusion
SOURCES

Introduction
Important though it might be, by dint of its resources and its legislative powers, as an integral forum where education issues may be discussed, the European Community is a relatively recent development. The United Nations' Education, Scientific and Cultural Organisation was set up in 1945, the Organisation for Economic Cooperation and Development, established to coordinate economic recovery in post war Europe, dates from 1948 and the Council of Europe, founded in 1953, anticipated the signing of the Treaty of Rome by five years.

Cooperation between the Community and the main international organisations with an educational remit — for example, the Council of Europe and the Organisation for Economic Cooperation and Development — was foreseen in the Treaty of Rome. The drawing up of the Community's Education Action Programme in February 1976 intensified it. With other bodies, the relationship rests more upon the development of long term contacts and exchanges of views than upon a formal legal basis. This is the case with non governmental organisations of an international nature. What have been the main areas of interest shared between the Community and other bodies of an international stature? How have these links developed? And what are the characteristics of such collaboration? To answer such questions, it is useful to distinguish between international governmental organisations on the one hand and international organisations of a non governmental type on the other.

Commission cooperation with international organisations of a governmental nature:
With international organisations of a governmental nature, collaboration is based on regular meetings between the Educational Services of the Commission and the Secretariats of the Council of Europe, of the Organisation for Economic Cooperation and Development (OECD) and the United Nations Educational, Scientific and Cultural Organisation (Unesco), both in Paris. Representatives of the Commission attend regularly the main governing bodies of all three organisations. The Commission also participates in the Standing Conference of European Ministers of Education. This meets once every two years, when it brings together the signatories of the Cultural Convention of the Council of Europe. In addition to the Council's 21 member countries, the signatories include Unesco, the OECD and the Council of Europe itself which, together with the Commission, send observers to these meetings. The purpose of the Standing Conference is to review various aspects of international cooperation in the field of education as well as discussing issues of major interest for all countries.

Over the past seven years, the Resolutions passed by the ministers during these events have covered such topics as models of educational planning and investment in education, educational research, admission to higher education, upper secondary education, the educational needs of the less able, the education of migrant workers' children, equality of opportunity for girls and young women and the role of pre-school and primary education. The Resolutions of this conference are passed on to the Committee of Ministers and, when it should be required, are further examined by the Council for Cultural Cooperation of the Council of Europe which then seeks to have them implemented insofar as they lie within its realm of competence.

The Commission participates fully in the Senior Officials Committee which prepares the Standing Conference. Progress reports of the Commission's activities are also presented. For instance, at the 12th session held at Lisbon on June 3-4 1981, papers dealing with the Community's development of priority areas of action in pre-school education were laid before the meeting. And, at the 11th session at the Hague (Netherlands) in June 1979, the Byrne Report, *Equality in education and training for girls (10-18 years)*, formed the Commission's major presentation.

Active participation in these bodies by the Commission's representatives, both on a formal and an informal level, has gone far in establishing a relationship based on mutual confidence.

The complementary nature of some of the Commission's activities with others being undertaken, *inter alia* by the Council of Europe and the Organisation for Economic Cooperation and Development has also developed into a mutually advantageous exchange of information and experience. Examples of this are to be found with the Council of Europe in the issue of mobility in higher education and collaboration with the Organisation for Economic Cooperation and Development in the area of pre-primary education, education for the handicapped and, more recently, in drawing up strategies for the application of the new information technologies. Conversely, repesentatives of the international organisations are invited, with observer status, to many expert meetings which the Commission organises in the context of implementing the Education Action Programme.

Particularly useful in developing these relationships has been the practice employed by the Education Service of pointing out to the Education Committee those areas of potential cooperation with individual organisations during the early discussion of various undertakings contained in the Action Programme. This practice is seen as valuable by Member State delegations to the Education Committee since many of them are also responsible for liaising between their own countries and the Council of Europe as well as the Organisation for Economic Cooperation and Development in particular. Thus, even prior to high level meetings organised by the various international organisations, there is increasing willingness to entertain the possibilities of acting together at the level of the Ten.

1. Council of Europe:

The relationship between the Community and the Council of Europe is based on article 230 of the Treaty of Rome. This article calls upon the Commission to *'establish all appropriate forms of cooperation with the Council of Europe'*. The development of such cooperation was laid out in an exchange of letters between the President of the Commission of the EEC and the Committee of Ministers of the Council of Europe. Dated August 18th 1959, the terms of this exchange still hold force.

The Commission has participated regularly in the meetings of the then Council for Cultural Cooperation, now known as the *Comité Directeur de la Coopération Culturelle*, in addition to a number of activities associated with specific projects organised by the Council of Europe. This cooperation has been intensified since 1979, particularly in the relationship between the Commission and the Directorate for Education, Culture and Sport. In the Autumn of 1980, further proof of the good relations between the two institutions was furnished through a series of meetings involving the Documentation Section of the Council of Europe and the Central Unit of EURYDICE, the Education Information Network of the European Community, with the participation of Directorate General XII of the Commission. Following an exchange of letters between the Directors General, an agreement was reached on the joint financing and development of the EUDISED thesaurus. This, as a result of a meeting in Brussels in May 1981, is now to be extended to cover the area of language teaching and research. Other examples of the close cooperation between the Commission and the Council are to be seen in the European Schools Day, the European dimension to teacher education, both of which are fields of mutual interest. Furthermore, as a result of an agreement reached on November 5th 1980 between the two Secretariats, representatives of the Council of Europe, now participate in the European Committee for School Television, operated from out of the Kreysig Fund.

Amongst other areas of active participation between the two institutions one may cite such mutual interests as the education of the children of migrant workers, continuing education and admission to higher education. As regards the first, the Council participated in the colloquy held at Odense (Denmark) on October 12th-15th 1980 whilst, reciprocally, the Commission took part in the colloquy held at Strasbourg on February 26th-27th 1981, where the education and cultural development of migrants was discussed in addition to the issue of the *livret scolaire*, (pupil profile card) further investigation into which is being financed by the Community. As regards the second, the Council was represented at the Berlin colloquium, organised by the European Centre for the Development of Vocational Training (West Berlin) between October 14th and 17th 1980 on the theme, 'New perspectives for an enlarged Community for education and permanent training *(formation permanente)*'. Conversely, the Commission attended the discussion that took place in Strasbourg on November 25 to 27th 1980 where the topic was 'Ten years of change: perspectives for the Eighties'. As regards the third area of cooperation between the two institutions, the Commission was represented at an experts' meeting held at Strasbourg on September 25th-26th 1980 which dealt with the issue of academic mobility. Likewise, an observer from the Council of Europe was present at the meeting of the Commission's committee for selecting applications for funding Joint Study Programmes, held on July 10th and July 15th 1981 at Brussels.

It is obvious from these examples that there is an area of complementary action undertaken by both the Commission and the Council. This is evident with the publication in April 1981 of the Student Handbook which covered admission to higher education in those Member States which, though signatories of the Cultural Cooperation Convention, are not members of the Europe of the Ten. The Council of Europe production used the same format as the Student Handbook of the Communities as well as the same editor from the *Deutscher Akademischer Austauschdientst* of Bonn who drew up the Communities' publication. Furthermore, both Council and Community, together with the European Cultural Foundation (Amsterdam) made a contribution to the publication of the British Overseas Students Trust, entitled *The Overseas Student Question: studies for a policy*, which appeared in 1981.

From the standpoint of long-term developments in higher education, the Commission, in discussing the issue of the academic recognition of diplomas on May 5th 1981, took fully into account the European Convention on the academic recognition of university qualifications of Devember 14th 1959 that the Council of Europe had laid down. The Community's activities in the field of higher education are then, to some extent, based on existing structures one of which is the Equivalence and Mobility Centres established within a framework established by the Council of Europe.

2. The Organisation for Economic Cooperation and Development:

Relations between the Organisation for Economic Cooperation and Development and the Community are based on article 231 of the Treaty of Rome. The Commission is called upon to *'establish close cooperation with the OECD, the details of which are to be determined by common accord'*. To this has been added a Supplementary Protocol No. 1. It provides for the participation of the Commission of the European Communities in the work of the OECD. Thus, the Commission is represented on the Education Committee of this latter organisation as well as on the Governing Council of the Centre for Educational Research and Innovation (CERI) which operates within the framework of the OECD.

From time to time, the Commission's representatives have also participated in various specialised OECD working groups whose activities correspond to priority actions undertaken by the Community. Amongst them one may cite the problems of transition from school to working life, the training of administrators in higher education, the development of educational statistics and the use of new information technologies in education.

At present the Commission is exploring the possibility of closer cooperation with the OECD, particularly at the level of officials in charge of specific topics of mutual interest. In addition to those already mentioned, interest has been expressed in having closer contact on such matters as vocational training and employment, education in changing demographic conditions, continuing education and the role it may play in the development of mainly rural areas, the education of handicapped young people. An inter-secretarial meeting took place between the two organisations in Brussels on January 13th 1982.

3. **United Nations Education, Scientific and Cultural Organisation:**
Relations between the Commission and Unesco are laid down in an exchange of letters which took place between September 2nd and 15th 1964. This exchange, described by two signatories as an agreement, was supplemented by a further exchange between the President of the Commission and the Director General of Unesco on February 13th 1972, December 12th 1972, March 10th 1976 and June 14th 1976. Amongst other matters, it set out provision for the creation of various mixed working groups dealing with such matters as the equivalence of degrees in higher education, and the development of aid within the general field of education, culture and information media.

A number of meetings have taken place between Unesco and the Commission, principally in the area of multi-language teaching, and the bi-cultural education of migrant workers' children within the framework of the Unesco programme in this area. These activities are of help to the Commission in orienting the latter's undertakings in this field.

International organisations of a non-governmental nature:
Importance has always been attached by the Commission to maintaining a dialogue with a range of non-governmental organisations to the interest of which lies in the field of education. Since the setting up of the Commission's Education services in 1973, it has been part of their policy to keep an 'open door'. This has encouraged the development of contacts, both formal and informal between the Commission and various organisations which, whether representative of teachers, parents or young people, all have a European-wide remit.

Prior to October 1981, the Commission met with each of the two teachers' unions organised at Community level. These were the World Confederation of Organisations of the Teaching Profession (WCOTP) and the European Teachers' Trades Union Committee (ETTUC). In 1978, the first of what were seen as a series of regular meetings to exchange ideas and information relating to the Education Action Programme took place. At this meeting, the Commission formally represented the Education Committee as a whole. In October 1981, the teachers' organisations joined together to form the European Trades Union Committee for Education.

This Committee brings together those European member organisations that are part of the International Federation of Free Teachers Unions, the World Confederation of Organisations of the Teaching Profession and those European members of this latter who belong to a trade union that is itself member of the European Trades Union Confederation (ETUC). The purpose of this new Committee is to represent teachers' interests both with the European Trades' Union Confederation and the European Communities. It acts as the sole spokesman for some 58 different bodies which, in turn, represent some two million members in 18 countries.

The Commission also maintains close links with the European Cultural Foundation, Amsterdam as well as with the European Institute of Education and Social Policy which the Foundation set up in 1975. The European Institute of

Education and the European Community

Education has offices in both Paris and Bruxelles. The latter administers two exchange programmes on behalf of the Commission in the field of higher education — the Short Study Visits for teaching staff, administrative staff and researchers; and the Joint Programmes of Study. This latter is divided into two sub-grants, the first intended to prepare later Joint Programmes of Study, the latter being the main programme involving exchange of staff and materials between higher education institutes across several Member States of the Community. (*For details of this see Chapter V pp.88ff.*). The European Institute of Education and Social Policy at Paris, as its title indicates, undertakes policy analysis mainly in the field of post compulsory education. The Commissioner in charge of Education is an ex officio member of its Board of Administration. Over the past eight years, the European Institute of Education has undertaken a number of comparative investigations on behalf of the Commission — amongst them a six country study of the links between higher education and regional development and another report on *Education and Employment: the problems of early school leavers*, presented in 1977. In addition, the Institute has worked with the Commission's Berlin-based European Centre for the Development of Vocational Training (CEDEFOP) on matters related, in the main, to the issue of 'alternance training' (*For this latter point see Chapter IV, pp.67ff.*).

Financial support is provided by the Commission each year for conferences, seminars and other activities designed to impart information on matters directly related to the Community's Education Action Programme. In 1978, for example, the Commission supported the investigation by the European Committee of WCOTP into the preparation of young people for life in society. This resulted in a number of publications, amongst which, *Preparation for life in Society*, brought out by the British National Union of Teachers in 1978 and *Preparation for Adult Life in schools in England and Wales*, produced by the British Association of Assistant Mistresses in the same year. A Commission observer participated in the annual European Conference held in Stavanger (Norway) in October 1980.

In the area of higher education, the Commission is represented at the meetings of the International Association of University Professors and Lecturers which are held twice yearly and at which the Commission notifies the Association of the latest developments of its activities relevant to this Association.

Commission representatives also participate in the twice-yearly meetings of the Liaison Committee of Rectors' Conferences of Member States of the European Communities. The Commission's activities of interest to this Committee of heads of higher education institutions (mainly universities) in the Member States, are presented and discussed in these regular meetings.

The Commission also makes a regular practice of inviting such bodies, where it is deemed appropriate, to send observers to expert seminars and conferences organised by the Commission. Representatives from various specialised interests such as parental or family organisations with a European remit are likewise invited under similar conditions. Amongst them are the Committee of Family Organisations in the European Communities (COFACE) and the International

Group of Catholic Parents Associations (GIAPEC). In more specialised areas for example, the European Committee of the International Federation of the Blind, Rehabilitation International, the European Association for Special Education and the World Organisation for Pre-School Education, contacts are maintained.

Close links exist also with those non-governmental bodies specialising in the study and development of a European content in education. Amongst these are the Centre for European Education (Brussels), the Association for Teacher Education in Europe (Brussels), the International Federation of Europe Houses (FIME) and the International Centre for European Formation (CIFE). Over and above these links, support of both a practical and a financial nature is provided to these bodies.

Support of a similar nature is also given to a large number of youth organisations or those bodies which include youth activities as part of their undertaking. The European Coordination Bureau of International Youth Organisations (BECOJ), the European Trade Union Confederation (ETUC) and the Youth Forum of the European Communities are prominent among them.

Youth Forum of the European Communities:

The origins of the Youth Forum may be traced back to the declaration of the Heads of State at the Hague Conference in 1969. Amongst the various points included in the statement issued at the end of this Conference was the conviction that *'European growth will be assured of a better future if the younger generation is closely associated with it'*. On this basis, the Commission put forward a plan for a 'Youth Council'. It was not, however, accepted by the Council of Ministers. Following a revision in 1976, supported by the European Parliament, the Council agreed that the Communities would make a financial contribution to enable the various youth organisations — amongst which the National Committees of the Member States and the International Non Governmental Youth Organisations — to hold discussions. The Statutes of the Forum were agreed upon at a meeting held in June 1978 at Ariccia (Italy).

The Forum is based upon three principles:
- an independent General Assembly;
- the equality of National Committees and International Non-Governmental Youth Organisations;
- three Permanent Commissions which deal with the following areas:
  . youth organisations and the political development of the European Communities;
  . the social position of young workers in the European Communities;
  . youth organisations and the educational and cultural position in the European Communities.

The Youth Forum of the European Communities is made up of Full Members, Consultative Members and Observers. Amongst the first are the National Committees of the Member States and some 22 International Youth Organisations which, fulfilling the criteria laid down in the statutes, have active national branches in more than half the Member States of the European Communities. The second category is made up of coordinating bodies — the European Coordination Bureau of International Non Governmental Youth Organisations and the Council of European National Youth Committees. Those included under observer status are the National Committees of European countries not members of the European Communities and those International Non Governmental Youth Organisations that do not fulfil the conditions for full membership.

The Forum acts as a focal point for the information, consultation and expression of opinion for the various groups of young people in the Europe of the Ten. It is a permanent body and started work in January 1979. Its three permanent Commissions have discussed such matters as Youth Rights, the enlargement of the EEC, alternance education, new technologies and employment, the campaign against illiteracy, access for foreign students to establishments of higher education, youth exchange and multi-cultural education.

Conclusion:

An examination of the relationships between the Communities and other international organisations, whether governmental or non governmental shows that there are basically three types. The first, which corresponds to that held with the international organisations of a governmental nature, involves comparatively close collaboration based on the existence of programmes and enquiries, technical development and personal contacts, often underpinned by formal agreements between the participating agencies. These areas of sustained interest, corresponding to the Education Action Programme, permit the experience of others to feed into the policy development machinery of the Communities and to assist in the development of actions undertaken by other international government organisations. Equally, it allows them in their turn to take into account current thinking in the Communities.

The second, which corresponds to the type of relationship entertained between the Communities and some non governmental organisations of an international nature is essentially maintaining an 'on going' collaboration by keeping them informed about the latest developments within the Community in areas of particular interest and concern to those bodies.

A third type of relationship involves support of both a practical and financial nature by the Commission to various specialised groups. These groups act as a focus for particular interests to discuss their concerns and the way these may both affect and contribute to the development of Community policy in education. Representative of this relationship are, for example, the Youth Forum or the European Trades Union Committee for Education.

SOURCES

i. Primary: internal Commission documents

'Information note for the Liaison Committee of the Rectors' Conferences of Member States of the European Communities on the developments at Community level in the field of higher education since the meeting . . . in October 1980', *Aide-Mémoire*, (n.d.), February 1981 (?).

'Evolution de la coopération entre la Commission et le Conseil de l'Europe dans le domaine de l'Education au cours de l'année 1980 à juin 1981: cas concret de coopération', *Aide-Mémoire*, May 26th 1981 (typewritten).

Rapport sur les activités communautaires en faveur de la formation culturelle et professionnelle des travailleurs migrants et des membres de leur famille 1975-1981, September 1981, (typewritten).

'Note succinte d'information sur la conférence permanente des Ministres Européens de l'Education', *Direction Générale de l'Emploi, des Affaires Sociales et de l'Education*, December 16th 1981, (typewritten).

'Commentaires de la Direction de l'Education, de la formation professionnelle et de la politique de la Jeunesse sur le programme de travail et le budget de l'O.C.D.E. pour l'exercise 1982', *Aide-Mémoire*, December 10th 1981, (typewritten).

'Report drawn up on behalf of the Committee on Social Affairs, Employment and Education on Activities of the European Youth Forum', *European Parliament Working Documents 1979-1980, Document No. 151/79*, May 7th 1979.

ii. Tertiary: pamphlets, articles of a non-official nature

Forum Jeunesse des Communautés Européennes, December 1980, p. 6.

The Echo, vol. XXX, No. 4, December 1981.

Franz de Paauw, 'DGXII of the European Commission — a report from May 1980 to March 1981', *IAUPL Communication Bulletin No. 12*, Autumn 1981, p. 24.

Olav Magnussen, *Education and employment: the problem of eary school leavers*, Amsterdam, 1977, European Cultural Foundation.

Guy Neave, 'Regional development and higher education: an issues paper', presented to Directorate General XII of the Commission of the European Community, Paris, 1976, Institut d'Éducation (mimeo).

Guy Neave, 'Higher Education and regional development: an overview of a growing controversy', *European Journal of Education*, vol. 14, No. 3, Autumn 1979.

Chapter Twelve
Conclusion

Structure:
Introduction
A policy model of Commission activities in the area of education
  1. The scope of the policy
  2. The Point of intervention
  3. Sphere of action
  4. The client group
  5. Objectives of the programme
The research model in Commission education policy
The place of education in Community affairs
Education policy in the Member States: the break up of consensus
Commission education policy in a contemporary perspective
Envoi
SOURCES

Introduction

The inclusion of education as one of the fields of the Commission's activities is relatively recent. In the course of this study, the major components of these activities, represented in the Community Education Action Programme of 1976 have been examined and some account of the activities, research and thinking that underlaid them, set out. This final chapter has the purpose of bringing the various strands contained in the earlier parts together thereby providing a broad perspective to the nature of Community education policy and its overall evolution, placed against a background of some of the long-term developments that took place at the same time in the Ten.

No-one looking at the range of activities that make up the Commission's educational responsibility can fail to be struck by their variety, by the difference in approach and manner of moving forward. Commission activities, in short, do not form a monolithic whole. There are considerable differences in administrative style and procedure from one programme to another.

A policy model of Commission activities in the area of education:

This raises the question of what type of policy model such activities imply. Community policy may be compared to a species of matrix, made up of a series of interlocking points and a number of separate dimensions. The interlinking nature of this policy can be seen in the case of the transition from school to adult life programme. This programme contains such subsidiary issues as compensatory education, education for girls, immigrants and the handicapped. Effectively, actions undertaken within one particular sphere of the Commission's preoccupations, have implications and repercussions on others. Thus the various projects and programmes have a mutually reinforcing function. To take a specific example, certain projects contained with the transition programme pilot studies were closely associated with the issue of education for the children of migrant workers and with vocational training.

Analytically, it is possible to see five dimensions in the Commissions educational policy model. These are:
— the scope of the policy.
— the point of intervention in the education system.
— the sphere of action.
— the client group.
— the objectives of the programme.

i. The scope of the policy

This particular dimension defines the territorial or administrative framework in which a given project or programme is located. It may, for instance, involve only individual communities — a proposal that was made in the early thinking about the type of action that might be undertaken on behalf of the handicapped.

Such communities are reckoned to be around 200,000 people. On the other hand, the territorial unit involved may cover a whole region as was the case for the project designed to strengthen links between compulsory and post compulsory education on the one hand and vocational education and the German secondary modern school (Hauptschule) on the other. The whole of the Land Baden Wurttemburg was involved.

A further distinction which lies in the carrying out of broad-range actions, is that of action at Member State level and action pursued at Community level. For the most part, the centre of interest of this analysis has been upon the latter.

ii. **Point of intervention in the education system**

Community action has tended to focus primarily on what might be termed the interstittal parts of the education system, that is, the link points between pre-primary and primary education, between primary and secondary education, between compulsory education and the transition to working life or the transition into the vocational training system in those countries where such systems exist outside secondary education. A similar interstittal intervention can be seen in the realm of higher education, as for instance the question of access to institutes of higher education and, at the other end, the recognition of academic diplomas. In certain instances, such as the proposal for teaching about Europe in schools or the stillborn Resolution on foreign language learning, the point of intervention involved main-line primary and secondary schools. On balance, however, Commission education policy has tended to place less emphasis on this area than upon the links between the various sub-systems of the educational enterprise.

iii. **Sphere of action**

The sphere of action corresponds to the substantial content of a particular project. It may involve specific aspects of individual development as in the case of compensatory education for the children of immigrants. Alternatively, it may involve specific pedagogical action an example of which would be the teaching of foreign languages to young nationals, induction into the language of the host country for children of incomers. A further sphere of action is contained in those areas of general education that may lend themselves to being treated from a 'European perspective' – history, economics, geography or civics. Vocational training as well as continuing education or re-training for adults may also be seen as constituting a sphere of action.

iv. **The client group**

Over the past few years, education policy – and in this the Commission is no exception – has tended to focus with increasing precision on a series of specific client groups – those categories of children who appear to policy makers or to representatives speaking in the name of such client groups, to be in a position of particular need. Commission education policy involves several – migrant families, women and girls, the handicapped, the unqualified school-leaver, children in inner city areas, those in sparsely populated regions, youngsters in search of a first job. Certain projects bring these groups together, arguing that the more individuals who fall into more than one category, the greater their degree of disadvantage. There is, then, a considerable degree of overlap as in the case of young immigrants leaving school without qualifications, or, within the immigrant population, unqualified girl school leavers. Generally speaking, there has been a tendency in Commission thinking to move increasingly towards action involving 'multiply disadvantaged' groups and away from broad categories of what might be termed 'single dimension' disadvantage. One exception to this is the disabled. In this specific instance, Commission activity has been conceived to follow and to assist their progress right through the education system and out into the world of work, in the form of a single programme.

v. Objectives of the programme

Objectives in Community education policy range from broad statements of principle — for example, the achievement of equality of opportunity through equality of access to education, individual self-development and integration into the community — which may be a culturally defined community in the case of immigration or a physically defined community in the case of the disabled — down to very specific and precise statements of intent. Amongst the latter one may refer to the aim of the transition school to adult life programme. Its purpose is to insert young people into working life. Other programmes aim at fostering exchange and cooperation between various groups such as school students, young workers and administrators at various levels of national education systems. The objectives of such programmes are multiple: on the one hand, they have a short term immediate objective which may be seen as complementary to the main programmes to which they are often attached. In such cases, their purpose is to promote the exchange of information in a particular field. The medium or long term objective, however, aims at setting up permanent self-sustaining networks for dialogue and discussion across the Member States. In this way, it is hoped, networks such as these will serve as a vehicle to sustain innovation and change at grass roots level and also act as instruments for long term cooperation.

Research model in Commission policy:

If these are the basic items in the framework within which Commission education policy evolves, no less interesting is the research model that underpins it. There has been much discussion in recent times about the role that research, both fundamental and applied, plays in decision-making and policy definition. The commonly held view on the matter is that research provides the basic information and understanding to enable policy makers to act. This presupposes a direct linkage between research and policy making which, recent research has suggested, is by no means as close as was once thought. Research, it has been argued, rarely influences policy in a direct manner. It serves to alter the intellectual climate or the perception that the policy-maker has of a particular issue, rather than providing a series of clear cut options amongst which the decision-maker makes his choice.

The commission of research as an instrument of policy is a particular feature of the Education services of the European Community. This is not to say that Member State administrations do not do the same thing. But, in the case of the Commission there are additional reasons why investigative enquiries are more than usually important in the policy-making process. The first and undoubtedly the most important, reason stems from the nature of the Community itself. Commission policy is faced with the fact that, whatever its objectives, its realisation has to take place across ten Member States whose systems of education, administration, financing and control differ widely from one another. For this reason, the way a particular issue may manifest itself and even the degree to which it may – or alternatively – may not be present in individual systems of education, is itself subject to variation. Hence, the need for cross national enquiry to ascertain the presence or absence, reach and extent of a particular area of concern. For example, the ways Member States seek to assist young immigrants adapt to the culture in which they find themselves, varies from one country to another. If some form of action is contemplated, the Commission needs to know the 'state of play' in order to devise means of attacking the problem that will be seen as relevant by individual Member States and at the same time, be effective. In short, recognition of the diversity that exists at Member State level both in the area of policy and practice places an added premium on research as a means of taking this into account. Those things that may be taken for granted within a single national system of education cannot be taken for granted when dealing with Ten.

A second reason for placing particular emphasis upon the research element in Commission policy is the fact that Education is still a relative newcomer in Commission affairs. This means, in effect, that the Commission cannot draw on an inherent stock of knowledge and insight which administrators in long-established national Ministries acquire by dint of being in them. National administrations, by their very nature of being long established, possess this acquired stock of knowledge which means that research is reserved for those issues which arise and which do not correspond to such accumulated wisdom. In the case of the Commission, research constitutes the stock-building knowledge which, because it is at a relatively early stage of its development, may have far more impact upon policy-shaping than would be the case in Member State administration.

A third reason for the importance placed upon research in the policy framework of the Commission is more in the nature of a latent than a manifest function. Most research undertakings, because they involve the exploration of issues across many Member States, are made up of multi-national teams of experts, themselves often members of national research organisations, teachers associations, parent groups etc. Engaging in research is often the first step towards creating a discussion forum on a more permanent and international basis. Thus research serves as an instrument for strengthening, indirectly, the Commission objective of drawing up diffusion networks, reinforcing thereby its strategic purpose of cross national cooperation between Member States at local level and Member States and the Commission itself.

Finally, there is the question of personnel. Contrary to most popular visions of the European Community, the Education Service is infinitely smaller in terms of its permanent civil servant personnel than any of the national Ministries with which it has to deal. Desk officials rely heavily on research and enquiry conducted by outside experts to undertake work that, at Member State level, would usually fall to various specialised Research and Intelligence Units inside the central Ministry.

This situation has important repercussions on the role that research plays in Commission activities. First, those that commission research are very often precisely those who have to deal with the particular problem to which it is addressed. Second, it follows from this that the dialogue between official and researcher tends not only to be more sustained but to take place with relatively fewer intervening instances than would be the case were the bureaucracy larger. For this reason, it is certainly arguable that the direct impact of research upon the initial stages of policy discussion inside the Education Services of the Commission is greater than it would be in the context of national administration.

Generally speaking, the type of research undertaken tends to be of an applied kind, the purpose of which is to inform or illuminate questions of immediate concern. This, of course, does not exclude fundamental research, but such fundamental research does not occupy a primary place. Work commissioned by the Education Services of the Communities may be said to fall into three categories. These are 'state of the art' reviews within a comparative perspective; examinations of current policy or practice as regards a particular issue; evaluative or monitoring exercises.

The first usually serves to outline and contribute to initial discussions both within the Education Service and between interested parties and interest groups in the Member States. The second tends to coincide with what may be termed the second stage of the dialogue, when the issue has been honed down to a relatively narrow series of topics which are subsequently investigated either with a view to defining the Commission's views on the matter, or as a position document for discussion within the Education Committee by the Member States. The third type of enquiry – monitoring and/or evaluation, provides feedback on the progress of particular programmes – for instance, Joint Study Programmes in higher education or the pilot projects in the transition school to work programme. This procedure allows both the Commission's education services and the representatives of Member States in the Education Committee to see what progress has been made. It also serves to give an overall perspective on the programme to those taking part in it at grass roots levels.

Grosso modo, the research model which underlines Commission activity is a complex form of Research-Development–Diffusion procedure. Particular emphasis is placed on close links between the research and development side by means of action research carried out in the field. The transition school to work programme, analysed in Chapter III is perhaps one of the largest undertakings of its type in recent times. Equally important is the fact that many of the major programmes themselves have an in-built mechanism for diffusion, in the form of news letters or regular publications for popular and professional consumption. In short, the Research-Development-Diffusion model works along two main paths which may be said to be vertical and horizontal. The vertical path leads towards Community action at an official level, through the Education Services, the Education Committee and ultimately, the Council of Ministers meeting in the Council. The horizontal path leads towards the dissemination of 'good practice' at grass roots level between the national research teams. A recent development which clearly underlines the importance of this latter aspect has been the appointment of a series of National Policy Coordinators within the transition school to work programme. Their role is to ensure coordination with other national agencies working in parallel fields, to develop dissemination of results, to work in conjunction with the Commission to review progress and development. The National Policy Coordinators occupy a crucial position athwart both the horizontal and the vertical routes of procedures.

The place of Education in Community affairs

However, the fact that the Commission opens up an area of interest is not always a guarantee that Member States will take up the suggestion. Education is still a highly sensitive area and Member States are very much aware – as indeed is the Commission itself – that there are tacit boundaries beyond which one should not be seen to go. Indeed, in education as in agriculture, moving forward on a particular issue requires prolonged negotiation, consultation and the laying down of positions before one may consider which are the more fruitful avenues for future development. But there are other factors, apart from the purely juridical, that make Education a delicate area. The fact that Education as such does not figure in the Treaty of Rome is perhaps only the most obvious. No less significant is that hitherto the field of education policy has not been subject to international *negotiation*. There are, to be sure, other forums for debate and discussion: the United Nations Education, Scientific and Cultural Organisation, the Organisation for Economic Cooperation and Development and the Council of Europe are amongst the best known. Where these organisations differ from the European Communities is that action taken at Community level not only has budgetary implications. Such action may, ultimately, result in legal action that is binding upon Member States and backed with the force of law.

Another factor contributing to the sensitivity of education as an area of Community action is the fact that, hitherto, most Ministries of Education have conducted their affairs within the confines of their own territorial area. Their main negotiating bodies have been, for instance, the Ministry of Finance, Labour, national and regional planning (where they exist) and the various municipal or regional bodies entrusted with the day to day running of education. Such negotiations follow set procedures, obey established conventions and pay due regard to the nature and quality of a relationship between central administration and its peripheral partners that time and practice have created. At Community level, though clear cut procedures exist, they are formal. Time has yet to set them in a pattern of tacit understanding and convention. The amalgam between

Conclusion

different national styles of administration and negotiation has yet to emerge. This, together with the fact that international negotiation has tended not to enjoy so prominent a place in the administrative hierarchy of the national administration of education, adds to the highly sensitive nature of the relationship between Commission and Member States in the field of education. And, finally, there is the issue which remains at the back of everyone's mind, namely the importance of education as a very real symbol of the nation's cultural identity.

So far, most of the mainline activity of the Commission has resulted in Resolutions. This means that Member States agree to work together to attain particular objectives, but the manner in which they may be attained is left open to the individual Member State to interpret and act upon as circumstances, administrative, financial and political, permit. The popular notion that the Member State proposeth and the Commission disposeth and imposeth has scarce, if any, grounding in fact.

Yet, power in policy-making is largely a function of the particular angle from which decision-making is viewed. From the outside, it may appear that much influence is wielded by Bruxelles. But the notion that the base is powerless is one which is rarely shared by those who operate at the point where all roads cross. Quite on the contrary, the impression one gets is that the actors inside the Commission's Education Services are very much aware of the limitations placed upon them. Caught in the net of counter-vailing forces, some pressing for rapid action, others counselling prudence, some eager to disseminate results, others advising further verification and validation, Commission officials, like King Agag in the Old Testament, must walk exceeding delicately. For theirs is the task of bringing together systems of education, of reconciling widely different patterns of administrative behaviour, fields of responsibility and methods of control. So too, their task is to seek a common way across organisations whose common feature is their difference and diversity. Thus it is that the major effort in the area of education policy at Community level is less the translating of thought into action than preparing common ground on which action itself may be envisaged. This is the reality of educational policy in the Commission.

Some may argue that the weight of daily administration has worn away the one essential goal of Community action in education – namely, to create a 'new Europe'. Others may point out that since there has been no agreement on what 'type' of Europe, it is hardly realistic to move towards something on which nobody is agreed. Either way, it is by no means unusual for visions of utopia to depart from their original form when placed in the sultry climate of day to day administration. The plans of the seer in his study or the politician on his tub rarely take into account the complex administrative realities into which their views have to be inserted.

Education policy in the Member States: the break up of consensus

Yet, the apparent failure to make headway in the ideological reconstruction of 'Europe' has to be set against other, broader developments in the general field of education policy. Over the past decade, education policy, whether at

Community level or at the level of individual Member States, has become infinitely more complex. Some have attributed this phenomenon of the break up of consensus. Others regard it as part of a more fundamental issue of 'legitimation'. (Weiler 1983, pp.259-277). Either way, it is apparent that citizens are less willing to permit action by central authority to substitute for action taken by participant groups, claiming to represent various interests. In education, the issue is no less developed than elsewhere, as witness, for instance the demand for accountability in the United Kingdom, or the demand, almost universal across Europe in the late Sixties or mid Seventies, for student participation in university affairs. As a result of this challenge to the legitimacy of central authority, decision-making in education has become less confident. It is less willing to espouse a broad strategic approach to such matters as notorious disadvantage and equality of educational opportunity that were the watchwords of the late Sixties and early Seventies. Over the past decade, education politics in Western Europe have been characterised by what one might term 'the fragmentation of the educational estate'. Symptomatic of this process has been the emergence of myriad pressure groups and interest groups, which hitherto, formed part of the overall consensus of social betterment through improvement in education.

It is a matter of personal choice whether one sees the emergence of a 'pressure group society' as an advance in political behaviour or a reversion to clientelism, as a testimony to the strength of pluralism or the renaissance of the pork barrel. Suffice it to say that so long as resources are expanding, the Gross National Product grows and personal incomes rise, consensual politics could be easily maintained. So too in education — so long, that is, as it appears to be delivering to its consumers those traditional and historic commodities of status, social mobility and knowledge — elements both tangible and intangible — that are held to accompany social progress.

The emergence of a Community action programme in education coincided, however, with this crisis and took place almost exactly at that moment when Europe's vision of education fragmented at the level of individual Member States. (Neave, 1982). It would, of course, be an interesting historical exercise to see precisely when the Indian summer of Neo Keynesian thinking in education began to draw a close and the effects this had upon policy development in the various countries of the Ten. Some, like France, adhered to this approach far longer than others like Britain and Belgium, which abandoned it relatively early on. Be that as it may, in its early declarations, Commission policy and objectives remained heavily impregnated by two particular ideologies. The first of these was to see in education a vehicle for the reconstruction of 'Europe', an instrument by which the citizens of the Community might be brought into closer understanding of each other's culture and society. The second was no less influenced by the thinking which had underpinned the expansion of the Sixties and early Seventies. The conviction that education remained central to the elimination of poverty, to the realisation of social justice and the advance of social progress in general, ran strongly in the various discussion documents leading up to the Ministerial Resolution of February 1976 which launched the Community Education Action Programme. There were, not unnaturally, sound reasons for this quite apart from the fact that such a conviction was genuinely and deeply shared by those involved in the discussions throughout the period from 1974 to 1976. Prime amongst these reasons was the need to justify the place of education as one of the Commission's formal concerns.

Commission education policy in a contemporary perspective

Placed against this backdrop, the two Resolutions of February and December 1976 which announced the setting up of the Community Education Action Programme, take on a slightly different perspective. They may, of course, be seen as statements of intent and plans for future action at both Member State and Community level. However, they may also be seen as the final echo of that consensus which, gathered about the tenets of Neo Keynesian policies, had carried before it the most dramatic growth and change in education this century will see. If Commission policy started off firmly rooted in the twin ideologies of Neo Keynesianism and 'European construction', it became quickly apparent that the broad front strategy, outlined in previous discussions and expert group meetings and contained in the 1976 Resolutions could not be executed in its entirety. Very quickly, the major issue that Member States had to confront was not so much the continued advancement of social opportunity, equality of opportunity as to prevent the erosion of those gains which had been acquired in a decade and a half of educational growth. The rise of youth unemployment, a deterioration in the economies of Member States, demographic decline and reductions in teacher recruitment were the main problems the Communities faced. This is a situation by now familiar to most in the field of education. It has had dire consequences in all domains of education. What is less appreciated are the consequences these same events had upon the orientation of Commission activity. Drawn up in the latter days of educational growth, Commission policy had, very rapidly, to adjust to the changing climate. It chose to opt for immediate action in certain areas in the Action Programme and to exclude others for the time being. Far more significant, however, was the effect of such pressure upon Commission thinking in general and upon the way in which it conceived cooperation between Member States and itself in particular. The main shift was one which took the Commission very quickly away from what one might term the pursuit of ideological goals and into a highly pragmatic approach to the issues of the hour.

The move away from what one writer has termed 'Europhoria' to pragmatism cannot be said to be the result of any deliberate and conscious act. Nor, for that matter has such a shift in operational thinking been confined to the realms of higher education, though it is perhaps most visible in this area of Commission policy. It is, rather, a general reorientation of administrative style.

The emergence of the pragmatic approach and the need to respond to unforeseen events is best seen in the importance, both budgetary and in terms of human resources engaged in that part of the Action Programme involving transition from school to adult working life. Though the details of its development have been presented in Chapter III, the long term significance of this particular undertaking lies elsewhere. It lies principally in the way in which cooperation between Member States and Commission was seen.

Hitherto, the concept of cooperation rested on the assumption that it stood as the first step along the long road towards 'constructing a new Europe'. This is not to say that for certain interests and in other areas of the Commission's educational activities, cooperation does not have this ultimate purpose. Yet, faced with an issue of over-riding common concern to all Member States, the transition programme became a vehicle by which cooperation itself shed a large part of its ideological overtones. Instead, cooperation became largely pragmatic, an instrument through which Member States could pool knowledge on ways to deal with the rising tide of youngsters out of work, share experience, evaluate each other's efforts and learn from them. In short, cooperation became a means by which Member State development could draw on the accumulated wisdom of its neighbours, thereby adding a further dimension and a further contribution to the intelligence on which national policy might be based.

Such knowledge-sharing is not unique to the European Communities. It underlies similar activities in education, principally those of the Council of Europe and the Organisation for Economic Cooperation and Development. From this perspective then, Commission policy may be seen as an extension of a form of cooperation already well-established. The difference between the nature of this exchange within the Member States of the Ten is to be found in its sustained nature — the transition project for instance is now in its sixth year — and in the fact that the participants, both as Member States and as individuals or teams are engaged in evaluating each others' efforts at the grass roots.

The pragmatic approach gathered weight with the transfer of the Commission's Education Services from the Directorate for Scientific Research and Culture (Directorate General XII) in 1981 and their relocation within the field of Employment and Social Affairs. (Directorate General V). This same move also ushered in a new approach to policy issues such as youth unemployment, transition from school to work, vocational training and the development of new information technologies in the field of education. The watchword of the 'second generation' projects, launched from 1981 onwards, is 'coordination'. Hitherto, Commission policy had emphasised cooperation between similar services in Member States, these being broadly understood as coterminous with Educational administration. Now, with Education part of a wider Directorate whose remit encompassed areas of national administration other than Education alone, a new perspective could be entertained. For example, those activities in the transition programme which hitherto involved Ministries of Education could now be extended to link up with parallel developments in the world of vocational training.

The arguments in favour of 'integration' or 'coordination' across administrative boundaries were many, and not least amongst them, the results of the various pilot projects dealing with the problems of young people moving from school to adult life. Difficulties in school are often liable to carry over into the training system and from there be perpetuated when the young person seeks entry to the labour market. It stems from this that if there are to be any durable remedies to be had to the problem of lack of formal qualifications, skills or knowledge, they are unlikely to be effective unless pursued in a sustained manner across the boundaries of the various administrations involved in school/training/employment.

The 'integrated' perspective is being progressively applied to such projects as the Community programme on New Information Technologies, action on behalf of the handicapped and to the second stage of the transition from school to working life programme. Nor is it confined to policy development inside the Commission's Education service. The new approach has been extended down to field level. It is reflected in the importance attached to linking the efforts undertaken within the framework of education to others of a similar nature falling under the responsibility of manpower training and social services as well.

There is, however, a further consideration that may have played a part in this qualitative shift in policy perspective, though it has to be said that its precise influence remains unclear at present. Education, as has been pointed out earlier, is a subtle area, one in which national sensitivities are often quickly roused. It may well be that by associating and coordinating activities of an educational nature with those where education and training coincide and overlap, a more substantial juridical base is being built up and one that rests firmly within those articles in the Treaty of Rome dealing with vocational training.

Envoi:

This study has looked at the various components, activities and programmes which, together, go to make up the major aspects of Commission undertakings in the field of education. The nature of Commission policy, though complex and the situations which it has had to face no less so, is one of considerable flexibility. It is the outcome of sustained dialogue between all levels of education and rests on a research basis which, though empirical, is itself highly innovative. All in all, Community policy, research and development cannot be said to endorse a 'top down' strategy in which the Bruxelles tail wags the Community dog. Rather the contrary. The highly pragmatic approach that underlies Commission activity means that the experience of the base is gradually filtered upwards through a system of colloquia, seminars, meetings, reaching upwards to the Education Committee and finally to the Council of Ministers. If such experience is to be a genuine contribution to future practice at Member State level, it must be seen to be successful on the criteria and in the context in which they are to take place. And this is firmly anchored in the framework of the particular Member State.

In a sense, this account is incomplete. Negotiation, administration, progress and debate go on. New areas of discussion are opened up. The Communities pursue their path after the enquirer takes his leave. The period with which this examination has been concerned is, in effect, a very specific phase in the development of Community education policy. The eight years from 1976 represent, in many respects, a period when such policies remained in a state of becoming. There are several reasons for considering the period in this light, not least of which the fact that for research to yield results takes time. For those results to be discussed, their implications agreed upon and the lessons retained, is also a matter for the years. During these eight years, the emphasis in education activities has been on laying down the structures of dialogue, setting up research teams, refining the areas of common concern. To use an agricultural image, these eight years have been the period of sowing. Today, Commission policy stands another crucial point in its development: that of disseminating, broadcasting and, where there is agreement, implementing the lessons learnt. But then, perhaps the agricultural analogue is misplaced. For as harvest time comes, so too does the winter sowing. New programmes are being considered, new issues arise.

The way in which education has developed inside the Commission has been the prime concern of this examination. But in taking this particular perspective, it has also sought to place them within a broader historical and contemporary standpoint. The view from one tree is often better balanced by a picture of the forest around it.

In the long run, at whatever level – local, regional, Member State or Community – the foremost task of education is to enable the individual to realise her – or his – abilities and potential within the resources and constraints of an organised and democratic community. What we have sought to describe here, is perhaps the first stage in bringing to bear transnational experience on this issue. In short, what has been presented, is the potential of working together in education beyond the level of the nation state. What the long term results will be, no-one can foresee. In policy, no less than in education, it is a hazardous business to predict the future of the mature man on the basis of the perceived potential of his younger self.

SOURCES

i. Primary: internal Commission documents

'Implementation of the Community Action Programme on transition of young people from education to adult and working life', *Information Note for the pilot projects*, Bruxelles, October 1983 (typewritten) pp. 2-3.

ii. Tertiary: pamphlets, articles of a non official nature

Guy Neave, 'Community policy and teacher education', *European Journal of Teacher Education*, vol. 5, nos. 1-2, 1982.

Guy Neave, 'Accountability and control', *European Journal of Education*, vol. 15, no. 1, 1980.

Guy Neave, 'Recent trends in education policy in Western Europe' in Colin Brock, Patricia Broadfoot and Witold Tulasiewicz (eds) *Politics and educational change*, London, 1982, Croom Helm.

Guy Neave and Sally Jenkinson, *Research on higher education in Sweden: an analysis and an evaluation*, Stockholm, 1983, Almqvist and Wiskell International.

Rune I.T. Premfors, *Social research and governmental commissions in Sweden*, Stockholm, 1982, Group for the Study of higher education and research.

Rune I.T. Premfors, *Researchers and policy-makers — how do they relate? Research and policy making in Swedish higher education*, Stockholm, June 1982, International Institute for Education.

Alan Smith, 'From 'Europhoria' to pragmatism: towards a new start for higher education cooperation in Europe?' *European Journal of Education*, vol. 15. no. 1, 1980.

Carol H. Weiss, 'Policy research in the context of diffuse decision-making', in D.B.P. Kallen, G.B. Kosse et alii (eds) *Social Science research and public policy making: a reappraisal*, Windsor (England) 1983, NFER Nelson.

Carol H. Weiss, 'The many meanings of research utilisation', *Public Administration Review*, September October 1979.

Hans Weiler, 'Legislation, expertise and participation: strategies of compensatory legitimation in education policy', *Comparative Education Review*, vol. 15, no. 1, June 1983.